EFFECTIVE INTERVENTIONS

Recent Titles in
Contributions to the Study of Education

Experiential Education for Community Development
Paul S. Denise and Ian M. Harris, editors

The People's Universities of the USSR
David Currie Lee

Getting Down to Business: Baruch College in the City of New York, 1847–1987
Selma C. Berrol

The Democratic Tradition and the Evolution of Schooling in Norway
Val D. Rust

Diffusion of Innovations in English Language Teaching: The ELEC Effort in Japan, 1956–1968
Lynn Earl Henrichsen

Improving Educational Quality: A Global Perspective
David W. Chapman and Carol A. Carrier, editors

Rethinking the Curriculum, Toward an Integrated, Interdisciplinary College Education
Mary E. Clark and Sandra A. Wawrytko, editors

Study Abroad: The Experience of American Undergraduates
Jerry S. Carlson, Barbara B. Burn, John Useem, and David Yachimowicz

Between Understanding and Misunderstanding: Problems and Prospects for International Cultural Exchange
Yasushi Sugiyama, editor

Southern Cities, Southern Schools: Public Education in the Urban South
David N. Plank and Rick Ginsberg, editors

Making Schools Work for Underachieving Minority Students: Next Steps for Research, Policy, and Practice
Josie G. Bain and Joan L. Herman, editors

Foreign Teachers in China: Old Problems for a New Generation, 1979–1989
Edgar E. Porter

EFFECTIVE INTERVENTIONS

Applying Learning Theory to School Social Work

Evelyn Harris Ginsburg
Foreword by William J. Reid

Contributions to the Study of Education, Number 42

Greenwood Press
New York • Westport, Connecticut • London

Library of Congress Cataloging-in-Publication Data

Ginsburg, Evelyn Harris.
    Effective interventions : applying learning theory to school
social work / Evelyn Harris Ginsburg ; foreword by William J. Reid.
        p.   cm. — (Contributions to the study of education, ISSN
0196-707X ; no. 42)
    Includes bibliographical references.
    ISBN 0-313-26768-5 (lib. bdg. : alk. paper)
    1. School social work.   2. Behavioral assessment.   3. Behavior
modification.   I. Title.   II. Series.
LB3013.4.G55   1990
371.4'6—dc20   90-3156

British Library Cataloguing in Publication Data is available.

Library of Congress Catalog Card Number: 90-3156
ISBN: 0-313-26768-5
ISSN: 0196-707X

First published in 1990

Greenwood Press, 88 Post Road West, Westport, CT 06881
An imprint of Greenwood Publishing Group, Inc.

Printed in the United States of America

The paper used in this book complies with the
Permanent Paper Standard issued by the National
Information Standards Organization (Z39.48-1984).

10 9 8 7 6 5 4 3 2 1

Copyright Acknowledgment

Unpublished papers of Robert A. Labak are used by permission.

This book is dedicated to Elsie M. Pinkston, who directed me,
guided me, listened to me, and inspired me every step of the way in
this and my previous publication.

CONTENTS

FOREWORD

The behavioral movement in social work has often been criticized for being dominated by academicians who write books and articles telling practitioners what to do. The complaint has been that behaviorally oriented academics and researchers are not familiar with the realities of practice in social work settings.

The present volume should help mute that criticism. It is the work of a social work practitioner who has used behavioral methods in her own practice. She writes from a knowledge of her practice domain—school social work—that is both intimate and extensive. As a practitioner who has used behavioral methods, the author brings to her work a sense of which methods are important for which purposes in daily practice.

At the same time, it is a book in the best traditions of scholarship. Her scholarship is most clearly seen in the extensive reviews of research she presents on a wide variety of approaches pertinent to school social work. At first glance these reviews seem more helpful to scholars and students than to practitioners. But some reflection suggests that practitioners themselves should benefit equally. The research presented documents effectiveness, or in some cases lack of effectiveness, of the methods presented. Those practitioners who use them have a better sense of what they are buying than is the case with the usual methods text. At the same time, users will find a rich array of up-to-date references to which they can turn for additional evidence of further detail on the practice methods.

The methods presented cover a wide variety of populations and situations dealt with by school social workers. The techniques for dealing with the most common problems presented to school social workers are outlined with clarity and detail.

Contrary to the stereotype of the behavioral practitioner as one whose vision is limited to the deviant behavior of the individual, Ginsburg takes a broad perspective of the school social worker as one who is concerned not only with the behavior of children but with the many relations that children have in school settings: to teachers, to families, and to the community. Contrary to the impression that behavioral practitioners in school settings force children to adjust to bad systems, Ginsburg makes clear that the behavioral school social worker needs to make ethical choices about when to help a child accommodate to a system and when not to.

Throughout the book, we see first and foremost a school social worker who uses behavioral methods rather than a behaviorist who happens to be in a school setting. As a school social worker, the practitioner is involved in many roles—as a child therapist, as a family practitioner, as a consultant to teachers, and as an expert in community resources. As Ginsburg well documents, in all of these roles and in others, the behavioral approach has much to offer.

The book is for all social workers who practice in school settings. It does not assume prior knowledge of learning theory or behavioral methods. Rather, it presents the essentials of a school-based behavioral approach from the ground up. Since behavioral approaches have the advantage of being systematic and specific—an advantage accentuated by the author's own clarity—social workers from all theoretical orientations can readily master the basic techniques presented in the book.

Among the many approaches used in clinical social work, the behavioral approach comes closest to achieving the goal of a scientifically based, accountable practice. It does not have answers to all problems but at least makes clear what answers it has and what its limitations are. Perhaps most importantly, it provides a framework of case accountability, scientific assessment, and practice evaluation into which not only behavioral methods may fit but other techniques as well.

It is now fashionable to speak of eclectic practice. But eclecticism presupposes that one uses methods drawn from different orientations. I hope we are reaching a point in practice beyond eclecticism. In post-eclectic practice there would not be a mix of methods clearly identified as behavioral, psychodynamic, family systems, and so forth, but explicit, systematic methods whose processes and effects could be carefully monitored—in other words, methods that would meet criteria of a scientifically based practice.

The present book provides a resource and technology for such a practice not only for practitioners in school social work but for all practitioners who deal with children in families. Read on.

William J. Reid
School of Social Welfare
State University of New York at Albany

PREFACE

This book is based on a compilation of works in applied behavior analysis related to school social work, from general research to studies focusing on problems of children. The history of behavior analysis in schools and in social work is presented. The daily concerns of the behavioral school social worker are shown throughout, then summarized in the Appendix by generously shared excerpts from the work of Robert A. Labak, a model behavioral school social worker. Settings favoring the use of applied behavior analysis related to schools are explored. Throughout this text, the social worker will be referred to as "she" and the child client will be known as "he."

This text is meant to serve as a working tool for the school social worker no matter what her experience is with applied behavior analysis. It is of equal value to the student social worker and the social worker already on the job. A copy in their school library or personal professional book collection would also be useful to other school personnel wanting to understand the functioning of the school social worker or to research appropriate interventions to assist their pupils. Behavior therapists working with children in other settings and wanting to understand school problems would profit from it, as well.

Materials have been drawn from many sources. Some have been published in books and scholarly journals, while others are as yet unpublished. The latter group includes materials that have been presented at conferences, were written to meet the requirements for a university degree, or were simply flyers, handbooks, or notes on the job. Some information was given to me verbally. Through it all, I have relied on the members of the Chicago Association for Behavior Analysis.

Many people have graciously given materials or supplied their thinking and encouragement in this task. Marla Kruglik gave me her personal support and applied her skill as an editor to every page. Robert A. Labak, Patricia Hanrahan, Susan Drager, Tim Thomas, Kathleen Westling, Bruce Townsley, Nancy Buechin McGill, Carmen Marcy, Arthur Sontag, Anastasia P. Graven, David Betts, Leonard Jason, Virginia Richards, and Kim DeLong generously supplied unpublished materials. Doug Carnine, Henrietta K. Sachs, Jamie Lilie, R. Douglas Greer, Robert Woll, Tom Budziak, Richard W. Couch, Renata

Slaughter, Fred Waltzer, Patricia H. Flanagan, William J. Reid, and Ann P. Streissguth supplied me with copies of their own and other related works. Guidance and encouragement were given by Charles Merbitz, Betty Goldiamond, Irene Montella, Bruce A. Thyer, Sarah H. Stuart, Sophie Black, and George Rosenbaum. The entire project would have been impossible without the support of Jack Ginsburg, who put so many things on hold and personally extended himself so I could write this book. A special thanks goes to Israel Goldiamond who introduced me to behavior analysis and has been a close friend throughout.

I

INTRODUCTION

1

REASONS FOR BEHAVIOR ANALYSIS IN SCHOOL SOCIAL WORK

Applied behavior analysis presents some unique advantages for the school social worker. The vast number of publications and other presentations based on empirical research are of obvious value. But there is more. This method addresses a client's unique and specific needs at the moment they are occurring. This means the child will be working with the behavioral school social worker on what is of prime concern to him at the time of intervention, and this can translate into powerful motivation to change behavior.

In the school setting, the social worker will address impediments to school success where they operate. The behavioral school social worker places priority on addressing these deterrents. She will be able to do this because she fits herself into the school situation. In doing so, she demonstrates that she has something to offer that is distinct from and recognized by other school personnel and members of the wider school community.

School success is a priority of every child, even though he may deny it because he is frustrated or discouraged. Because behavior analysis places great emphasis on the environment and a client's uniqueness, the behavioral school social worker will be in a strategic position to evaluate a student's situation. She should try to shape the environment for the child's benefit. If she cannot, she should let him know that the only solution is for him to adjust his behavior to accommodate it. If the pupil does not want to work on these problems himself, the behavioral school social worker has the option of enlisting the aid of other school personnel, his friends, or his family.

Since learning theory is the basis of applied behavior analysis, the school social worker using these methods will share common theory with other school personnel. This will make it possible to fit behavioral treatment programs naturally into the school milieu. Also, the social worker will be seen as having the same goals as the rest of the school, which should enhance her acceptance there.

The behavioral school social worker can also use preventive methods. The use of such methods with children has been widely researched by behavioral scientists (Jason and Bogat, 1983; Roberts and Peterson, 1984; Rickel and Allen, 1987; Rhodes and Jason, 1988). Americans have a long tradition of expecting the public schools to prevent (or at least correct) all manner of social ills through their educational programs. The school social worker makes herself valuable when schools are required to carry out such programs by helping school personnel consider the validity of suggested approaches.

Applied behavior analysis is one of a number of emerging models of intervention design with an empirical base. Task-centered treatment is another one of these, and it has the distinction of evolving from and relating its research to social work (Reid and Shyne, 1969; Reid and Epstein, 1972; Reid and Epstein, 1977; Reid, 1978; Epstein, 1980). Thomas (1984) sees several research methods, including applied behavior analysis, as making serious contributions to this end. They are behavioral science research methods, studies of research utilization, models to retrieve literature and to generate intervention guidelines, program evaluation, experimental social innovation, action models, empirically oriented practice, intervention planning, and models of research and development.

IDENTITY OF SOCIAL WORKERS

Will social workers ever have their own identity? Should they? They have divided themselves into medical social workers, school social workers, psychiatric social workers, group workers, community organizers, policy specialists, etc. They have had separate professional organizations as well as umbrella professional associations. Some of the groups, such as the state associations of school social work, continue to this day.

And perhaps it should be so in a profession that has to be on the front lines of social problems. It is social work's unique function among the helping professions to deal with people in the context of their relationships to the world around them. A therapist, who does not address the effects of society on a client, is not a social worker.

Social workers must deal with the problems inherent in being attached to another discipline. Many take on the identity of the other professionals with whom they work. In hospitals, they emulate the medical profession. In group-work agencies, they take on the aura of recreational personnel. Social workers in private practice assume the trappings of psychiatrists. In the community they resemble business people. And in education the pattern is the same. How the social worker relates to the environment and yet retains her identity as a social worker with unique skills to offer is a test of her understanding of and strength in her chosen profession.

Unfortunately, the basic skills of social workers have not always been clearly defined or appropriate in the setting in which they were being practiced. Social workers have too often been trained to look at problems and their possible causes rather than how to treat them. They have been so involved with the idea of the uniqueness of each person that they have been convinced that scientific method could not be applied to treatment. It took psychologists to lead the way in the opposite direction.

Social workers were seduced by the "Freudian and neo-Freudian principles that took American social work by storm in the 1920s" (Sheldon, 1982, p. 9), and some have stuck with them in varying degrees to the present. They have viewed human behavior in terms of neurosis, sickness, or abnormality. With such an approach, submitting their practice to scientific evaluation seemed to them too difficult or impossible, irrelevant, and hardly worth considering.

Degree programs in social work first appeared in the 1920s in universities that offered graduate programs in the specialty. Sophonisba Breckinridge and Edith Abbott at the University of Chicago wanted to create social workers who could deal with clients as well as conduct research on social issues of the day (Leiby, 1978). At that time, schools of social work in New York, Boston, and Philadelphia were focused mainly on developing a generic pattern for social casework. Breckinridge and Abbott did succeed in incorporating casework into the overall scheme of policy formulation, research, planning, and administration.

But the United States was on the brink of the Great Depression and the New Deal with its many welfare programs. When the Social Security system was adopted, it was seen as the great answer for people in need. Examination of other solutions to client problems was put on hold. It took until the 1960s for the schools of social work to receive training grants and money for research.

Much of the funding came from the National Institute of Mental Health. But eventually grant programs were developed by public and private agencies interested in the aged, children, the handicapped or retarded, delinquents, medical patients and their families, alcoholics and drug abusers, and public health.

Psychologists were getting many of these grants because they were producing massive evidence that there could be a scientific research component to individual psychotherapy. And they were able to show effective and lasting results. Increasingly, graduate schools of social work have been addressing the need to incorporate scientific method into social work practice. As a consequence, bitter debates have ensued, with alumni associations threatened by unfamiliar research methods and wanting to retain the ego psychology or psychodynamic model they are comfortable with.

The universities have been further encouraged to engage in empirical studies by government sources and private foundations that have strongly favored such research when awarding grants. In the schools of social work, it has been research in behavior analysis, task-centered treatment, and similar modalities that have brought in the funds to the universities. As a result, academics have had to take a hard look at the professional integrity of social work and the value of programs in the field.

Meanwhile, social workers in private practice and private agencies were marshalling their resources to defend their nonscientific approach. They financed their efforts by accepting funds from the United Way or similar community sources or by opening private offices. The United Way raises billions of dollars annually through employee payroll deductions, promoted as a way to give to all worthy charities "once and for all." This has insured funds to perpetuate private agencies that were designed early in the twentieth century to service new immigrant groups, yet very few of the targeted clientele require such social services any longer.

Meanwhile, pressing needs were going unmet in the community among groups not serviced by such agencies. As new demands arose for help with such problems as substance abuse, child abuse, wife abuse, gang problems, and homelessness, even governmental bodies turned to the private agencies already in existence. This has only compounded the problems, because such agencies saw answers to all problems in using the same old methods with new phraseology.

In private practice, social workers have survived by treating upper-middle- or upper-class individuals on a fee-for-service basis. Often they share offices with psychiatrists, medical doctors, or psychologists in private practice who turn over some of their patients to the social workers. This has often meant working nights and weekends. Inevitably, it has forced such social workers to hustle continuously to have enough clients to support themselves in the style they prefer.

With regard to private practices with well-to-do clients, the question of whether this is social work has to be raised. With such clients, used to the methods of psychiatrists based mainly on ego psychology, social workers do not have to consider submitting their practice to scientific evaluation. They have become a subculture in the field of social work.

This state of affairs has had its effect on school social work. Trained in the Freudian model, school social workers proceeded to try to fit what they knew to their new setting. This was not possible. Public schools educated people from all classes, not just the upper classes. In fact, children from families who can afford it are often sent to private schools, leaving those in the middle and lower classes predominant in the public schools.

Strict laws requiring children to attend school were enforced by truant officers, insuring that the middle and lower classes would attend. The problems of such people were not those of the upper classes. The social workers in schools had to revert to the methods of the founders of the profession, who served the underclasses.

Another barrier to the usefulness of the psychodynamic approach in schools is that it is based on a medical model. It depends on the labeling of clients as having a disease or disabling condition defined in medical terms. Typically, those who would be clients of social workers were seen as mentally ill, and traditional social workers often went about determining this without empirical data. As O'Leary and Wilson (1975) succinctly explain:

Much of abnormal behavior is developed, maintained, and can be modified in the same manner as normal behavior. "Normal" and "abnormal," "healthy" and "sick" are labels which do not reflect intrinsic differences in social behavior as much as they represent arbitrary decisions by mental health professionals about whether or not the behavior of any given person is appropriate at that given time and place. Deviant behavior cannot usually be traced directly to any physical or psychic disease processes; the underlying intrapsychic conflicts which are assumed to cause maladaptive behavior can only be inferred from behavior itself. (p. 9)

It should also be noted that the social work researchers and practitioners have experimented with methods other than ego psychology and research-based therapies. Social workers have tried such therapies as the family-systems approach, Gestalt therapy, Adlerian psychology, and nondirective therapy. Some have even decided to use all of them, considering themselves eclectic.

This great variance among the methods of social workers has made it difficult to explain the goals and functions of the profession to others. In fact, social workers have had problems with defining their difference from other professions operating in the same settings. They need textbooks and leadership to help clarify their roles.

The medical approach and some of the others are quite foreign in the setting of public education, which has its own philosophy and methods in dealing with children. It has been a challenge to school social workers to find more suitable and compatible ways of serving children. Behavior analysis, an educational method, is a more logical approach in the school environment. It is within this context that applied behavior analysis will be examined in this text.

COMPATIBILITY OF APPLIED BEHAVIOR ANALYSIS WITH SOCIAL WORK

There is ample evidence of increasing use of applied behavior analysis in social work. A bibliography of textbooks and other publications was compiled by Thyer in 1981 that dealt with general principles of behavioral social work in psychiatric social work, school social work, medical social work, community social work, group work, child and adolescent treatment, marital and family therapy, casework and program evaluation, social skills training, gerontology, and education and training. And there have been many more publications in the field since then.

A look into some of these publications offers reasons for the growth of interest in applied behavior analysis among social workers. It can be assumed that social workers find the techniques useful and compatible with their objectives. It should be noted, however, that there is evidence of incompatibility between the stated goals of the profession and the actual practice of social workers.

Thyer (1987) writes that the official picture painted for the profession

is one of individual social workers carefully studying developing practice theory, criti-
cally evaluating the empirical evidence corroborating these various perspectives, and
then basing their direct service activities on this evolving body of theory and practice
knowledge. This Utopian state of professional accountability does not exist, and there
is little hope for significant improvement in the immediate future. (p. 150)

The "picture" referred to is "painted" by the National Association of Social
Workers and the Council on Social Work Education.

Another critic writes that "the profession of social work today faces a crisis
involving a credibility gap between its aims and its achievements. There is little
evidence to indicate that the profession is either efficient or effective" (Arkava,
1973, p. 1). Social work research has relied on practitioners using their own
judgment in assessing client change. This is far from reliable data. Applied
behavior analysis could improve this situation.

The field of "behavior therapy," a term coined by H. J. Eysenck and his colleagues in England around 1958 (Wilson and Franks, 1982) now covers a
number of different but similar approaches to treating behavior problems.
One of these is "applied behavior analysis." This term was used to distinguish
behavior analysis from use of the method in practical situations. "Behavior
analysis" has been used to describe basic operant animal research in controlled laboratories, usually in universities. Applied behavior analysis refers to
treatment of human beings, usually in the everyday world.

Applied behavior analysis, now often referred to as "radical behaviorism,"
takes the position advocated by B. F. Skinner that visible behavior is the only
variable that can be reliably measured. Also, he sees individuals as free to control their own destinies if they work at it correctly, a notion social workers
commonly hold close to the heart. A position of behavior analysis that has
wide support is that behavior is produced or shaped by the variables in a person's environment.

In an important, thoughtful, and inclusive textbook, *Effective Social Work
Practice* (Pinkston et al., 1982) we are told, "Social workers need to learn a
scientific methodology for conducting direct practice" for their clients to receive

the most effective assistance possible. Behavioral scientists determine how people function within a laboratory or within the context of the social environment, whereas social workers encourage people to function at their maximum potential by helping their
clients obtain training, personal support, and material services. Because the goals of
behavioral scientists differ from those of social workers, social workers cannot depend
on these scientists to conduct the research for and the evaluation of the improvement
of social work methods. Thus social workers must arm themselves with a scientific
practice-research methodology that will advance their field systematically and scientifically. Behavior analysis is such a methodology. (p. 1)

In discussing the use of behavioral methods by social workers, Sheldon (1982) speculates that the widespread application and concurrent evaluation of these methods would be a useful and dramatic event in social work. The behavioral techniques that will add up to a significant difference include close specification of goals, built-in evaluation methods, concentration on doing instead of talking, focus on the here-and-now of the client's complaints, and inclusion of research on the factors in the environment that perpetuate the client's problems. These will be strong elements for success because they are not contrived. Instead, they are integral components of the method.

In pointing out the need for a unified theory of social work practice, Thyer (1987) concludes that many of the typical targets of social work intervention are a function of their consequences. An example might be when students are rewarded with a great deal of parental attention when they do not do their homework, or when teacher attention is increased on the child who talks out of turn in class.

Consequence is one of the fundamental components of behavior measured in applied behavior analysis, and it is operative no matter what approach is taken. The question becomes whether the social work profession will recognize this fact and use the well-developed behavioral methods to achieve their goals. In other words, goals of social work seem to be universally similar, but too many practitioners use ineffective methods.

Schwartz and Goldiamond (1975) write:

Operantly oriented social work has not only much proven value, but also much promise for the development of future intervention models. While the contributions of applied behavior analysis include many that are new and innovative, they also include many points of agreement as well as disagreement with more traditional models. Social workers can choose these points of disagreement as occasion for future battles, or can seize them as the entering points for a dialogue that could lead to development of future practice models that could combine the best elements of the current and yet-to-be-developed approaches. (p. 4)

In examining reactions of social workers to behavior analysis, it is instructive to distinguish between those in private practice or private agencies, and those who work with disadvantaged clients. It is common for social workers serving the upper-middle and upper classes to think of behavioral techniques (if they think of them at all) as acceptable for limited use among the institutionalized and other profoundly handicapped persons. But they do not want this "short-term" therapy for their clients. On the other hand, those working with the underclasses and the severely handicapped have seen behavioral techniques as a lifeline.

It should be noted that social workers serving the underclasses or the severely handicapped are often those who have received training in behavior analysis. Since there have not been enough of them to do the entire job, agencies in such fields as rehabilitation have turned to other disciplines. They have hired rehabilitation specialists or behavior therapists who do jobs that social workers could have done had they been following the objectives of their profession, which require that they work with the least advantaged populations in real-life situations. Surely the rehabilitation field, which deals with health, vocational, and attendant problems of handicapped individuals, fits this definition. Behavioral social workers are trained to work with any population needing service, as were the founders of the profession.

In 1873, Jane Addams wrote *The Subjective Necessity for Social Settlements*, a pioneering statement of American social work. In it she stated that she wanted American society to move to "actual social democracy ... acting together in a common life, not divided by snobbish distinctions of class, race and religion." She thought the advantaged, especially social workers, should have the "willingness to experience the great common interests and the problems of human existence" (Leiby, 1978, p. 129).

Early in the twentieth century, social institutions began to employ people as caseworkers. Hospitals hired caseworkers for the nonmedical problems of illness, and mental hospitals hired them to take social histories and do extramural work. Schools began to employ "visiting teachers" and truant officers. Courts (especially juvenile courts) and correctional institutions relied on probation officers. The clients of these institutions usually needed money, but this was not the core of their problems; rather, they needed "help in managing their personal affairs" (Leiby, 1978, p. 182).

Typically, behaviorally trained social workers follow in the tradition of the early pioneers in social work by being equipped with skills that enable them to work with all classes, including the disadvantaged. But until they emerged in the 1970s, the social work profession overwhelmingly used the psychodynamic model or relied on federal welfare programs employing workers who were not usually professionally trained and had no skills to improve the underclass. From generation to generation, impoverished families remained in their miserable state, without hope and with little attention to their needs.

Behavioral social workers usually have been trained in undergraduate and graduate school in basic skills that enable them to work with any population needing service, as were the founders of the profession. This responsibility was detailed by Charlotte Towle (1947), who saw the need for social workers to involve themselves with all populations in all types of problems. In this spirit, social workers elect the behavioral sequence because they have thought through the purposes of social work. Some even selected the university they attended because it offered such a sequence.

In contrast to the behavioral social workers are the social workers who prefer the psychodynamic orientation. They chose the profession of social work because they could be certified as clinical social workers and work as therapists in private practice, removing themselves from social problems. Many see their function as getting people to express their feelings, which they regard as therapeutic. They can do this comfortably because they are under no pressure to use scientific methods that specify outcomes for what they achieve.

There are social workers employed in various settings who fall between the two groups. Some work in hospitals, where they address problems of families of patients or are involved with discharge planning. Others attached to governmental bodies such as courts, police departments, welfare programs, or child protective services, do social investigations or follow-up of parolees or neglected and abused children. Many school social workers fall in this category.

It is not uncommon for hospitals or public agencies to hire holders of bachelor's degrees along with, or instead of, social workers with master's degrees. The line between the responsibilities of the two groups is not finely drawn. In many instances the less-trained workers render the more pragmatic services, including those requiring behavior analysis. Some social workers holding master's degrees are offended by this.

Another group of social workers see themselves as eclectic and use a variety of methods. For example, they might use behavioral techniques for institutional settings and psychodynamic methods for outpatients or combination psychodynamic diagnoses with behavioral treatment plans.

If their responsibilities on the job do not demand that social workers take a clear position on behavioral versus psychodynamic therapy, they tend to be content doing just the routine tasks required of them. Since most are in public service positions involving pensions and seniority, they tend to remain on their jobs for most of their careers.

There are, of course, some who join with the behaviorists, the psychodynamic professionals, or advocates of other models. Behaviorists are finding that the ecobehavioral approach has come into prominence because pragmatic services in addition to behavior therapy are required for clients from the underclass (Couch, 1989).

A problem that continues to trouble behaviorally oriented researchers on the faculties of universities is the difficulty in getting practitioners to make use of current findings. Researchers are invariably available to make verbal presentations, backed up by printed material, at conventions, seminars, panels, or workshops. Also, they publish widely and frequently. When the behaviorists hold their conventions, they tend to offer many more choices, starting early in the day and going later into the day, than do other conferences.

On the other hand, audiences of professionals in the applied area have not been forthcoming in numbers that are at all comparable to the presenters. However, when behaviorists do attend, they take advantage of what is presented. Some work diligently at absorbing as much information as they can from the meetings. They collect materials, confer with presenters, and consistently gather new resources for their jobs.

Non-behaviorally oriented social work practitioners rarely publish, read technical reports, or seek out viable research. They seem mainly to respond to trends publicized in the media, using the same techniques with new phrases and passwords. Usually they are drawn to the profession because they prefer hands-on activity and want to be identified with the mainstream. These things have been a handicap to the profession in defining their real purposes and in providing suitable training for the workers.

The social work profession needs to take a hard look at what is being offered to clients. Perhaps it is time for the differing factions of social workers to stand up and recognize that they are not operating under the same goals. There may have to be a separation into two professions. Then, people wanting services from either group could be clear about what to anticipate.

Now, difficulties are compounded when social workers are hired to give service they are not skilled in or advice in areas in which they are not knowledgeable. Clients often refuse services or spend money unproductively because they are not clear about what is available from social services. This situation is diminishing the regard in which the profession is held.

COMPATIBILITY WITH EDUCATION

Behavior analysis or behavior therapy is based on learning theory. It has been applied to learning in the classroom as well as to changing a person's behavior. In fact, changing a student's behavior in order for him to learn is an integral component of all teaching. In this sense, a classroom teacher may be a behavior therapist. Alan Ross (1967) writes that there is a rapidly accumulating literature suggesting that

the application of behavioral principles is as relevant to education as it is to the treatment of patients with psychological disorders. This makes it possible to speak of a *therapeutic educator* with training in the application of behavioral principles that can be brought to bear on the teaching of children with psychological problems. Behavioral principles indeed have already been successfully applied in a variety of areas where modification of behavior is sought. These include the training of the mentally retarded, the rehabilitation of the physically handicapped and the treatment of children and adults with psychological disorders. This last application has come to be known as *behavior therapy*.... Behavior therapy differs from traditional psychotherapy in that it starts from the premise that psychological disorders represent *learned* behavior and that known principles of learning can be applied to their modification. (p. 275)

Ross believes that behavior therapy is more closely related to education than to traditional psychotherapy because

There is basically no difference between learning arithmetic and learning how to control one's temper, between practicing one's multiplication tables and practicing one's interpersonal skills. The principles underlying the teaching of academic subjects are the same principles that underlie the teaching of how to live one's life adaptively and constructively. (p. 284)

Indeed, one school social worker introduced herself to the high school setting where she was assigned by advising that she was there to teach the students social skills and how to manage their lives, just as others were there to teach their subjects.

This raises an interesting challenge for the school social worker: she has to determine where the teacher leaves off and she begins. If the teacher is not skilled in the use of behavior therapy, the social worker may have an opportunity to teach her some skills, provided the teacher is open to this. In any case, the school social worker has to confine her use of behavior therapy to whatever format is possible under the circumstances.

Possible formats range from individual work with only the child to cooperation from the teacher, parent, child, and whoever else has a direct bearing on the behavior to be learned. The school social worker always controls and directs the treatment plan, no matter who is carrying it out. She may or may not be the one who collects data or performs other needed steps. But she is always the one to see to it that all the necessary operations are undertaken in achieving whatever goals are sought.

The use of behavioral methods could also include classroom teaching, activities around the school and in the community, or behavior maintained by the family. It is rare for a teacher to ask a school social worker about teaching methods. However, these have been carefully developed and some are even available in packaged programs, such as Distar, a carefully structured reading program. Direct instruction, personalized system of instruction, programmed instruction, and the consulting behavior analysis model are the major behavioral methods in use (Selinske et al., 1989).

The behavioral school social worker should be knowledgeable about classroom methods should an opportunity be presented to advise the teacher about their use. A likely time to advise teachers is while collaborating on an individualized treatment plan in a multidisciplinary staffing for a child who may need special education services (Ginsburg, 1989). However, the school social worker should also look for opportunities to use these resources for instruction in regular classes as well.

There should be frequent opportunities for the behavioral school social worker to fit her techniques into the school setting. "The conceptual basis of behavior modification lies within learning theory, and to understand most of the techniques of behavior modification, one *must* understand modern learning theory" (Lovaas and Bucher, 1974, p. 1).

B. F. Skinner (1968) describes two principles involved in controlling learning behavior:

First, the Law of Effect has been taken seriously; we have made sure that effects *do* occur and that they occur under conditions which are optimal for producing the changes called learning. Once we have arranged the particular type of consequence called a reinforcement, our techniques permit us to shape the behavior of an organism almost at will. . . . A second important advance in technique permits us to maintain behavior in given states of strength for long periods of time. Reinforcements continue to be important, of course, long after an organism has learned *how* to do something, long after it has acquired behavior. They are necessary to maintain the behavior in strength. (p. 10)

Skinner explains that before this theory (known as progressive education) came into acceptance, teachers were instructed not to "spare the rod and spoil the child." In effect, positive reinforcement had not come into substantial use by teachers. Now there is another form of aversive treatment which includes "teacher's displeasure, the criticism or ridicule of classmates, an ignominious showing in a competition, low marks, a trip to the office 'to talk to' the principal, or a word to the parent, who may still resort to the birch rod" (Skinner, 1968, p. 15).

Of course, a teacher with thirty or more pupils cannot provide immediate feedback to each one, which is what is called for in behavioral learning theory. A solution can be found in learning machines, such as computers programmed to tell a child right away whether he has a correct answer. Observation of pupils using computers in this way usually reveals their satisfaction with the method. The rule of thumb in using interactive machines is to use them to complement human interaction, not to substitute for it.

The school social worker and the teacher using behavioral learning techniques can readily blend their services. In such a case, the social worker's advantage would be that she can be an objective observer of the interaction between student and teacher. The teacher's advantage would be that she has more continuous contact with the child and knows the intricacies of his behavior patterns.

If the school's policy and personnel both support the use of behavioral techniques, there should be great compatibility and ease of operation. If only the school social worker supports the modality, she may be frustrated but still get a chance to introduce her colleagues to the literature of behaviorism. This would be especially true after the school social worker establishes credibility and respect on the job.

RELIABILITY AND ACCOUNTABILITY POSSIBLE WITH BEHAVIOR ANALYSIS

Integral components of interventions using applied behavior analysis insure reliability and accountability by the user. These can be shared readily with whoever referred the child or with anyone else who would profit from knowing the outcome of treatment.

Data is collected in a behavioral intervention from start to finish. The problem to be solved is carefully targeted and succinctly stated. The steps to be taken in correcting the problem are specifically recorded and followed. The goals are observed in detail, charted, and eventually made into easily under-stood graphs. The entire operation is concerned with how the targeted behav-ior will be maintained and generalized after the course of treatment is over. Long-term follow up is planned. All of this helps ease communication with all interested persons.

As Polster (1977) stated so clearly:

Participation properties of applied behavior analysis contribute to its usefulness in school social work. Operational problem definition, consistent data recording, and outcome evaluation make possible efficient interventions for school settings. This is of particular importance to the majority of school social workers with over-sized case loads. (p. 17)

2

STATUS OF SCHOOL SOCIAL WORK IN THE FIELD OF BEHAVIOR ANALYSIS

Applied behavior analysis has yet to establish itself as the modality of choice for school social workers. The introduction of behavioral methods by any professionals working in schools preceded the introduction by social workers by only a decade. Literature on interventions by behavior analysts in the schools starts in the 1960s. Publications about social work related to behavior analysis begins in the 1970s, with one or two in the late 1960s. Even to this time, there are few articles or books that relate to the use of applied behavior analysis in school social work.

In fact, there is very little literature of any description on school social work. The book edited by Constable and Flynn (1982) containing a number of articles by other authors is already out of print. Allen-Meares and associates published a well-researched book that deals mainly with history and laws. The first book detailing procedures appeared in 1989 (Ginsburg). Typically, social work practitioners do not publish. This is unfortunate; it creates a situation where information is imparted by word of mouth, hastily written notes, handbooks, or flyers.

However, as will be shown in the case studies and other materials later in this book, the use of applied behavior analysis by school social workers is growing. Although these practitioners have not published, successful projects are detailed in handouts prepared to accompany talks to various school-related groups. Training courses or problem-related groups are held for parents or others in the community. In-service training is presented to school faculties.

School social workers are in a unique position in relation to applied behavior analysis because they do not have to develop interventions from scratch; they can start using procedures that have been researched, developed, and published by behavior therapists in other disciplines. The quantities of literature available on a wide variety of problems are listed as they appear in the monthly *International Journal of Behavioral Social Work and Abstracts* (Thyer, 1981). The school social worker can familiarize herself with these interventions and then adapt them to the unique requirements of each client.

When a school social worker finds herself in a setting where there is little use of behavioral interventions by school personnel or the community, she should find out why this is the case and try to educate those she encounters. Usually, educators have heard of "behavior mod." Some are quite sophisticated in its use and achieve good results with it. Others have used it incorrectly or are not willing to give it the careful scrutiny and detailed follow-up that it requires. If the behavioral school social worker aligns herself with school personnel who are adept at behavior analysis, together they can help others learn and apply these valuable techniques.

The children who become clients will be open to trying behavioral interventions, and some will even ask if other children in the school can use them. They are usually responsive to the positive, fair approach and the rewards that are integral parts of behavior analysis. And usually pupils who have behavior patterns that are giving them problems want to improve them.

There are, of course, those who have become discouraged about any good coming to them from school. Also, the hard, sometimes boring, work of changing behavior and the resultant lack of familiarity with new habits are sometimes uncomfortable. In addition, if children are being reinforced for not improving behavior, they may not be receptive to change. All of these possibilities have to be considered by the behavioral school social worker.

Parents are not always receptive to behavior therapy for some of these same reasons. However, there is an additional possibility that they have already encountered social workers and are either turned off to the profession or really do not want to change their life-styles. Once they agree to trying behavior analysis, busy parents may resent having to collect data and consistently practice new ways of handling their children. Other parents, often observed among the underclasses, are very isolated and have no support system to encourage them to develop and maintain new behaviors. They are so overwhelmed by so many pressing needs that school problems do not take the priority that other, more stable parents are able to give them. (Wahler, 1980)

The lack of training in behavior analysis in schools of social work has been a problem for the social work profession. Thyer and Maddox (1988) studied the behavioral coursework currently being offered in schools of social work. A letter requesting a current bulletin of courses offered and a student application form was sent to each of the ninety-nine accredited schools of social work in the United States. All but eight responded.

Thirty didactic courses on the practice of behavior therapy or the principles of learning theory were offered in sixty-seven schools. Forty-four survey courses with a behavioral point of view were available. Only in thirty-six schools were both types of courses offered. Only six complete and thirteen survey courses on research methodology were available in fifteen schools. Most schools of social work providing behavior therapy courses offered one course; fewer offered two or more.

Certainly there is a need for more extensive training in behavior analysis. Extension courses are needed for those already in the field who are not trained and who may have set on-the-job patterns of operating that the schools they serve have come to expect. Like others mentioned, school social workers may resist change and not be willing to put forth the efforts needed in behavior therapy. Also, they may not have thought through what they are doing on the job.

In some cases, the idea of using research methods with each intervention—a necessary component of behavior therapy—has been threatening. School personnel or parents have been known to see this as making a "guinea pig" of the child.

This, of course, is not the case. Research methods are used to measure what is happening to the child before, during, and as a result of treatment. The purpose is to know exactly what is occurring and what success has been achieved. Like an X ray or a blood test, the research is beneficial to the child and not to be used as part of a scientific experiment. Interventions are usually based on the findings of experiments already completed and found helpful in another setting.

Much of the initial research carried out in classroom behavior management was conducted in laboratory preschools. One of the advantages of working in such an environment was that a more precise control and examination of the variables to be manipulated and studied could be achieved if several adults and only a limited number of children were present. The extension of the basic operant principles into more typical classrooms awaited their validation in these relatively restricted settings. (Klein et al., 1973, p. 102)

Clearly, applied behavior analysis in school social work is still very much in a pioneer stage. The potentials are limitless. Behaviorally oriented school social workers have access to behavioral interventions designed by other disciplines. These usually work very well with some adaptation. There are only a few programs developed by social workers and even fewer by school social workers. These will be noted throughout the book. However, it remains for school social workers to adapt the method to the unique needs of their profession.

HISTORY OF BEHAVIOR ANALYSIS

While behavior analysis may be said to have started with the psychologist J. B. Watson (1878–1958), its widespread application to real-life situations did not become common until the 1960s. Since the school social worker using applied behavior analysis will draw on the vast research before, during, and since the 1960s, it seems important to briefly review that history.

The behavioral field is very new and already factionalized, as reflected in the school social worker's ability to choose which interventions to use. The major line of disagreement centers around whether to use only behavior analysis or to combine it with cognitive treatment. The studies of behavior analysis used by therapists outside the school in treating children with school problems probably are the most useful and available for school social workers interested in issues in the field (Graziano and Mooney, 1984).

During the first quarter of the twentieth century, Watson worked at the University of Chicago and Johns Hopkins University.

He advocated the use of "methodological behaviorism" in the scientific study of human behavior. While he is best remembered for what is popularly labeled "radical behaviorism," or the reduction of the human organism to a bundle of responses, it was his emphasis on methodology and his scientific approach to the study of behavior that makes him truly the founder of behavior modification. (Craighead et al., 1975, p. 7)

Watson was committed to the idea that hard research in human psychology could measure only behavior because only behavior could be observed. He did not discount internalized behavior, but ignored it because it could not be reliably measured. It took B. F. Skinner to take the position now recognized as *radical behaviorism*: that there is no basis for a science of psychology using internal factors.

Skinner sees human behavior as the only variable that can be considered. As Epstein (1982) observed:

Though he is interested primarily in observable behavior ... [Skinner] does not *deny* that there are "thoughts" and "feelings" and so on. He simply regards them as physical states of the body, as opposed to metaphysical or psychical entities. He also questions their causal status. Just because you felt afraid and thought to yourself, "I'm getting out of here!" at the approach of a tiger doesn't mean that either the thought or the feeling *caused* you to run away. Rather, says Skinner, the thought, the running, and the feeling that you would report as fear are *all* caused by the approach of the tiger. It's not that the inner events don't exist; it's just that they aren't necessarily the causes of your behavior though it often seems that way. Activity inside your body is as strictly determined by your genes and the environment as is the behavior others can see. (p. 2)

Skinner's work had been in basic research with animals. In 1953, he initiated the field of psychology into use of behavior therapy with humans with the publication of his landmark book, *Science and Human Behavior*. He was more interested in observing, predicting, and controlling behavior than in the study of the human mind. The thrust of those trying to change behavior then becomes one of changing a person's environment. This is compatible with the traditional approach of social work in working with individuals (Pinkston et al., 1982).

This new approach to human behavior was considered a learning theory, in contrast to the widely used psychodynamic approach, which was based on the medical, or disease model. Graduate schools of psychology used the behavioral approach with its strict scientific methods. These contrasted with the medical or medical-influenced settings in which they could complete their practicums.

The advent of behavior modification was marked by its challenge to the prevailing status quo and the presentation of a systematic and explicitly formulated clinical alternative that attempts to bridge the gap between the laboratory and the clinic.... Behavior therapy grew out of the dissatisfaction with traditional psychodynamic procedures which had completely dominated psychiatry and clinical psychology. (O'-Leary and Wilson, 1975, p. 7)

Meanwhile, in the field of education, Skinner was proposing programmed learning and teaching machines. These caught on.

Publishers produced more than 350 new programs in 1963 alone, and variations in teaching machine hardware seemed to abound. Work continued amid a good deal of controversy that seemed much like that which would involve behavior therapy just a short time later. Controversy notwithstanding, programmed instruction became a regular part of many school systems across the country. (Graziano and Mooney, 1984, p. 19)

The teaching machines have turned into sophisticated interactive devices, such as computers, that are now common in public and private schools. Programmed instruction and precision teaching have formed the basis for many teaching systems that have followed. It was in the schools that behavior analysis, more commonly known as behavior modification, was introduced to work with children.

While behavioral theory has become more prominent in teaching systems, it has also been used to deal with the behavior of children in class and around the school. In the 1970s, many publications appeared that dealt with how to control a classroom, how to correct the behavior of individual children, and how to involve parents to improve a child's functioning in school. All of these are areas in which school social workers should be involved.

R. Vance Hall (1971), who has published extensively on applied behavior analysis in the field of education, tells us:

Applied behavior analysis has its basis in modern learning theory. According to psychologists and educators who take this approach, behavior—whether it is appropriate or deviant—is learned. In contrast to traditional approaches, attention is focused on the subject's behavior and his interactions with the immediate environment. Although the developmental history, physical status, intelligence and other such factors are still considered to be important, primary attention is given to the subject's ongoing behavior ... and on what consequences are provided as a result of his ongoing behavior in his own environment—in the school and the home in most cases.... A parent, an educator or a psychologist who has knowledge of the principles of learning can often restructure the environment so that more acceptable patterns of behavior can be learned. (p. 6)

It would seem the stage was set for applied behavior analysis to be recognized as the logical modality for school social workers. And yet it has not progressed rapidly in all areas. There seem to be pockets of use rather than a universal acceptance. Where there are workers trained in behavior analysis, the choice is clear. In some cases where other methods were tried and failed, it has been instituted.

A further obstacle to its use lies in the separation between special and regular education and in the way teachers regard the students in their classes. College students preparing for special education usually receive sophisticated behavioral training, but those preparing for regular education receive much less. Later, the two kinds of teachers view their pupils differently. The special education teachers see applied behavior analysis as useful, while the regular teachers think it should be reserved for their more difficult students. It is not clear which came first, the attitude or the college training. The low regard in which the public holds the handicapped, if not the cause of the problem, certainly compounds it.

The lack of behaviorally trained social workers and the tenacity with which social workers oriented to psychoanalysis and other modalities hold on to their beliefs and facilities are also great obstacles. Hope for the expanded use of applied behavior analysis by school social workers lies in the effectiveness displayed by the method, its clear relation to the educational field, and the support available from the graduate schools of social work.

SUPPORT FOR PROFESSIONALS USING BEHAVIOR ANALYSIS

Professional organizations that support behavior analysis have played an important role in its growth. There is a sense of excitement and mission about behavior analysis that binds behaviorists together. Perhaps it is related to the certainty they gain from empirical findings. Behaviorists work with concrete, provable methods. An added plus is the rapidity with which clients improve their behaviors.

So it was natural that behaviorists would want to get together in professional organizations. Often they were working as the only behaviorist in a setting. Also, they wanted to share their results and gain the support that comes from seeing eye-to-eye with another professional. In the mid-1970s they joined together into the Midwest Association for Behavior Analysis (MABA), holding conventions in Chicago which were real "happenings" for the mental health field. The denim-clad, backpack-toting young behaviorists who crowded into the Blackstone Hotel in 1976 gave the impression of being with the times and having the energy for the job.

Within a few years, the Midwest Association blossomed into the national Association for Behavior Analysis (ABA) and eventually became an international association. Its meetings were moved out of Chicago because Illinois did not support the Equal Rights Amendment. However, in Chicago there remained a devoted group of behaviorists led by Israel Goldiamond and Elsie M. Pinkston, University of Chicago professors of behavioral medicine and social service administration, respectively. Wanting to meet more often than once a year, this group became known as CABA, the Chicago Association for Behavior Analysis (Jason et al., 1985). It was apparent to them that MABA was primarily an organization for psychologists, who were the first to use behavior analysis. Goldiamond and Pinkston were teaching social workers and medical personnel. They advised extending CABA to professions other than psychology. And so it became the first task of CABA to enroll such people (including social workers) in the association.

Eventually, other ABA chapters formed throughout the country—in California, Georgia, Florida, Tennessee, Texas, Minnesota, and elsewhere. The international organization decided to incorporate them into its structure, so they became formal chapters. These chapters have incorporated themselves as not-for-profit organizations and have taken on a number of functions, such as bringing the latest research in behavior analysis to the applied sector through annual conferences, frequent seminars and workshops, and informal social gatherings.

Through the chapters, people in the research area have sometimes joined forces with others doing research, and those in the applied field have worked with others in the same setting. Some chapters have extended their work to the political arena in an effort to standardize qualifications for those using behavioral methods. Other services offered have been bringing job seekers together with employers and announcing new publications of members through regular bulletins.

In the spring of 1988, CABA joined with faculty from the University of Chicago, the Illinois Institute of Technology and representatives of the applied sector to conduct an advanced for-credit seminar at the School of Social Service Administration of the University of Chicago on alternatives to out-of-home placement of children classified by the Illinois Department of Children and Family Services as abused or neglected.

Other chapters have put on major annual conferences in their states that do not coincide with the annual ABA conference. Through these and other interim programs, they have attracted many people interested in learning more or expanding their services through behavior analysis. Those involved with basic research have joined those in the applied settings to strengthen their programs. All chapters and the ABA issue newsletters regularly.

Through ABA and its chapters, much has been written and published. ABA publishes *The Behavior Analyst*, which contains articles on outstanding developments in the field and reviews recently published books. ABA's annual international convention serves as a meeting place for exchange of ideas, an employment service, a stimulus for reporting recent research, a display center for new books or machines or gadgets useful to the membership, and a place to make new friendships or continue old ones. It has always focused on university students training in behavior analysis and has endeavored to make the program relevant for them. Indeed, they have a full voice in ABA affairs.

ABA has a number of task forces, including one on the right to effective education. Matters of current concern in the field have been researched and findings presented at the ABA conference. There is also a special interest group on behavior analysis in education. These could offer some direction to behavioral school social workers.

Applied behavior analysts have been dedicated to the service of all populations. They have taken on groups such as the autistic, the developmentally delayed, institutionalized persons of all descriptions, the elderly, the head- and spinal-cord-injured, substance abusers, victims of AIDS, Alzheimer's patients, and abused and neglected children and their families. Previously untreated populations are being cared for, their afflictions are being researched, and hope is being generated in places where it never was before. For the school social worker who must deal with all of the above populations and more, the associations offer important support and training.

II

WHEN TO USE BEHAVIOR ANALYSIS

3

BEHAVIOR PROBLEMS RELATED TO SCHOOL

A major component of a behavioral school social worker's job is using the resources of the school and changing the environment there for the benefit of a pupil. Key to the environment of any school is the principal. Applied behavior analysis provides answers to dealing with the principal and the school environment. For example, Copeland and associates (1974) experimented with methods whereby the principal could be positively involved with the students in reinforcing their good behavior.

Since it is a major concern in her practice, the behavioral school social worker wants to evaluate the school environment by observation in several areas. The following criteria, all indicative of a positive environment, are offered as a guide:

The primary concern of all who work in the school, nonacademic employees as well as teachers, is for the good of all of the children.

The faculty and staff enjoy working with children and take pride in their accomplishments with them. They consider their work to be of major importance.

The school has positive relations with the parents and the community.

Well-understood and carefully followed rules and regulations based on behavioral principles truly govern the school.

The school principal is clearly in charge of all aspects of the school.

Everyone in the school shows respect for everyone else there, as evidenced by ongoing courtesy and consideration. A test of this is the treatment received by persons who are handicapped; in a racial, religious, or ethnic minority; or in a lower socioeconomic class.

The school functions as a *home* for all of the children and adults there. Each feels that he belongs in that school and that he is liked and understood.

The school offers stability that may not be available in the community or in the student's family home.

Continuous emphasis is placed on a positive learning atmosphere in every classroom. Children are in learning situations where their unique needs and ability levels are taken into account.

The teacher attempts to stretch the student's parameters beyond his surroundings so that he knows there is more to life than what he sees at home and in the neighborhood. Enrichment is especially needed for disadvantaged pupils.

A positive approach to life is taken, with emphasis on generating hope to each child.

These standards are very high and no school is able to live up to them at all times. However, it should be clear whether or not these are the goals of everyone in the school.

Many referrals to the school social worker are related to children's behavior problems. Others involve family problems and social conditions that have created problems for the child in school. The school social worker has to deal with all of them. Dealing with social conditions requires knowledge of their current status and resources available for coping with them. To be treated in school, family problems should be limited to those affecting a child's in-school behavior. Behavior problems, however, lend themselves to behavior therapy when working within the jurisdiction of the school. The school social worker who uses behavior therapy will work with individuals, families, groups, or a combination of any of these.

Behaviors that have been studied by behavior therapists will be examined here. This will not be an exhaustive list. However, those types of problems to which the field has addressed itself will be considered, along with case studies and directions on how to proceed.

If there is a place where behaviorally oriented school social workers seem to naturally fit, it is in the area of serving misbehaving children. "Give me your worst behavior cases," they have said, endearing themselves to school personnel, who happily give them these "worst" cases. A few exceptions are those faculty members who want to control the student or are suspicious of anyone who would want to work with such a child. Too often, they expect the social worker to immediately find another place for that child, preferably at another school. This cannot be accomplished so easily and, more important, is usually not in the pupil's best interest. Behavioral school social workers can work successfully with these children when given cooperation from the school; then it is not unusual for good results to occur in a few weeks. But they are unable to help when, as is so often the case, behavioral treatment has been initiated, only to have the child snatched out of the school and sent to another setting.

The school social worker has several things to consider before deciding how to proceed in correcting behavior problems. A major factor is the circumstances under which the negative behavior occurs. Is the child reacting to difficulties with academics? Or is he being provoked by someone? "Someone" could be his teacher, another child, a bus attendant, or anyone else he encounters in school. Are the philosophy and methods of the school conducive to poor behavior? Sometimes the behavior is being reinforced by circumstances outside of the school.

In judging a child's primary handicap, a requirement in special education multidisciplinary conferences, school personnel are often baffled by candidates for programs for the behaviorally disordered. They try to make a case that the child has certain established behavior patterns that make this labeling necessary. However, it usually becomes clear that the child behaves one way in one setting and another way in another (Wahler, 1969). The child might even be observed acting differently in the course of a day if he goes from one teacher to another for different subjects or special help. Often, major changes are observed from one year to the next when a new teacher works with the student.

Likewise, if a behaviorally oriented school social worker has used a successful intervention, it could be observed that the child has now changed his behavior and so can no longer be considered handicapped. Whether or not a pupil is legally found to be handicapped could be a major determinant in any child's life. When a duly authorized multidisciplinary team designates that a student is handicapped this judgment carries the weight of law.

While schools vary and always have internal problems, they are generally good settings in which to determine if a child's behavior is appropriate or not. Public schools are open to all residents of the school district, so a cross-section of the children residing there is available. School personnel often come from the community or surrounding area and also reflect the local mores. While it is possible that inappropriate judgments would be made, by and large, the school setting is more likely than any other to provide a picture of the student's adjustment in relation to the norm.

The school social worker is in a good position to assess whether a child referred is behaving within normal bounds. She should be mindful that this is not always the case with other school personnel who are involved with the student in one capacity or another. School personnel usually see the child from the point of view of their specialty as administrator, nurse, truant officer, lunchroom attendant, library teacher, or whatever.

The behaviorally oriented school social worker's approach is to take a full view of the child and what is happening to him. She considers what is occurring from his point of view. Every so often she has to point out that the child's behavior *is* appropriate or the best that can be expected from him under the circumstances and that he should be so treated by the referring person.

Students with learning disabilities have difficulties with academics. Too often, this is not clearly understood by adults and children in the school who, not really understanding the handicap, think that learning disabled students also have difficulties in peer interactions. Ormsby and Deitz (1989) explored the social behavior with peers of twenty-four learning disabled students in grades one through five in seventeen classrooms. The five categories of interactions studied included positive/neutral social initiation, positive/neutral response, negative initiation, negative response, and no response.

The five categories were analyzed, after observations, to determine the percentage of time each was displayed. This revealed that "the response patterns of peer interactions of elementary-aged students with learning disabilities within school settings varied according to peer type, interaction role, response type, and structure" (p. 2). While the learning disabled students seemed to be interacting in a positive, appropriate manner, the experimenters thought more study was needed to generalize their conclusions for all learning disabled students.

Unfortunately, there are some schools that approve aversive and even, in some cases, damaging treatment of children. The school social worker, of course, has to weigh whether she wants to serve such places. As a behavior therapist, her role inevitably requires helping the child to adapt to such a setting. She should be aware of the fact that behavior analysis is a powerful method for change, and that a moral judgment is required here (Hall, 1971). If she teaches a child to adjust to a destructive environment, she may be doing him irreparable damage (Graziano and Mooney, 1984; Hall, 1971). The behaviorally oriented school social worker has a major decision to make here and it is very important that she do so responsibly.

BEHAVIOR PROBLEMS OF INDIVIDUALS IN THE CLASSROOM

A basic decision that a school social worker has to make in deciding to change a child's behavior relates to his academic performance. There are many instances where a misbehaving child at the same time is doing poorly academically. Since the primary purpose of attending school is to learn specific subject matter, a student who is not succeeding academically inevitably reacts to this, often by resorting to negative behavior. The school social worker has to decide if the primary focus of treatment should be on the pupil's academic performance or his presenting behavior.

Ayllon and associates (1972) dealt with a classroom for thirteen educable mentally retarded children in an elementary school. The class had four of the most troublesome and unmotivated children in the entire school. To effect positive change, the academic program was restructured to reinforce achievement, and a token economy was instituted. After this, all four of the troublesome, unmotivated children improved in reading and mathematics, and their levels of work showed advancement over baseline. Behavior then improved as a by-product of academic success.

Next, in a now-classic study, Ayllon and Roberts (1974) obtained similar results with children in regular classes; again, behavior improved following academic gains. First, the researchers developed a token economy rewarding academic achievement in the classroom. In a class of thirty-eight pupils, they focused on five highly disruptive students and found that their behaviors improved as their academic achievement rose. Treatment was not focused on the behavior of the children but on academic gain for the entire class. Improvement of the behavior of the five highly disruptive students was only a by-product of the research, although it was the precipitating problem. Thus, the two

studies by Ayllon and his associates showed that improved academic performance could also create better social behavior in children.

Graziano and Mooney (1984) cite several studies dealing with improved behavior resulting from academic gains: Winett and Winkler (1972) "argue that
decremental approaches may only serve to underscore the teacher's power to
force children to remain quiet, orderly, docile, and obedient, which might not
be either appropriate or ultimately beneficial" (p. 248). Ferritor, Buckholdt,
Hamblin, and Smith (1972) found that "academic achievement does not necessarily improve when disruptive behavior is successfully reduced" (p. 248).
Marholin and associates (1975) "provide a rationale for aiming interventions
at increasing academic behavior through positive reinforcement, and then observing if disruptive behavior decreases as well" (p. 248). Page and Edwards
(1978) and Hundert, Bucher, and Henderson (1976) further supported the
work of Ayllon and his associates.

School personnel have pointed out that improving behavior through academic success is different in the 1980s because the social milieu has adversely
affected children, and not all teachers have the skills to use the necessary methods. They advise that some pupils come from circumstances in which nurturing is so inadequate that they can succeed only in smaller classes, where more
teacher attention is available. But with class size too often reaching between
thirty-five and forty pupils or more, they think the teacher has other priorities
forced on her. They contend that often she first has to deal directly with the
disruptive behavior of these children and their current social problems not
being addressed elsewhere before she can address academics. This point of
view, commonly observed, requires documentation.

What then are some of the specific problems presented by pupils in the classroom that should lead the school social worker to consider treatment by behavior therapy? Several studies suggest what these problems are.

Ability to Stay on Task and Complete Work

The ability to stay on task and complete work is of major concern to teachers, who tend to evaluate such activity as related to the child's learning. For
many teachers this is the main teaching method. It therefore follows that if this
is the predominant learning experience a child has, it could become the teacher's daily measure of how he is progressing. However, there are sometimes
other methods by which a child learns. Since on-task usually refers to in-seat
individual work related to repetitive information that the child writes down in
various alignments on paper, it is possible that it is not the procedure that
teaches him the facts or skills sought.

A pupil may master a concept through intellect alone, for example, and be
able to apply it thereafter as needed with very little practice. On the other
hand, he might be able to write information and work on a problem without

understanding the concept involved. But such considerations are sometimes overlooked by teachers dealing daily with large classes.

Ninnes and Glenn (1988) advance the position that negative effects come from a teacher's preoccupation with on-task behavior. They reason that the appearance of being on task can cover up poor study habits or lack of learning. They go on to state that youngsters have been misdiagnosed as learning disabled by the teacher on the basis of on-task behavior, rather than on the basis of what he has learned. In this context, it should be observed that the final decision about whether a child is learning disabled rests with a multidisciplinary team that considers a number of different types of evaluations presented at a multidisciplinary conference (Ginsburg, 1989). Any teacher is on shaky ground if she takes it upon herself to label a child as learning disabled without following the federal laws concerning handicapped children. A school social worker could clarify this for the teacher if necessary.

Keeping on task and finishing assignments are indices of the ability of the child to conform to expectations. The social worker's help is usually sought when a problem is perceived in this area. If the child does stay on task and complete assignments but does the work incorrectly, other questions arise related to study habits or ability to learn and follow directions. Of these, study habits are sometimes seen as proper reasons for referral to the school social worker.

Aaron and Bostow (1978) report a strong relationship between on-task behavior and academic productivity. On-task and work-completion behavior is looked on by school personnel as indicating desired social adjustment. Another study by Van Hasselt and associates (1979) established that high social status in children is related to superior academic achievement. Therefore, if favorable on-task and work-completing behavior in the classroom are an integral component of high social status there, they could be effective in helping a pupil achieve in the superior academic range. In studies reported by Ginsburg (1989), significant academic gains were accomplished by students serviced by behavioral school social workers when treatment changed off-task behavior to on-task.

Verbal or Physical Fights with Classmates

The behavioral literature is replete with studies of aggression in children. They have been methodically and thoroughly reviewed by Ninnes and Glenn (1988), whose work has provided valuable guidance to those treating aggressive pupils. But the victims of aggression have not been studied as much, and treatment is not universally agreed upon. However, it is common for aggressors who fight successfully and for their victims who retaliate to reverse roles frequently. These students are often vying to prove who is the best fighter. They usually enjoy a good fistfight and have been encouraged in this outlook at home or among their friends. Often good fighters have athletic ability. Others are cultivating a macho image.

But this does not account for those who really are not aggressors, the children who are picked on often because they present themselves as weak or different and unwilling to defend themselves in a fair fight. Some actually precipitate the attacks by negative behavior (tripping, pinching, insulting, taking possessions, etc.) that they, of course, try to conceal from the teacher. Others just sit there and pity themselves or even sustain the physical injuries inflicted by the aggressor.

In fact, there now are youngsters who are fascinated with tattoos, writing on themselves, and breaking their skin with pins or knives to write a word or symbol. Some even lightly slash their wrists. If the skin mutilator wants to do the same thing to other children, there are some who welcome it. This behavior can quickly spread through a classroom or school. Teachers, principals, and social workers need to be alert to such happenings and develop both school rules forbidding such activity and cooperation from the home. Meeting with pupils in a group to get them to pledge to stop doing this has been initially successful, but it is too early to judge long-term effects.

Self-mutilation can often be traced to violent television programs and hard rock bands. However, those who have worked with self-injurious behavior point out that there is someone in the child's environment reinforcing him for doing it, even if the reinforcement is negative (Graziano and Mooney, 1984; Liberman, 1972; Lovaas and Bucher, 1974). Very little behavioral research has been carried on with children who are functioning in a regular class but exhibiting self-mutilating behavior. Perhaps it is because educators and others are quick to label the self-mutilator as mentally or emotionally handicapped and therefore ineligible for placement in a regular class.

A great deal has been done with retarded, psychotic, and autistic children who are placed in special classes or institutions. Ross (1981) observes that

Some milder forms of this behavior are also encountered among less profoundly disturbed individuals. In a sense, nail-biting, eyelash-picking, and excessive scratching are forms of self-injury. The hair-pulling, technically known as trichotellomania, that results in large bald areas on the child's head should also be viewed as falling into this category. (p. 354)

Osnes and associates (1989) studied interactions of children in a classroom of mixed pupils labeled normal, emotionally disturbed, and at-risk, for one year. The setting was a two-class public county school with sixteen students from three to seven years old in each class. One class had equal numbers of normal and emotionally disturbed pupils; the other had equal numbers of normal and at-risk students. All participated in the regular curriculum, however, and teachers had been trained to work with both of the populations they served. Every student in the school was observed in this study.

When the emotionally disturbed children entered the school, they were said to present one or more of the following behaviors: aggression, destruction, masturbation, self-stimulation, echolalia, spitting, out-of-seat, off-task, noncompliance, cursing, and social withdrawal. On admission to the school, the at-risk children were described as presenting out-of-seat, off-task, noncompliance, social withdrawal, and verbal disruption.

Applied behavior analysis was used to instruct the pupils in academics and social adjustment. A major ongoing emphasis of the classroom teachers was to promote "nondiscriminatory, integrated play" by providing teacher attention for such interactions. Each child was observed twice a week for initiations that were appropriate or inappropriate, verbal or nonverbal.

Results demonstrated that in all categories the students used appropriate initiations approximately twenty times as often as inappropriate initiations. Differences between groups were insignificant in all areas. "The distribution of initiations by all groups of children toward at-risk and emotionally disturbed children appeared consistent with a primarily integrated, nondiscriminatory, early childhood play setting" (Osnes et al., 1989, p. 12). This study supports the idea that environment can control behavior no matter what a child's behavior is elsewhere.

When schoolchildren engage in fights, behavior therapy does have things to offer the victims. Social skills training, including assertiveness training and desensitization, are possible choices; the behavioral school social worker should be skilled in all the choices. Social skills training is used to help a client change behaviors that are limiting him socially, such as negative interactions with peers or other age groups, aggressive behavior, disturbing mannerisms, and withdrawal. Treatment would involve targeting the problem and proceeding as in any behavioral intervention. Assertiveness training could be included in social skills training (see chapter 6 for details of this method).

Working with the Teacher

A pupil may find himself at odds with his teacher for any number of reasons. Being "turned off" to school because he has not achieved academically has already been mentioned. Or he may not have developed social skills needed for classroom interaction. He may just be following the examples of other students in the class who are aware that the teacher is not in control there.

It could also be that the teacher reacts negatively to the pupil because of some stereotype he represents to her, the poor behavior observed in an older sibling, or a rumor she has heard from other school personnel. Some children react negatively to the entire school because their parents have derogatory attitudes towards the school system generally, the neighborhood, or a particular teacher, based on her reputation or the parents' previous experience with her.

Whatever the source of conflict between teacher and child, it may become the school social worker's responsibility to help right the wrong. In some cases a different teacher could be the answer; this would have to be worked out with the principal. The principal might be reluctant to transfer the student to a different classroom for fear of setting a precedent resulting in other parents or teachers asking for a child to be transferred. In other cases, the parent, teacher, or child might be the appropriate change agent. But if the contingencies cannot be changed, the child will have to alter his reactions to them.

A number of behavioral resources are available to the teacher having trouble managing her class. She may want to study these herself, having been exposed to the behavioral resources by the school social worker. Or the teacher might choose to work with the social worker in instituting and monitoring the needed change. Either approach is appropriate, and the school social worker should be prepared accordingly.

Should the teacher want to improve classroom behavior, Buckley and Walker (1978) offer this set of procedures:

1. Develop individual behavioral and academic goals for each child in the classroom.
2. Decide how often the behavior is currently occurring.
3. Set daily steps.
4. Involve the child.
5. Decide on the environmental change.
6. Record the behavior.
7. Change the program if it is not producing the desired effects.

Maintaining appropriate control in a high school could present special problems, given the gregarious nature of the age group. McAllister and associates (1969) used social reinforcement and social punishment to help a teacher elicit appropriate behavior from the students in her class. Four behaviors were observed: inappropriate talking by students, inappropriate turning around by students, verbal reprimands by the teacher for inappropriate talking or turning around, and praise dispensed by the teacher for appropriate behavior. An experimental group and a control group were determined. Twenty-seven days of baseline were used to record the four behaviors without any restrictions.

On the twenty-eighth day, the teacher applied aversive social consequences for inappropriate talking.... She called the student's name and made a direct, verbal, stern reproof.... When periods of quiet occurred, the teacher socially reinforced the entire class.... Social reinforcement occurred during the first two minutes of class, after each 15-minute period when a lecture or class discussion was taking place, at the end of silent seatwork assignments, and at the end of each class, as appropriate. (p. 279–280)

On the fifty-fourth day, she began socially reinforcing or punishing turning-around behavior in the same way as the talking behavior. The talking behavior was reduced to 5 percent from 100 percent and the turning around reduced to 4.1 percent from 100 percent.

It should be noted here that negative reinforcement was used in the Mc-Allister studies. The students were trying to escape doing their classwork. However, the teacher did not let them do this, so their talking behavior and turning-around behavior were reduced.

Many behavioral studies are available that show how teachers affect the in-class behavior of students. Other studies show how students who come to class with poor behavior can be changed for the better in the classroom. Environment is the key to change, and the change that develops in one setting is not guaranteed to replicate itself in another setting (Wahler, 1969). In other words, behavior in class can be improved, but change may have to be reinstituted as a pupil moves from that class to another one.

McKeown and associates (1975) conducted a study to determine the effects of a behavioral training course on elementary school teachers and the eventual use of the learned techniques in improving children's behavior in the classroom. Results were good in both areas. With reading and participation in a study group, the knowledge of the teachers improved. With the additional information, they were able to increase good behavior in the classroom. Those in a control group who were given no instruction on behavior modification did not obtain such results.

Some of the factors that can improve relationships between the teacher and the entire class or an individual child warrant mention here. Brophy and Good (1970) showed that differential teacher expectations of individual students was a significant factor in academic achievement. O'Leary and Becker (1967) conducted an early study using a token economy to improve deviant behavior of pupils. Token-reinforcement programs have been used frequently and successfully since then to improve classroom behavior. There are many other important related studies, but they are too numerous to mention all of them here.

O'Leary and associates (1970) showed that soft reprimands were more effective than loud ones in dealing with second-grade students. They conducted research on asking a teacher to change just one type of reprimand that she used. This involved substituting a soft reprimand made to a child at his desk for her usual reprimand made in a loud tone of voice so that the entire class heard it.

Two second-grade boys in the same class were studied. Nine types of oppositional behavior were noted during the baseline period when the teacher was asked to use her regular methods. These included such things as out-of-seat behavior, aggression, noise and time off task.

During the first treatment phase the teacher used only soft reprimands. There was a second phase for reversion to baseline (loud reprimand) followed by a third phase, which resumed the soft reprimands. The mean level of disruptive behavior was consistently higher for both boys when loud reprimands were used.

Carter (1972) identifies three types of reinforcers that influence and increase behavior: tangible rewards, social reinforcement, and self-reinforcement. He sees children as progressing from tangible to social and finally to self-reinforcement, the highest level. The classroom teacher should use all of these reinforcers when she can. For maximum effect, the reinforcement should be customized for each child. But this is not always possible when the teacher is dealing with thirty-five to forty pupils on a regular basis. This could be the point where the services of the behavioral school social worker are sought to attempt to move each child from stage to stage.

Tangible rewards are obvious; they are objects given to students, such as stickers, smiley faces, stars, and the like. Social reinforcers include a teacher's smile, a parent's hug, a few words of praise. Self-reinforcement usually occurs when a student thinks an activity is fun or may have previously been disciplined to engage in it. This will vary from individual to individual. Each type of reinforcer may be needed with the same child.

An interesting twist was shown in a study by Graubard and associates (1971) when students tried to change the teacher's behavior. The researcher worked with special education and minority children who were poorly received by both teachers and regular-education, non-minority pupils. Within the school where the experimenters worked, teachers scapegoated these children and the other students ridiculed them.

Seven students between the ages of twelve and fifteen were chosen from the special education and minority groups. They were trained as behavioral engineers. For half a day, the behavioral-engineer pupils were trained in keeping records of comments by teachers and students which they then sorted into good and bad comments.

The first phase of the intervention was to improve relations with the teachers in the regular classes they attended. The children were trained to make eye contact with the teacher and say such things as, "Gee, it makes me feel good and work so much better when you praise me," or "I like the way you teach that lesson." They learned to show up early for classes, sit up straight, and ask for extra work. They learned to break eye contact when a teacher scolded them.

In four weeks, the relationships between teachers and students changed dramatically. There were an average of eight positive contacts between them during baseline and thirty-two after four weeks of intervention. The opposite scores were seen in negative comments, which had been eighteen per week during baseline and became zero after four weeks of intervention.

The second phase of this study involved the students in the experiment working with regular students. The special education and minority children had been called such names as "retards" or "rejects from the funny farm." These project participants listed the names of students who harassed them, their troublesome behaviors, and those they wanted to spend more time with. They followed this with training in breaking eye contact and ignoring the remarks of the harassers. They were also taught to share candy or toys, give compliments, and initiate activities with students they liked.

As had the teachers, the students responded well. The average number of positive contacts between special and regular pupils increased from four to eighteen. Hostile comments decreased from twenty-six to six. Teasing and negative physical contacts decreased, and positive behaviors, including such things as invitations to parties and ball games, increased.

Competition is a basic motivating force in Western society, and it can be seen among children at very early ages. The identification of members of communities with their sports teams has been likened to civil religion. Therefore, teams organized in classrooms represent an appealing and usually successful technique for improving children's behavior. Teams put the teacher fully and effectively in control, helping her in her efforts to establish positive working relations with each student in the class.

In 1989, Daoust and associates studied the use of behavioral methods by coaches of twelve-year-olds playing on baseball teams. Behavioral interventions are emerging as important techniques for the rapidly increasing numbers of coaches of amateur teams and coaches showing interest in issues beyond the physical skill of their players. The techniques could be especially helpful for coaches who see concentration, perseverance, showing respect, and cooperation as important traits to be fostered in amateur athletics.

Daoust and associates examined twelve-year-olds in two teams of twenty-four members each. One team served as a control group and the other as the experimental group. A behavioral "Code of Conduct" which contained positive programming and a decelerative component was central to the research with the experimental group. At the start, the control group's record of runs scored, games won, games tied, and games lost by one, two, or more runs was better than the experimental group's. After the experiment, the two teams reversed their records.

Treatment was conducted during the regular baseball season. At the outset of the season, both teams received the same treatment, which included reinforcement and reprimand procedures. The head coaches heavily praised the teams in public and in private. The Code of Conduct had not been written yet, so the coaches explained it in detail to members and to the entire team in meetings following the games. Also, the coaches verbally reprimanded players inconsistently during and after games.

At midseason, the control group continued as described above, but the experimental group adopted a new plan. The written Code of Conduct was formally introduced at a meeting with all players and coaches present. Ten sporting behaviors were identified, and the players were told that a violation would result in their being benched or moved to a less-preferred position on the team for a minimum of three innings. After the meeting, the code was conspicuously posted inside the dugout at the start of every game, while the coach reminded everyone that the rules were in effect. Those observing the code were reinforced with praise given in public and private.

The researchers emphasized several points. They noted that it is important to enforce the behavioral conditions during the playing season because just using them during practice will not generalize to the actual games. Also, the intervention greatly reduces tensions during the play-offs, when tensions usually run high. When used with a reinforcing procedure and clear rules of conduct, the deceleration program of benching or changing position was helpful. The experimenters see this study as an initial one in the area of using behavioral techniques in sports, but they think it holds promise for the future.

Possibly the most popular in-class behavioral interventions to date have been the Good Behavior Game (Barrish et al., 1969) and the Spelling Game (Delquadri et al., 1983). Team competition in the classroom is an integral factor in each. In the Spelling Game, team competition is effectively combined with peer tutoring.

Greenwood and associates (1987) conducted a large-scale study of 211 inner-city pupils in four schools during their first- and second-grade school years, using the Spelling Game.

Analysis of group and individual results indicated that (a) both teacher instructional procedures and classwide peer tutoring were effective in increasing spelling performance above pretest levels, (b) peer tutoring produced statistically greater gains relative to the teachers' procedures for both low and high student groups formed on pretest levels, (c) these outcomes were representative of groups, classes, individuals, and years during the project, and (d) participant satisfaction with the program was generally high. A separate analysis of the social importance of treatment outcome revealed differential findings for low and high groups related to pretest levels. (p. 151)

Slaughter (1988), a school social worker at the LaGrange Area Department of Special Education in LaGrange, Illinois, suggests several pitfalls to avoid when using the Spelling Game as well as solutions to them should they occur. She advises preteaching the words before tutoring, because some students do not know how to say them. To avoid the students' being inaccurate or dishonest in totaling points, she recommends collection of all the papers and spot checking points earned, giving extra points to those who have added accurately and reported points honestly. If pupils cheat, record a zero for the day. If the students take too long to get ready to tutor, wait a reasonable length of time, reset the timer, and begin the game. This will teach them that they lose points if they waste time.

In case there is an uneven number of pupils on a team, fill in with a tutor or an aide, Slaughter advises. Another way to handle uneven numbers on teams is to prorate the points. For example, find the average (mean) score for the team and add that to the total. Should a team member be absent or have to leave the room, prorate the points and assign a tutor to the team.

If a tutor makes critical comments about the tutees, counteract this by awarding bonus points for both good tutoring and praise offered by the tutor to the tutees. In fact, the teacher should be sure to train the tutor in detail in all aspects of his job, preferring overtraining to undertraining him.

Harper and Mallette (1989) experimented with using peer tutors to teach spelling to mildly retarded students in the primary grades. They specifically addressed three issues. (1) What additional skills are needed by tutors who are classmates and have mastered the spelling being taught? (2) How much training do children in a class for the mildly retarded need to implement the procedures successfully? (3) In view of the competitive nature of classwide peer tutoring, would there be negative social outcomes among tutors, tutees, and the rest of the class?

Basically, the same procedure outlined in the Delquadri Spelling Game (1983) was followed by the tutors. Six male and six female tutees were involved over thirteen weeks. It was established that classwide peer tutors can be used with primary mildly retarded students. The only skill needed by the tutors is the ability to read words and match tutee performance to the sample. Training was easily accomplished and there were no negative social outcomes. Spelling accuracy increased sixty percent among tutees.

The school social worker may want to meet with small groups needing behavioral improvement. Hinds and Roehlke (1970) studied forty children in grades three, four, and five who had behavior problems. They were divided into eight groups of five students each. Four groups received treatment and the other four served as controls. They attended counseling sessions in a setting inside the school building but away from the classroom. Each group held biweekly sessions for ten weeks. During this time, the control groups remained in the classroom and did not come together in groups.

The behaviors to be changed were considered interfering behaviors. They included inattention or physical activity not related to classroom activities, nonparticipation or restricted class participation, verbal behavior not related to classroom activity, negative interaction with peers or teachers, and submission or domination in small groups. Adaptive behaviors were also measured, covering attention to activities, concentration, participation, appropriate interaction with teachers or peers, and small-group behaviors such as initiating interactions with others, not interrupting or dominating others, supporting others, and paying attention.

Treatment consisted of systematic reinforcement to shape the children's behaviors in favor of adaptive responses and to extinguish inappropriate behaviors. A specific problem to work on during group sessions was targeted for each student and explained to him. He then earned points for working on his own specified problem, having been briefed ahead of time on exactly what he had to do to acquire the points. The point system was like playing a game for many. During the ten weeks the groups met, emphasis was shifted from point reinforcement to social reinforcement, resulting in intermittent schedules of reinforcement.

Although there were no significant differences between the two groups at the start, by the fourth and tenth weeks and at the end there were distinguishable increases in adaptive behaviors in the experimental group. Also, behaviors interfering with learning were diminished for the experimental group after counseling.

Stedman and Peterson (1971) studied eight boys aged ten to 12.5 years. Some of the boys had serious acting-out behavior in the classroom and others exhibited withdrawn behavior. Every meeting started with a brief discussion of plans for the session and moved quickly into a planned activity. Tokens were given at predetermined intervals for predefined good behavior. Data showed that in-class behavior was improved as a result of the intervention.

Inordinate Demands for Attention

Children who are constantly demanding attention from school personnel fall into several categories. There are those who are hyperactive, those who do no academic work unless they are given one-on-one attention, and those who persist in breaking school rules. All are suitable referrals for the school social worker.

That hyperactivity can be controlled by adult attention was shown by Allen and associates (1967). However, medication has often been prescribed for these children by physicians encouraged to do so by the children's teachers, parents, or both, clouding the results of behavioral research. In fact, whether to use behavioral intervention or medication has become such an issue that research has been inhibited.

School personnel are not anxious to cooperate in research that requires children who have been medicated to be taken off the medication in order to be observed in their natural state. Likewise, behaviorists have not wanted to interfere with a medical prescription. There is much debate about the circumstances under which these children can best achieve academically. While some research has come forth on the use of behavioral methods rather than medication, still more is needed to be convincing (Mash and Barkley, 1989).

Evidence that focusing on academic skills will decrease hyperactivity has already been alluded to in the discussion of the Ayllon and Roberts (1974) study that established that academic achievement could improve behavior. In 1975, Ayllon and associates had focused on academic improvement decreasing hyperactivity. Both studies depended on systematic reinforcement by teachers and parents. Graziano and Mooney (1984) found that "building up identified skills in specific deficit areas rather than reducing the generalized hyperactivity as decremental approaches have . . . may prove to be effective alternatives to medication" (p. 259).

The problem of the child who will work only with one-on-one attention has to be explored in terms of what is really happening. Some such pupils are simply being called on to do work for which they have no background because they have had little enrichment at home or they have moved frequently. Frequent moves usually result in gaps in a child's education and time missed from school. Others just do not have the ability to measure up to the level of the classes they are in. In such a situation, a change of class placement or remaining in the class and receiving individual tutoring may be the answer. Otherwise, special education or reading or mathematics clinics might be indicated.

However, some children also have been trained at home or in school to do academic work only in one-on-one situations with an adult attending to them. The school social worker can help these children by setting up behavioral interventions such as contingency management or peer tutoring that will gradually wean the child away from the one-on-one situation. Back-up by the parents is also usually needed for such a problem.

Children who constantly break rules in class will have to be handled by the teacher who makes the rules and enforces them. The school social worker can be useful to a teacher in this position, most often by helping the teacher set up a contingency contract to deal with these behaviors (Homme 1974).

Stealing and Lying

According to Patterson (1976):

There are two problems that often go with stealing: wandering and lying. Most children who steal are allowed to spend a great deal of time roaming around unsupervised by adults. They are often out late at night, sometimes overnight. Most of the weekend they are off on their own.... There are a small number who do not wander about stealing from the community. They steal mainly from their parents.... The problem there is not so much a child given more freedom than he can handle, but instead a battle between parent and child. (p. 106)

Patterson advises handling these problems by setting up a contract with the child and parent in which stealing and lying require doing prespecified amounts of work, and not engaging in these activities is rewarded. Limiting the child's opportunities to be outside on his own is also a major part of Patterson's program. Jehu and associates (1972) also advise using multiple techniques in treating such problems as stealing, lying, and cheating.

Reid and Hendriks (1973) studied the families of fourteen boys who stole. They found that the families had "an incredible level of family disorganization and diffusion, a near-total absence of family activities, and a lack of general parenting skills" (p. 218). They had to teach parents and children to relate more closely to each other before they could deal with issues of stealing. If the stealing occurred outside the home, parents tended to ignore it. However, when it was brought closer to them by such circumstances as the authorities' taking the boy to a detention center until the parents picked him up, it became more real.

Switzer and associates (1977) worked with three second-grade classes in which two or three thefts by pupils were reported every day. A lecture approach was used by the teacher to no avail. This was followed by a group contingency intervention in which the teacher told the class every morning that they could have ten minutes of free time after their snack if she found that nothing was missing.

If nothing was stolen she would praise them. However, if something was missing the teacher would tell the class what was missing and say that she was going out of the room; if the items were placed on her desk by the time she returned they could have free time as usual. On the other hand, if they failed to return the items, they would have to sit quietly at their desks and eat their snacks and then put their heads on their desks when they finished. The teacher left the room for two or three minutes as scheduled. The stealing behavior was immediately reduced and eventually discontinued.

Parsons (1989) considers lying a complex issue. He distinguishes two components of lying: misinformation (falsification) and non-information (concealment). "Verbal lying takes place in many contexts," he says, "notably where there is competition or conflict involving positive consequences such as money or sexual gratification, or involving negative consequences such as damage or even death" (p. 2).

If several people witness an accident, their stories will differ, sometimes dramatically. This is very clear when children fight on a school playground. It could be out of fear of reprisals, the excitement of the moment that clouded their perception, poor memory or comprehension, or a rich fantasy life. Whatever the reason, there usually are many versions of reported events where misbehavior could be involved. In such circumstances, it is important to clarify what really happened should there be a violation of school rules requiring punishment.

Some school personnel are quick to say a child is lying or brand him a liar without taking into account what is precipitating the story being told. There are some children who come from homes where facts are clouded even when no evil purpose is involved. However, some children could be so embarrassed, frightened, or threatened by parents or by what occurs at home that interrogation by an adult will cause them great stress or even pain. The school social worker might be able to intercede in such circumstances and offer the child support as well as to try to elicit understanding on the part of school personnel. However, the social worker must be careful to sort out what course to follow to best improve the child's functioning in school.

Speech Problems

There are several conditions characterized by limited speech, such as echolalia, reluctant speech, and elective mutism, that have been observed among schoolchildren. They typically occur in the early school years. The school social worker might want to consult with the speech therapist in some of these cases. However, all have been dealt with in behavior therapy.

Echolalia is a condition in which a person repeats a word or phrase many times after it has been spoken to him. Often the repetition does not respond to what the other person is trying to interact with him about. Echolalia is common among developmentally delayed persons and is said to be one possible clue in diagnosing their condition.

Reluctant speech refers to underdeveloped speech. The person may not have matured to the point of using correct interactive speech. This is not a selective condition on the child's part. It is just an ability he does not yet have. With careful training, development can be accelerated.

Elective speech refers to children who may carry on an intelligent conversation in one setting but then choose not to do so in another. In school, it is seen among bright pupils who talk fluently at home. They are usually above-average students who perform well in other academic ways but refuse to speak. This is usually very frustrating to a teacher who wants her more capable students to excel in all areas.

Echolalia and reluctant speech are often developmental conditions in profoundly handicapped children. Ross (1981) states that "unlike the language problems of autistic and retarded children . . . elective mutism is a performance deficit in that the child fails to emit verbal behavior only under specific stimulus conditions" (p. 85).

Elective mutism is sometimes ignored by the teacher because the child is performing well in all other areas in school. But such a pupil is more likely to be referred to the school social worker anyway, as soon as someone in authority interprets his speaking only in certain circumstances as oppositional behavior. However, except for the elective mutism, he is typically well-behaved and handles written work well. In fact, his life outside school is usually in good order.

Individual cases of elective mutism have been handled by behavior therapists with varying success. However, these interventions have been unsystematic, uncontrolled single-case designs; no conclusions can be drawn about the overall success of the method.

One study by Scott (1977) did have good results in the treatment of an electively mute girl, and it eventually was generalized to her school situation. This intervention started with the girl's talking alone into a tape recorder in a relaxed setting. The therapist then entered casually as the girl continued talking. Eventually, more individuals were introduced into the setting. One of these was her classroom teacher. Through small incremental steps, she was eventually able to speak in front of the class and in front of guests at home.

Reluctant speech is usually related to a delayed stage of a young child's speech development. Contingency-management techniques have been successfully used to treat this problem (Williamson et al., 1977). Often it is treated outside school before the child is of school age. If it is treated in school, the encouragement of the rest of the class can be helpful, so long as it does not overwhelm the child. Once treatment is initiated, progress is usually rapid.

Echolalic children show ability to use words, but not necessarily as a basis of communication. The child will repeat a phrase of some statement or question made to him. He might even say it again and again throughout the day. In the development of speech in echolalic children, Risley and Wolf (1967) summarized their methods as

(1) shaping and imitation training for the development of speech; (2) fading in of new stimuli and fading out of verbal prompts to transfer the speech from imitative control to control by appropriate stimulus conditions; and (3) extinction and time out from reinforcement for the reduction of inappropriate behavior in conjunction with the differential reinforcement of appropriate responses which are incompatible with the inappropriate behavior. (p. 73)

Most of the speech problems discussed here that arise in the classroom can be behaviorally treated by the school social worker. They must, of course, be brought to her attention first. Next, a person or persons from the child's environment who will work on the problem has to be identified. Then, with data collection, targeting the problem, and following through on the agreed-on program, good results can usually be achieved.

Withdrawn Behavior

Just because a child is withdrawn is no proof that he is socially maladjusted. However, if such behavior is being caused by something harmful in his life, it is a matter for concern. A rule of thumb for the school social worker in determining if treatment is needed would be whether such behavior is creating problems for the child. Some people just prefer to be this way and are not troubled by appearing withdrawn (Ross, 1981). Some teachers worry about these children, especially the bright ones.

The school social worker should consider possible inhibiting factors in children who appear withdrawn. Some of these children could be responding to a culture pattern wherein the child is expected to sit quietly and do what he is told. Others come from homes where another language is spoken and are not proficient enough in English to respond comfortably. Still others may be bused to enhance integration and feel out of place because they are in a racial or ethnic minority in their school.

Should the school social worker decide that a withdrawn child is to be worked with, there are examples in the behavioral experience. A case in point was described by Liberman (1972). In his study, an extremely withdrawn and adult-oriented four-year-old girl was reinforced with praise by her teacher for child-oriented responses. To increase her opportunities to interact, the teacher had her go with other children into her play area.

With these interventions, the pupil's interactions tripled. When reversal to baseline was resumed, her interactions dropped precipitously, even in the play area. When the program was reestablished, her interactive behavior improved rapidly. Finally, "the girl's playing and cooperating with other children was solidified by switching to intermittent reinforcement and by the children and the social games taking over the reinforcing function from the teacher" (p. 279).

Similarly, Sheldon (1982) cites the case of a class where one black child joined a class of white students. The teachers did not see him as fitting in, and he sat alone in the class. When the teacher's approach changed and the other students began offering approval and sweets (candy) on a regular basis, his interactive behavior improved.

A variety of other techniques have been used by teachers and behavior therapists to modify withdrawn behavior in children in school. These have included filmed modeling, flooding, direct social skills training of children, and teacher training (Graziano and Mooney, 1984). However, it has not always been clear in the research that the children considered withdrawn have really found their behaviors problematic to themselves.

BEHAVIOR PROBLEMS AROUND THE SCHOOL

Violation of school rules is the usual kind of behavior problem out of the classroom but on school property that the school social worker addresses. If the rules and the consequences of not observing them have not been made very clear to pupils and teacher, chaos results. Most schools do communicate the procedures, but some better than others. Also, some rules are better conceived and presented and therefore more effective than others.

If a child willfully chooses to disobey the rules continuously, he is certainly a case for the school social worker. In some instances, such children will work with her and make efforts to improve. In other cases, it is necessary to work with the family. Some children who move frequently or live in chaotic circumstances may simply need to learn what the rules are and then get specific training in observing them.

Law enforcement authorities usually become involved when children disobey the rules of society. If this happens to a child in the school where the school social worker is assigned, she will want to work with the police, courts, and other community agencies that may or should be involved (see chapter 5).

When a student breaks criminal laws inside the school, the principal has to report the incident to the police. Unlawful acts might include defacing school property, bringing illegal items such as weapons or drugs to school, major thefts of school property or an individual's possessions, and threatening or inflicting injury on other people.

Sometimes residents of the neighborhood where the school is located will come to the school and ask for its cooperation in controlling the out-of-school behavior of a student or students. The school should be interested in good relations with the community. However, an illegal act must be reported by the person against whom it occurred or who witnessed it. Before advising helpful procedures to the neighbors, it is important to know both sides of the case.

Fights are probably the most common problems encountered on a daily basis in school. Children usually follow their own unwritten rules governing school fights. These rules are understood among the students, even though they have never been discussed or arrived at by mutual consent. However, when brought to the school office to account for themselves, children reveal certain information about the mores of fighting. For example, an insult to one's mother is an unconditional reason to retaliate.

There are a number of other guidelines followed in relation to fights. A male aggressor's striking a younger child or a girl is cause to retaliate, especially for the victim's relative. However, some girls are able aggressors. Children who are overprotected by their parents, especially if their parents are visible on a regular basis (such as children of parents who hang around the playground and even fight with other children themselves) are seen as fair game.

If the child picked on reacts by crying or answering taunts with similar taunts he will become a constant target. He is less apt to be picked on if he does not react to such provocation. Also, if a group attacks just one individual, it is considered unacceptable, and that individual has the right to collect his own group of fighters to help him retaliate. Often parents will defend their children and encourage them to fight back on the basis of such rules.

Pupils who engage in physical and verbal fights inevitably require the time and skills of school personnel. In fact, a designated member of the faculty, such as the assistant principal, is often known as the school disciplinarian. The disciplinarian typically has to deal with pupils sent to the school office by teachers or anyone else who witnessed the disruptive behavior. If the misbehavior is severe enough, such as injuring another child or teacher or bringing illegal weapons to school, the police may have to be called and a suspension issued.

When a student is continuously breaking the law or getting suspended or sent to the office, he might be referred by school personnel for a case-study evaluation for special education and placement in a program for behavior-disordered students. His teacher will be asked to keep an anecdotal record, which is a daily log of his unacceptable behaviors. The keeping of such a record usually emphasizes the child's unacceptable behavior, and the extra attention might even encourage it.

When a school social worker is asked to work with a student involved in fights in school, she has to determine where the impetus for fighting is originating. It could be that the classroom is poorly controlled or that a teacher has designated the child as a "problem" to divert blame from herself. Or it might be that the pupil is underachieving and is more successful in fights or disruptive behavior than in academics. He could be seeking to divert attention from his lack of academic achievement.

Some students come from homes or cultures where fights are modeled continuously or are needed for survival. Others are responding to other pressures as already discussed. Whatever the source, the school social worker has to go to the designated pupils to implement an individualized treatment program to correct the problem.

There are some non-behavioral social workers who reason that they should not take a position against the behavior of a person in treatment. But the social worker's job is precisely to help a person adjust to society. The school social worker must ever be mindful that she is there to teach and train children to live in the world. To forget this would be irresponsible.

The research in the field provides guidance for working with aggressive children. The study (Pinkston et al., 1973) of treatment of a preschool child who made continuous verbal and motor attacks on other children "demonstrated the existent role of contingent teacher attention in maintaining a preschool child's aggression to his peers, as well as an imposed use of contingent teacher attention to increase his low peer interaction" (p. 115).

Bernal and associates (1968) dramatically decreased abusive behavior in an 8.5-year-old child. He was described as engaging in "tantrums, assaultiveness, threats, etc., which are highly aversive and serve to render others helpless in controlling him" (p. 1). The researchers assumed that the behavior was learned from and reinforced by the parents, and the treatment plan was designed with this in mind. The mother systematically ignored his poor behavior and told him specifically what behaviors she approved, then warmly praised him for his compliance. Eventually the boy's behavior improved.

Sheldon (1982) observes that sometimes a child's behavior is in response to contingencies that the social worker cannot change, such as peer pressure. The focus of treatment then has to be on changing the child's reactions to the contingencies. He points out that "although it makes sense to attack the problem of bullying at school . . . quite often this is impossible, and so we are left with the option of changing the client's own responses so that bullying and exploitation become less reinforcing for those who engage in it" (p. 181).

Some children exhibit nervous habits that their classmates, teachers, or parents find annoying. These sometimes cause the child embarrassment and difficulties in school. Azrin and Nunn (1977) detailed treatment of these habits. They dealt with nail biting, cuticle biting, nail picking, hair pulling, stuttering, nervous tics, lisping, thumb or finger sucking, shoulder or head jerking, eye blinking, squinting, nervous blushing and perspiring, teeth grinding, tongue thrusting, gum sucking, trembling hands, head shaking, hand and foot tapping, and doodling.

They created a basic method for dealing with all of these. However, they caution that while they have had success with the method in treating lisping, tongue thrusting, teeth grinding, cheek biting, and nervous blushing, their experience at the time of publication was not sufficient to claim it as a proven method for dealing with these problems.

Usually only one session was held with a person wanting to cure his habit. The average reduction was about 99.5 percent at the end of six months. What few relapses occurred were handled by the client himself, or by the client's phone call to the counselor. But more than 80 percent of the more than 300 people treated had no relapse.

To minimize the need for advanced skills in treating such people, Azrin and Nunn's clients were asked to bring a friend along. That friend was then given written instructions and was able to administer the treatment. It was suggested that a person with a nervous habit ask for help himself. If he appeared to need help, he would likely become embarrassed if a friend mentioned it.

Treatment follows a basic behavioral model. The client first reviews all of the times he has been inconvenienced by the habit and becomes sensitive to its details. He keeps a record of times the habit occurs throughout the treatment period. He is then taught a behavior incompatible with the nervous habit and uses it to interrupt the old habit as soon as it starts. He practices the new habit often, so that its use is easy. Also, he uses the new habit whenever it seems the old one will resume. To do that, he must learn what antecedents set the habit in motion. The client learns how to relax when nervous, especially in situations where the habit was used in the past. Then he asks his friends to support him with encouragement when he has overcome the habit. The client rehearses the new behavior in imagined situations and then seeks out situations where he will have to put it into use.

4

HOME BEHAVIOR PROBLEMS
RELATED TO SCHOOL

The school social worker deals with home problems as they affect the child's functioning in school. Some school faculty members get curious about events in a child's life that intrigue them or about which they are judgmental. At times the school social worker has to refuse to enter a situation at home because it is not related to the student's in-school behavior. Also, at times school personnel erroneously assume that because a pupil experienced something at home or in the community, he will have a particular reaction. Again, the school social worker will have to address this problem.

In handling home-related problems, the school social worker has to be aware of the changing nature of families in Western society. No longer can it be expected that children will be living with their natural parents and siblings, surrounded by loving grandparents, aunts, uncles, and cousins. A school social worker will come across every possible variety of home setting.

There will be some intact, stable families, but many of the cases referred involve children living in makeshift, deteriorated, or demoralized circumstances. Many children are even raising themselves. Some families move frequently, changing their children's schools. Others simply have no homes.

Some critics see the "crisis in parenting" as the number-one problem for American schools. The permissiveness of American society towards everyone, including children, the high value placed on consumer goods, the need to have at least two incomes to support a family with children, the fractured family, and the lack of affordable housing are only a partial list of factors underlying this crisis. Parents are unsure of themselves when it comes to dealing with their children. They may also be trying to raise their offspring without a proper environment or adequate physical and moral resources.

The conflicts in home life constantly challenge the social worker's ability to deal effectively with some students. George is a case in point. He is an exceptionally intelligent ten-year-old. But he was born with fetal substance abuse syndrome, including some neurological damage, causing him to be hyperactive and disorganized. Still, he learns very quickly and is a handsome, appealing child able to get most things he really wants. For example, he managed to attend three camps one summer by arranging full scholarships at all of them.

George is much more personable than his mother, who suffered brain damage and diminished intelligence from her substance use; she operates on a much lower intellectual level than does her son. However, George's mother really cares for him, and she will cooperate in anything that the school asks of her. George's father is an alcoholic with no respect for education. The nearest he ever gets to George's school is when he drives the mother there on rare occasions. But even then he refuses to enter the building.

George's father is totally irresponsible at home. His work is erratic, and George never knows if his father will be there when he returns from school. Since his mother works long hours to bring in a regular income, she is there only very early in the morning and at night. She does consistently encourage him to bring home his books and homework assignments and even phones the school social worker daily to discuss the homework. But when the father is at home with George, he discourages him from doing homework and takes him places on impulse. As a result, George rarely brings home the books and assignments needed to do his homework.

In school, George resists doing his classwork, and his desk is so disorganized that he spends a great deal of time looking for what he needs. He has received help from a program for the learning disabled; that teacher provided him with one-to-one teaching when she was able to manage it. He responded to it and did the work required. Otherwise, he did not do schoolwork with any consistency.

In spite of all the obstacles, George scores very high whenever a test is given in class. School personnel have worked hard to get him to improve his study habits, but without success. He enjoys playing a game with his mother and his teachers, the objective of which is to pass the tests without studying, thereby keeping the adults working on him. The only person from whom he gets approval for this is his father.

The substance abuse by his parents that has resulted in his mother's diminished intellectual functioning and his father's irresponsible behavior are clearly factors in George's school adjustment. These present challenges to the school social worker, who must avoid getting caught up in George's game plan.

Some problems that affect behavior in school can be treated in the home. When a behavior observed in school is also occurring at home, treatment at home and in school are the best approach (Wahler, 1969). Home-based conditions that affect in-school behavior on which there has been research in the field of applied behavior analysis include truancy and school phobias, enuresis and encopresis, problems with homework, transferring schools, child abuse, and sleep problems. Parent training, a home-based procedure that can greatly influence academic achievement, is explored in chapter 7 on parent training.

TRUANCY

Truancy is an ongoing problem for public education in the United States because school attendance is mandated by law. Truant officers are employed by school districts to enforce this law. They know many of the families referred to the school social worker and can be very helpful to her as they work together for the benefit of children.

A number of these families are so deteriorated and malfunctioning that a child's school attendance becomes just one more problem to overwhelm them. Therefore, the pupil often must get himself to school or be overseen or accompanied by his older sibling. The older sibling may be a school dropout already or barely managing to get himself to school, let alone his younger brother or sister. Sometimes a pupil is kept home to baby-sit a younger child.

SCHOOL PHOBIAS

Behavior analysts have distinguished between truants and school phobics. Wilson and Franks (1982) indicate that "the school phobic is usually characterized by fear and anxiety, whereas the school truant is characterized by delinquent behavior" (p. 461). School phobias have fascinated behavior therapists and comprise their largest area of research into children's fears.

Before 1960 there were very few published reports of child fears. Since then, most of these studies have been single-subject designs (Graziano and Mooney, 1984). Of papers written on behavioral treatment of fears from 1960 to 1984, seventy-seven of the 125 children studied had school phobias. This indicates a higher number of children referred for school phobias than for other fears, possibly because of the legal requirements and strong cultural values attached to school attendance.

The case of Valerie, an eight-year-old black child suffering from school phobia, has been widely studied (Ayllon et al., 1970). She was considered to have zero chance of improvement at the start of the intervention. But school attendance started quickly after the onset of treatment, and it was maintained with no "symptom substitution" noticed through the nine months of follow-up.

The first step in treatment was to get the mother to withdraw very pleasant home reinforcers that kept Valerie from going to school. These included sleeping an hour later than her siblings after they left for school, following mother to work until she was out of sight, staying at the neighbor's house where she pored over a mail-order toy catalogue, or playing outside. Sometimes she had money that she could spend on candy, gum, or soft drinks. After the home reinforcers were noted, a home-based reinforcement program for school attendance was instituted. It featured ignoring and greatly reducing rewards for refusal to go to school.

Valerie's return to regular school attendance was accomplished by full cooperation between school and home. The needed interventions could be carried out in both settings. A great many rewards pleasing to the child were used in both places when Valerie met expectations.

At one point, when her mother waited for her at school, Valerie did not arrive. Her mother trudged back home in the rain and was so angry when she got home that she spanked Valerie. After this, the return to school attendance behavior was accomplished. Once back in school, as Valerie attended regularly, her academic functioning improved. The interventions used with Valerie could be adapted to other cases by the school social worker and truant officer working together. The effect of the spanking by mother can be seen as negative reinforcement that had very important results in achieving treatment goals (Iwata, 1987; Townsley, 1989).

Houlihan and Jones (1989) took a somewhat different approach in treating a thirteen-year-old boy's school phobia. This boy, William, had not attended school for a year, and previous treatments for school phobia had failed. He was a seventh grader of average to high-average ability. He was treated with *in vivo* desensitization, "the graduated exposure to items on the fear stimulus dimension in the actual situation" (p. 6).

William's presenting problems were "excessive and unrealistic concern about competence in social and academic areas" (p. 8). He frequently reported somatic (abdominal) complaints, was tense and unable to relax, and refused to attend school, which he related to great anxiety in that setting. At home, he seemed to engage in ritualistic hand washing when he thought about school and social performance. The goals of the intervention were to "increase school attendance to normal levels and decrease William's depression" (p. 10).

The first day of treatment started with William and his behavioral therapist sitting on the steps of the empty school outside school hours. The therapist saw this as only mildly anxiety provoking. Next, William and the therapist walked the halls of the school while class was in session and a few people were there. From there, they went to the therapist's office to talk for five minutes about the fun aspects of attending school. At that time, William's homeroom teacher joined them and continued talking for another five minutes about the positive aspects of school.

For the next four days, the second phase was implemented. William's time in school was gradually increased to three hours. During this time, he and the therapist sat in the rear of the homeroom teacher's class with the students present. All subsequent treatment was with the students there.

During the four days, the therapist left the room for increasingly longer periods of time. He was there for fifty minutes the first day, thirty minutes the second day, and ten minutes on the third and fourth days. William remained in the same classroom during class changes. During this time, he was in attendance for the last three hours of school so that he could be dismissed with the rest of the pupils.

The third phase lasted five days. It began with the therapist eating lunch with William in the school lunchroom, which added a half hour to the time they were in the school building. During lunch, the therapist engaged William and some other students in conversation. After lunch, William sat isolated from the rest of the class for three hours a day in his homeroom with the therapist.

On the second day, William did not appear for lunch. He was found wandering in the hall and told the therapist he had forgotten his lunch money and was afraid of a confrontation with the lunchroom personnel. An arrangement was made with the principal's office for William to go there whenever this happened again.

During the last three of the five days of phase three, the therapist faded his attendance at lunch. As with the time in back of the class, the therapist spent thirty minutes at lunch the first day; twenty minutes the second day; and ten minutes on days three, four, and five.

The fourth phase of treatment lasted five more days. William spent seven hours a day in school, with all in-class time in his homeroom. Having explained what he would do ahead of time, the therapist spent the first ten minutes of two class periods each day with William.

The fifth phase was five weeks long. William attended one new additional classroom besides his homeroom each week. Teachers who would be supportive were chosen and prepared for his arrival. The therapist walked him to class for the first ten minutes of each new class. The same day, the therapist attended another class with William for ten minutes, as well as for the five-minute break between classes, on an intermittent basis.

During the fifth level of treatment, by the end of the first quarter William was spending two class periods in his homeroom and five in other classes. William then asked for a regular schedule without the therapist being there. For the rest of the school year, from time to time the therapist attended a randomly selected class for a ten-minute visit.

William's attendance in seventh grade was 152 out of a possible 180 days. A year's follow-up showed that he spent 166 out of 180 days in school during eighth grade. His grades went from C's in seventh grade to B's in eighth grade. In addition, his depression and hand washing were decreased.

The researchers considered the intervention with William a success. However, they point out that it will need replication to assure validity. They also recommend more careful pretreatment evaluation and more careful data collection throughout. This treatment appears to be a procedure that a school social worker could change or moderate for a client.

Last (1985) also reported using *in vivo* treatment with a school phobic child. Careful testing led to a diagnosis of separation anxiety in a sixteen-year-old girl named Mary. She was chronically avoiding attending school not out of fear of school but rather fear of being away from her mother.

Mary had been able to attend elementary school regularly, but at age fourteen, after having experimented with marijuana, she had a panic attack. After this, her fears of leaving her mother became apparent and worsened over time. She had refused to attend school and was being tutored at home. She underwent family therapy, individual psychotherapy, and relaxation training over two years, but none was effective in alleviating her fears.

Last initiated treatment by telling Mary she would have to expose herself to the very things she feared repeatedly and for long periods of time. She was reluctant to do this, but after several lengthy sessions she agreed to exposure therapy. She then participated in twelve treatment sessions of two and a half hours each. The time was divided between being exposed to increasingly difficult situations and discussions of homework and treatment progress.

Mary's mother's help was enlisted to modify her daughter's behavior. Her mother had been reinforcing Mary's avoidance behavior by attending to it. She was told instead to ignore her daughter's negative behavior (such as crying and sobbing to avoid situations) and to reward her positive actions with attention and praise.

The exposure therapy gradually increased from easier to more-difficult tasks. Mary was asked to remain in situations that evoked high anxiety until she could relax. This was done to help her associate escape responses with relief from discomfort. Along with this, Mary was required to engage in structured homework sessions at home, using her mother as therapist.

Thus she exposed herself to situations at home as well as in the therapist's office to generalize the effects of treatment. She began by getting dressed for school, then driving there with mother and entering. After three weeks of this, she attended her mathematics class with her mother waiting outside. The next week she did this without her mother being on the school property. Two weeks later, she attended school full-time on a regular basis.

Mary continued to expose herself to other fearful situations. After twelve weeks of therapy, weekly sessions were discontinued by mutual consent. Mary was then encouraged to practice exposure to fears on a daily basis. After six weeks, her mother reported that Mary was showing some reluctance to attend school. It turned out that the mother was attending to signs of fear and anxiety in Mary out of her own fears. When she stopped this, progress resumed. After six months, the therapist checked and found that gains had been maintained.

Waltzer (1984) used a behavioral group approach with chronic truants in a junior high school. Usually, such students received some form of punishment for repeated unexcused nonattendance, such as in-school and out-of-school suspensions, grade reductions, or additional school hours. Waltzer hypothesized that this punishment led to more nonattendance and unintended learning of other dysfunctional behaviors. This might result in the truants' associating punishment with their teachers, the school building, their school work, and other school-related items. These could result in temporary withdrawal from school, dropping out, and avoiding involvement with other formal education.

A behavioral group program was implemented with the goal of increasing attendance. A single-case design was used instead of a control group. This program focused on increasing desirable behaviors. While in the group program, the members received no punishment for nonattendance. Participants (three females and five males, all truants who missed twenty percent of the previous trimester) were selected at random. All had received suspensions for past unexcused absences and fighting, functioned below grade level, and had frequent verbal conflicts with teachers.

Intake interviews were held with each group member when the school social worker conducting the group assured them that no punishment would be given during the study. All of those interviewed volunteered to be in the group and agreed to continue for the planned eight weeks of the program. Group meetings were scheduled for twice a week, fifty minutes each.

A token economy was developed. The goal was to increase each student's attendance by an average of at least 0.75 of a day for five days. Each subject recorded attendance on a daily chart signed by teachers for validation. Points were awarded once a week for attendance by a member selected by the group. No points were awarded for those who lost charts or whose charts were not validated by teachers.

The group could earn a possible 1,280 points (a 20 percent increase in attendance) per week. If they earned 1,040, all members received a soda and a bag of potato chips. If they did not, the leader initiated a discussion of which behaviors were responsible. This was followed by role playing at meetings and practicing desirable attendance-inducing behaviors between meetings. During the second week of treatment, the members adopted a group goal (20 percent improvement) to be achieved after eight weeks. Achieving the goal would earn them a trip that would include roller skating and a picnic.

Waltzer collected data throughout the intervention and checked reliability against central school attendance records. Correlation was at 98 percent. During baseline, the group had a 3.6 day per five-day week attendance. At the end of eight weeks, they had a 4.5 days per week attendance. After eight weeks of observed post-treatment they maintained an average attendance of 4.2 days per week.

ENURESIS AND ENCOPRESIS

Two related problems seen at home and in school are enuresis and encopresis. These have also been widely studied by behaviorists. Children with these problems are often referred to the school social worker because teachers are troubled by their "smell." Or the school social worker is the person who keeps a supply of dry clothing at hand. Also, some people in school settings, who are not familiar with the research think that enuresis and encopresis indicate serious psychiatric problems. There is *no* body of reliable research to sustain this position.

Before undertaking treatment of pupils with these problems, the school social worker should always check to find out if there is a medical reason why the student cannot be retrained in his urination or defecation habits. Usually, the child client is very eager to overcome these habits and appreciates the confidentiality of the school social worker in treatment. Pupils have even successfully worked on such a problem unknown to their parents, although the parents had given permission to the school social worker to target any problem she deemed necessary.

In 1969, Bruce L. Baker at Yale University recruited through local newspaper advertisement ninety enuretic elementary school children. All but four had not stopped wetting their beds after infancy, and more than half were wet seven nights a week, though no organic problems had been diagnosed.

Thirty children were given controlled intervention at home. The other sixty, serving as controls, received no treatment. The intervention consisted of

two foil pads, with holes in the top pad, separated by an absorbent sheet, and placed under the subject's lower bed sheet. The pads were connected to a white plastic box which contained two 6-volt batteries, a sensitive relay, and a buzzer. Within seconds after the child began to wet, a circuit was completed and the buzzer sounded. The buzzer continued to sound until the subject got out of bed and shut it off (p. 44.)

During the Baker studies, the child was kept on the bell-and-pad gadget until he had fourteen consecutive dry nights. In the end, 74 percent of the children treated were cured and 15 percent were greatly improved. Follow-up studies showed changes were sustained.

Following treatment, substitute symptoms were not observed in any of the children. In fact, social gains were achieved without all the former embarrassment. In 1969, psychodynamic therapists were saying without empirical data that bed-wetting was a symptom of some deeper problem; if it was eliminated, a new symptom would occur. Baker's work was one of the early scientific studies that destroyed that theory (O'Leary and Wilson, 1975).

The bell-and-pad training method used by Baker had been established by Mowrer and Mowrer in 1938 and had been frequently used thereafter. In 1977, Doleys summarized twelve studies of the use of the bell-and-pad method on 628 children. The follow-up studies showed that 81 percent of the children treated had not wet the bed for an entire year.

In 1970, Kimmel and Kimmel introduced three enuretic children to a daytime method of control. The procedure was simply to get the child to extend the waiting time between the urgency to urinate and actual urination. They did this by asking the child to let the parent know when he had to eliminate. Then the parent would ask him to wait a stated time until he went to the toilet. He was given rewards decided upon in advance for doing this successfully. The time period between urgency and elimination was consistently extended, and in a matter of a few days the children were waiting up to thirty minutes.

Two of the children studied by Kimmel and Kimmel were four-year-olds with no other problems; they stopped bed-wetting in seven days. The third was a ten-year-old being treated for emotional problems at an outpatient clinic. It took her two weeks to accomplish being dry at night, using the same method.

Dry Bed Training is a procedure developed in 1974 by Azrin and his associates. They used the bell-and-pad method but added a variety of techniques to it, including specific operant interventions such as positive reinforcement for a dry bed, nighttime urination in the toilet, practice and reinforcement for getting out of bed to urinate, and punishment for any accidents. The punishment consisted of having to get out of bed and remake the bed and being scolded by the parent.

The 1974 findings of Azrin and associates were similar to the results observed in previous studies of the bell-and-pad method. In their further studies in 1978 and 1979, the bell and pad were eliminated, and only operant procedures were used.

At first, they trained the parent during a single night session at home that lasted as many hours as seemed needed. In the second study, they had the parents come into their office for training in how to proceed. In the second study, all of the forty-four children participating stopped bed-wetting. There were no dropouts, and the relapse rate was only 7 percent. Parents actually seemed to prefer the in-office training to the night-at-home session.

Several findings have been reported about encopresis which should be useful to the school social worker in planning her work (Walker et al., 1989). Approximately 50 to 60 percent of the children who have encopresis, or soiling, after the age of four have previously been successfully toilet trained. Encopresis is four to five times more prevalent in males than in females. Most researchers believe that parents underreport encopresis, revealing it only when questioned about the appearance of symptoms.

While there has been extensive and continuing research on enuresis, there has been comparatively little on encopresis. This compounds the school problem because encopresis will typically occur during the day, while enuresis may well be confined to nighttime at home. Because it occurs during the day, it is soon noticed in school, and the child is quickly ostracized, embarrassed, and even tormented by his classmates. Teachers also will sometimes be short of patience with such pupils.

Unfortunately, this negative reaction is not successful in curing encopresis—or it would stop right there. Ross (1981) reported that "the fact that these negative social consequences do not lead to a cessation of the soiling behavior reflects that the problem results not from an excess response that must be suppressed but from a deficit in a skill (sphincter control) that must be acquired" (p. 142).

When children are punished by peers or parents for soiling, they do not cease defecation but find creative ways of avoiding those who are punishing them. Therefore, studies by behaviorists have pointed to the need for skill training in bowel movement as well as encouragement and rewards to the child. In an early study of four institutionalized children, Neale (1963) used learning theory to cure them. He achieved "rapid success" in three children and attributed the failure to cure the other child to "faulty application of learning theory rather than defects in the approach" (p. 149).

Subsequent researchers have used a combination of behavioral techniques with notable success. Crowley and Armstrong (1977) used in-home training, but did not isolate specific methods. So it is now commonly recognized that behavioral contingencies are effective in treating encopresis, but which ones are best have yet to be established.

Graziano and Mooney (1984) conclude that "functional analyses in each case are important because several possible major issues appear to be involved.... Parent training and home behavioral intervention appear to be the treatments of choice" (p. 351). The school social worker usually has an opportunity to use these methods with encopretic children who are referred to her.

Walker and associates (1989) relate encopresis to three causes and advocate determining which is operative before instituting behavioral training. The most common cause is retentive encopresis, which is characterized by chronic constipation. A second cause is chronic diarrhea or irritable bowel syndrome. The third is manipulative soiling.

Behavioral methods for retentive encopresis have been reported in many single-case or small-sample research projects. Positive reinforcement and ignoring of accidents have been used favorably. A few researchers have used punishment in the form of having the child sit on the toilet for increasing amounts of time or requiring the child to clean himself and his clothes with potent soap in cold water.

More comprehensive procedures have included periodic pants checks, frequent toileting, positive practice, token systems, and cleanliness training. Progress monitoring and charting along with positive and negative reinforcement have been used.

For chronic diarrhea or irritable bowel syndrome, Walker and associates recommend control of symptoms and reduction of stress and anxiety in the patient. Medical and psychological measures could be needed. Such interventions as hypnosis, relaxation training, and assertion training have been used. Manipulative soiling is rarely seen and not considered in the behavioral literature.

PROBLEMS WITH HOMEWORK

Probably the most frequent interventions that a behaviorally oriented school social worker uses concern homework. These could range from encouraging parents to read to their nonliterate children for pleasure to giving them direct instruction or behavioral training. In between are procedures to keep parents posted on what homework is assigned, how to become more nurturing parents, and how to change the child's study habits.

Unfortunately the advice from teachers to parents is sometimes given in negative or even threatening terms. Also, teachers often fail to suggest specific steps in curing the problems and do not take the home situation into account.

The skill of the school social worker is needed here to provide workable programs for the teacher and parent.

To eliminate problems in developing successful homework procedures, the idea has even been put forth that there should be no homework assigned, so that the school can totally control the child's learning (Townsley, 1989). This might necessitate that school personnel work much longer hours. But the child may be better able to do academic work in only one place. This would eliminate such commonly encountered problems as the child's forgetting to bring assignments, worksheets, or books home, or denying that he even has work to do. Townsley suggests this procedure for students who try to avoid or escape learning situations.

However, although homework is the child's responsibility, teachers often want parent involvement. But there is little consistency in what teachers want from parents. Some depend heavily on the home for such things as enrichment, social skills training, and even direct academic instruction. There may be formal, informal, or no arrangements between parents and teacher. The work with the child could be carried out at home by parents, siblings, specially employed tutors, other relatives, or friends.

Families place varying degrees of importance on academic work. Some think a child is not getting enough homework at school, so they assign work to him which may not be related to what he is doing in school or to his ability level. This often makes academic work distasteful to the child and could even undermine his self-confidence.

Some children within a family are regarded as fine students and others as poor learners. Some parents even tell their average-ability (often learning disabled) children that they are dumb or stupid when they are having difficulties with academics. This is devastating to the child so labeled.

The school social worker should firmly tell such parents to stop depreciating their child and reassure the student that he is not dumb or stupid. Parents often attach great importance to advice from school personnel. This places a great responsibility on the school social worker to be on-target with parents. But at the same time it offers an opportunity to improve a child's environment.

A survey (Polster, 1977) of research concluded that student underachievement can be "successfully modified across academic subject areas when environmental contingencies are altered" (p. 5). Focusing on counseling or motivation has not been productive. But, "reinforcing academic performance and emphasizing the expectation for high achievement rather than low achievement may be essential to improving academic performance" (p. 6).

Studies by Ayllon and associates (1972, 1974) previously discussed have concluded that changing the atmosphere of the classroom from one of predominant concern with poor behavior to one of positive emphasis on academic achievement has improved both achievement and behavior.

The study by Polster (1977) of underachieving seventh-and eighth-grade students in a Chicago public school used a home-based model. There were two experimental groups and one control group studied in a multiple-baseline-across-subject design. The experimental groups followed the same procedures throughout, except that one group used self-monitoring and the other used parent monitoring.

Polster succeeded in raising students' performance in both experimental groups to expectancy levels. To do this he used a daily assignment report card filled out by the student and initialed by teacher and parent. If the pupil forgot the form, he made a duplicate copy on a plain piece of paper. If no homework assignment was given in a subject, the student gave himself an assignment in line with the class's current studies, and the teacher approved it with her initials on the daily report card.

In addition, each participating pupil had a cleared-off study area at home to be used for nothing but homework. He never studied anywhere else. The student was required to study for a specified amount of time daily. For all of this, he was monitored on a daily point system which earned him carefully predetermined rewards from his parents. Data was kept throughout by parents and students. This eliminated the demand for extra teacher time to improve school functioning.

Self-monitoring was found to be more productive than parental monitoring. The pupil monitors recorded more time studying. Had self-monitoring alone been used, the social worker's time with the family and student could have been decreased. Less social worker time was seen as important here, because this program was designed to fit into the busy schedules of school social workers (Polster and Pinkston, 1979).

As a result of these studies, students in both experimental groups studied at a higher frequency during treatment than during baseline. In group 1 the increase was 51 percent between baseline and program conditions with parent control (figures are percentage of total checks when students were observed to be studying), which improved to 60 percent with self-monitoring. The students in group 2 increased studying from 24 percent during baseline to 92 percent during treatment.

In terms of grade point averages, the experimental groups showed higher achievement than the control group. Fifty-eight percent of the experimental groups achieved grade point improvement of at least 1.5, or one-half of a full letter grade. Nineteen percent of the control group fell within this range. Forty-two percent of the experimental group and 62 percent of the control group fell in the range of slightly positive to no change. Nineteen percent of the control group and none of the experimental group showed negative changes in the range of -0.6 to -2.5, or one-sixth to five-sixths of a full letter grade. Experimental group 2 showed a trend toward more grade point average improvement than experimental group 1, with a difference of .43, or one-sixth of a letter grade.

Schumaker and associates (1977) used a daily report card and parent-managed privileges with problem junior high school students in three experiments.

In the first experiment, home privileges and parental praise were contingent on improved school conduct, classwork, daily grades, and teacher satisfaction. Three students were studied, and their performances improved considerably.

Another two students were studied in the second experiment. A similar report card system was instituted, but parental praise was contingent on improved school performance. As a result, the students did not bring the report card home. Class performance was not improved for one of the students until home-contingent privileges were added. The other student improved with the report card and praise. But classwork declined over time for both.

In a third experiment, an instructional manual describing the report card program was written for the school guidance counselors. Two counselors read it and each used it with one student. As a result, the school performance of both pupils improved.

TRANSFER STUDENTS

Transfer students present problems with which the school and the school social worker must deal. They have been growing in number and in frequency of moves, especially in urban areas. In 1983, Cornille, Bayer, and Smyth estimated that there were about six million children between the ages of five and thirteen who transfer to a new school each year.

The problems of transfer students are many. They are often from families who are homeless or constantly moving in search of affordable, suitable housing. Some families respond by parceling the family members out to members of the extended family or to friends because there is no other place for them in view. Other times, they rent a better place than they can finance. Then they do not pay the rent but instead save up for the day they will be evicted so that they can pay for moving expenses.

There may even be times when such families move because an apartment becomes available which appears to be better, but on moving in they find it is not. Sometimes the rent is precipitantly raised so high they simply cannot afford it any longer. These parents usually do the best they can to solve the problems they face because of inadequate affordable housing.

Other families are involved in drug use, violence, or crimes that sometimes lead them to be disturbing to other tenants in the building; they are asked to leave. Or perhaps a family has a child who is stealing, defacing property, fighting, or otherwise creating a ruckus in the community. Such children lead landlords to evict their families. And such families rarely have leases, so they are subject to the rules of the eviction courts. Some of these parents do not have sufficient funds or do not budget well enough (especially if they are addicted to drugs or alcohol), so they miss rent payments.

There are also families with more stability who move often. A parent in the military or employed by a large corporation is subject to being transferred on short notice. Upwardly mobile families move to improve their social status or quality of life. Many families move as their neighborhoods change. For such families, having children does not act as a deterrent to moving.

The school social worker must recognize that there is no guarantee that a child will continue to live with the same people as when she first encounters him. Children are being transferred from place to place by their parents or guardians. Perhaps their natural parents never actually lived together or established a home. Numbers of children are unplanned-for and their parents or grandparents have to find makeshift arrangements to accommodate them. For some children, school may be the most stable environment in their lives.

The transfer student has been studied by Leonard Jason and his associates (1989). They have developed innovative programs to help such children adjust better and attain more academic success in school. The basic component of the remedial program has been regular tutoring sessions held in school. Their organization and history will be described more fully in chapter 8 on settings. The study of Quenton that follows is illustrative.

A transfer student, Quenton was a ten-year-old white male in fifth grade. He was living with his mother and an aunt since his parents had recently separated. Finances were a problem since the divorce. When he entered the transfer program, Quenton was a year below grade level in spelling and mathematics and two years behind in reading. Data was collected regularly in each tutoring session so that progress could be measured and his program adjusted if necessary.

The nature of Quenton's performance in all below-level subjects was studied and work instituted to improve it. For example, it was found that his phonics were at the first-grade level. He was given consistent help from the tutor on this problem until he finally reached the fourth-grade level.

In mathematics Quenton did not know his multiplication facts, and this was also worked on with his tutor until he mastered all of the basic tables. With extra practice, he improved his spelling scores. Reading also was carefully monitored. With feedback and practice, his reading accuracy and comprehension also improved.

Eventually, Jason and associates considered problems beyond the tutor-to-pupil teaching procedure. For example, poor attendance was worked on with other school personnel. Parents were trained to help children at home by providing extra tutoring. Eventually, the researchers recognized that services going far beyond routine academic tutoring were required. These transfer students needed help with social problems.

CHILD ABUSE

Child abuse seems to fall into two major categories in the minds of the public—sexual and physical. Other categories not so easily defined are psychological abuse and educational abuse. The school social worker sees all four categories.

The school social worker has many opportunities to deal with abused children. Usually a school social worker is seen as the person on the faculty who should be working with the "worst" cases, the children considered by school personnel, other children, and the community to be abused. Also, because she is available in the school on a regular basis, children, friends of children, parents, community members, and school personnel will often mention child abuse when they might not speak to a social worker or therapist elsewhere.

Child abuse comes to the attention of the school social worker in the most obvious way when a pupil has visible scars and bruises. Other times, a child tells his teacher, the social worker, or another person on the school staff that abuse has occurred. Or, it will be the friend of an abused child who comes alone or with the abused student to report it to the social worker. The pupil or his sibling may speak to another member of the school faculty. In some instances, people in the community, either professional or lay, come to school and tell the school social worker or another adult there. Sometimes, a group of students, usually in the upper grades, report suspected abuse.

In most states, child abuse must be reported to the child protective services. Reporting child abuse presents a dilemma for the school social worker. Since the abuse is usually reported in confidence, it may be a violation of trust of the client to make an official report. Usually it is because the school social worker is a professional that the reporter feels comfortable in telling her. She can always agree to look into the matter, but if reporting appears indicated, the school social worker will have to confront the reporter early on with this eventuality. The school social worker also has to consider the specifics of the state laws related to reporting child abuse. These vary a great deal from state to state.

There are few behavioral studies available that deal directly with how to treat abused children. Most behavioral studies have limited themselves to treatment of mothers (Graziano and Mooney, 1984; Wahler, 1989). Only recently has the role of social conditions or mores been considered in studies of child abuse.

The courts, social agencies, hospitals, and residential care facilities for children have reacted case by case. In fact, most literature now available on child abuse is dependent on individual case studies. To make matters worse, therapists from many different backgrounds deal with abused children, so that agreement on techniques often is lacking even within the same agency.

Corsi and associates (1989) involved one family judged neglectful by the state authorities in improving personal hygiene to reduce one of the charges against them. The study proceeded on the theory that a factor in a neglect judgment is the quality of a child's personal appearance, and this family was being reported because of their lack of personal cleanliness, among other things.

The family members' hygiene in eleven body areas, such as face, hands, clothing, teeth brushing, and hair washing was observed weekly by the researchers. Scores were determined by family members and the experimenters until they achieved high levels of cleanliness. Four of the family's six children who had been placed out of home by the state authorities were returned home. Also, all family members remained consistently clean for an extended period after treatment, as determined by unannounced visits by the experimenters. And, the families were no longer charged with child abuse.

CHILD SEXUAL ABUSE

Attempts have been made to estimate the prevalence in society of sexual abusers. By national statistics, fifty-seven of every one-hundred thousand females were raped in 1977; the majority of victims were children. But other sexual crimes are not reported on the national level (Abel et al., 1981). They may include incest, exhibitionism, voyeurism, sadism, masochism, frottage, homosexuality, transvestitism, fetishism, obscene calling, bestiality, public masturbation, and others. In most cases, the offender will not admit to all of the types of crimes he or she has committed.

In their study of 411 paraphiliacs, Abel and his associates (1985) took every sort of precaution to assure the offenders of confidentiality. With this assurance, they were able to determine that the average paraphiliac committed forty-four crimes a year, usually starting at the age of twelve. Of the victims, 87 percent were female. Their age range went from younger than fourteen years (56.5 percent), fourteen to seventeen (33.3 percent), and older than seventeen years (43.2 percent).

In the same study, there were eighty-nine rapists who attempted or completed an average of 7.5 rapes each. The same number of child molesters, whose victims were under fourteen years of age, attempted 238.2 molestations and completed 166.9 on 75.8 victims. Another difficulty in securing accurate statistics is the fact that nearly 50 percent of the paraphiliacs commit multiple sex crimes.

The actual incidence of incest is unknown. A major bar to accurate statistics is that child victims of sexual abuse in and out of the home are counted similarly. It is known that incest is not a rare phenomenon and that the majority of perpetrators are male. Investigators of these crimes against children do not differentiate fathers from stepfathers (Becker and Coleman, 1988).

Sexual abuse of children in their homes has become newsworthy since the early 1960s. There has been a tendency to suspect the wife and child as having encouraged the abuse, making the offender in the case less to blame. At least a partial explanation of this phenomenon could be the embarrassment of women involved and their fears of what will happen to them if they report the abuse.

Much has been made of the possibility that self-proclaimed victims of child abuse are lying. But Jones and McGraw (1987) estimate that no more than 2 percent of reported cases of child abuse are false.

Although there are not reliable statistics on incest, it does appear to occur in all racial, religious, cultural, and socioeconomic groups. Becker and Coleman (1988) conclude that "incest is not a rare phenomenon, and that the majority of perpetrators are male . . . father or stepfather and daughter incest . . . appears most often in legal reports and clinical studies" (p. 189).

Often it becomes necessary to place the father or stepfather out of the home, away from the victim, to break the pattern of incest. Some of these fathers, of course, will spend time in prison or be given parole with the requirement that they enter treatment. Returning home then becomes a goal and the offender becomes ready for treatment in order to reunite with his family. Once he leaves prison, if he does not participate in the therapy, the therapist must put it in writing and the offender will have to return to prison.

Becker and Coleman recommend cognitive-behavioral treatment programs based on social learning theory as the most effective for the offenders, provided they are not retarded or psychotic. This therapy is based on the premise that the sexual drives of a perpetrator have become associated with deviant sexual behavior, namely, a sexual interest in a child. Therefore, the sex offender of children needs to be retrained in acceptable behavior in relation to his sex drives.

Covert sensitization and satiation have been the most effective treatment methods, according to Becker and Coleman. The offender is taught to associate the consequences of his behavior with the precursors of engaging in sexual contact with a child. Though he might deny it, there are identifiable antecedents that lead up to every assault. Once the offender has defined these, a list of possible aversive consequences which might befall him has to be made on at least ten videotapes covering no less than ten minutes each.

Then the perpetrator takes part in satiation therapy that pairs deviant sexual fantasies with masturbation for fifty-five minutes after orgasm. He does this for twenty sessions while the therapist listens to the tapes. If the offender objects to masturbation on principle, the satiation can be conducted without it.

The offender is also taught communication skills followed by family therapy around the incest. Sex education is used with the client to be sure he really understands what constitutes an acceptable relationship. Social skills and assertion training are used throughout the therapy, as needed by the offender.

Becker and Colemen report a number of behavioral studies of offenders but only one of a victim. This four-year-old victim was treated with contingency management. A victim's therapy should also contain treatment for the mother, even if it has to be court ordered.

Mothers are hard to engage unless they believe that the events did take place and they do not blame the child (Salter, 1988). Of course, the effects of the incest will vary with each child, and it should not be assumed that because some specific thing occurred, the client or her parent will react in a prescribed way.

Those treating the children usually proceed as in any other child therapy they normally use. However, assertiveness training and communication skills to teach the victim how to refuse to get involved in a future sexual molestation are most important. Sex education is indicated so that the child will understand what has occurred and what the consequences might be.

Judith Becker (1989) has conducted large-scale studies of teenaged sexual offenders in New York. Her findings indicate that sexual abuse can be a learned or relieving experience that developed in the home. It is not all abusive or aggressive, and child victims do not necessarily experience sexual abuse as bad. They can experience it as pleasurable because of their relationships with the offenders. Some people start engaging in sexual abuse because of their anxiety and need to relieve tensions. Afterwards, the abuser may feel guilty and not disclose the act.

Becker found that teenaged sexual abusers often had been abused themselves. Many had been "batted-around" children. If they had been in foster homes or institutions, some of the adults they encountered there may have been sexual abusers. Sexual abuse for them was not an isolated criminal act; their background led these abusers to think that if they wanted something, they could take it. After such experiences, younger children become fair game for the teenaged abuser. Still, a social worker treating such abusers should be aware that each client will have different values, and his sensitivities should be respected.

A teenaged sexual abuser could come from a home where substance abuse was evident. Or the abuser could have become sexually abusive in his irrational state. Other sexual abusers may have been encouraged by magazines or movies with sexually explicit scenes. Or a youngster may be on a delinquent path where he is doing bad things anyway, so why not add sexual abuse, which could be enjoyable, he reasons.

Although most adult sexual abusers started in their teens, little research is available on treatment of teenaged abusers. Which behavioral methods are used seems to be related at least in part to a cognitive approach. Behavioral treatment includes covert sensitization, satiation, social skills training, assertiveness skills training, sex education, and cognitive restructuring.

Among the helping professionals, social workers and nurses tend to treat reported incidents of sexual abuse as much more serious than do psychologists, physicians, and psychiatrists (Snyder and Newberger, 1986). In a study of literature on sexual abuse, Kurkjian and Scotti (1989) suggest that "social workers are concentrating a large share of their professional efforts on child sexual abuse issues, while psychologists are perhaps ignoring the issue" (p. 4). Of the 118 studies reviewed by Kurkjian and Scotti, only seventeen were treatment studies.

SLEEP

The school social worker will encounter pupils who say they are tired because they did not or could not sleep. Others come to school late or not at all because they overslept. They relate this with an air of finality indicating that they are unable to control their sleep patterns.

Indeed, some families and youths develop poor sleep patterns related to their life-styles. Some families do not follow regular patterns in their daily lives. Sometimes there is no family member who has to report regularly for a job. This could be because no one in the family has been able to hold a job, and the adult in charge is on a disability pension or receives welfare.

In some cases, substance abuse or violation of the law may be involved. If the family follows no schedules, they might not incorporate the fact that a child is on a schedule for school. Some children struggle to get themselves to school, but the environment of the home works against them.

Then there are youngsters who are into bad habits themselves. They may be involved with substance abuse, delinquent behavior, or preoccupation with violence or deviant subcultures. However, there are some who play games around sleep because they are not successful in school and prefer to remain at home, watching television with the family.

Some students have simply developed poor sleep habits and feel trapped in them. Others will be worried about not sleeping. There are also parents who demand that their children sleep more hours than they require. The behavioral school social worker has to identify environmental factors at home in attempting to treat children's sleep problems.

Ferber (1985) treated Jimmie, a four-year-old boy with very irregular sleep patterns. He went to sleep between seven and eleven o'clock at night and often awakened in the middle of the night, staying up for hours playing happily. He took naps at irregular times during the day for thirty minutes to four hours.

Jimmie's family were caring and had a satisfying family life. They led a very unstructured life typical of their community. His parents were not troubled by Jimmie's daytime sleep patterns, but they were concerned about his nighttime habits. They did not relate their unstructured lives to his sleep patterns.

Treatment for Jimmie's sleep problems included setting up regular times for going to sleep and waking up. A pleasant bedtime ritual was established. Jimmie was required to sleep only in his own room. If he awakened during the night, parents could go into his room but not allow him to play with toys. If he had trouble sleeping, they were told to sit with him if necessary but to engage in little discussion. Jimmie had to sleep alone. Nap time was established and adhered to. Parents were also told to set regular meal times.

Jimmie's parents charted his sleep patterns for two months, although they were required to do so for only two weeks. They found charting helpful in establishing the new routines, and they liked to see the progress shown on the chart. At the end of two weeks, Jimmie was sleeping according to a regular acceptable pattern. It turned out that he did not need a daytime nap. Ferber points out that irregular sleep patterns can be easily reestablished; parents must be careful to maintain a newly established effective sleep schedule.

There have been some studies of sleep by other behavioral researchers (Bootzin and Nicassio, 1978; Spielman et al., 1987). Spielman and associates base their treatment on the patient's keeping a log to determine his total sleep time. He then is advised to limit his time in bed to what he has found from his log. Next, he gradually extends his sleeping time until he is comfortable with his sleep patterns. Good results were obtained, but more research is needed for verification.

Bootzin and Nicassio use more extensive procedures. They also start with a log to establish a baseline to determine treatment. They advise sleeping only when tired. If a person cannot sleep, he is told to get up after ten sleepless minutes and not return to bed until he is sleepy. He must use his bed for nothing but sleep and sex. Telephones, games, television, food, books, or other objects that would stimulate him should not be brought to the bed. The client is also told to establish a reasonable sleeping time and hold to it until favorable patterns are set. He should not take a nap because this would spoil chances of conforming to regular hours.

Hauri (1982) sees Bootzin and Nicassio's procedures as usually taking two weeks to establish desirable sleep patterns. However, he thinks clients need a lot of encouragement during the change period, such as calls from the therapist twice a week. He also sees the client's keeping a daily graph as reinforcing. An exception to the reading-in-bed rule would be made for people who try too hard to sleep.

Bootsin (1973) studied seventy-eight severe insomniacs recruited through newspaper advertisements. Each received one of four treatments: stimulus control instructions, relaxation training, relaxation scheduling, or no treatment.

The stimulus control subjects were given six instructions: (1) Lie down to sleep only when sleepy. (2) No reading or television in bedroom. (3) If unable to fall asleep, get up and leave the bedroom, returning only when you feel like it. (4) Repeat step 3 as often as necessary if unable to fall asleep. (5) Set alarm and get up every day at the same time to acquire consistent sleep rhythm. (6) Do not nap during the day.

The relaxation training group was taught to relax deeply twice a day. Those in relaxation scheduling received no training but were told to relax twice a day. The no-treatment group was told to keep extensive records, to be followed eventually by treatment. Every participant kept daily records of the time it took to fall asleep, number of hours slept, and the quality of sleep.

Before the study, everyone averaged more than ninety minutes a night to fall asleep and slept about 5.5 hours a night. The stimulus control group showed the most improvement, reducing to sixteen minutes to fall asleep and sleeping an hour longer per night. Relaxation training resulted in fifty-two minutes to fall asleep and an hour more of sleep. Relaxation scheduling reduced to seventy-five minutes to fall asleep and no change in length of time slept. No treatment resulted in sixty-six minutes to fall asleep and no gains in length of time slept.

Weil and Goldfried (1973) treated an eleven-year-old girl with insomnia. She was so fatigued in school that the school nurse sent her to them for help. She was so sensitive to noise that it took her two hours to fall asleep every night. If her parents went out and she was left with a baby sitter, she did not sleep. Weil and Goldfried treated her with relaxation therapy.

The therapist went to her house at bedtime and, using alternate tensing and relaxation methods, helped her fall asleep in one hour. He put the same instructions on a thirty-minute tape recording. She used it for two weeks and improvement was noted. The therapist then changed the tape, eliminating the muscle tensing and leaving only relaxation. She then fell asleep between fifteen and thirty minutes after the tape started. Next she got a fifteen-minute version of the tape. After two more weeks, she was given a five-minute tape. In one more week, the tape was removed and she was told to concentrate on relaxing. In a few weeks, she fell asleep upon going to bed. After six months there was a follow-up and all of her previous difficulties were gone.

Pointing out that most recommended treatments for pediatric sleep problems have not been systematically evaluated, Piazza and Fisher (1989) undertook a study of four developmentally delayed individuals with severe sleep disturbances. Using a faded bedtime procedure with response cost, they made such an evaluation.

Each child's bedtime was systematically delayed to increase the probability of short latency to sleep onset. Response cost (removal from bed for one hour) was used when the individual did not show short latency to sleep onset. A fading procedure was introduced to advance bedtime, gradually increase the length of time asleep, and decrease night waking and inappropriate daytime sleep.

Both biological and environmental manipulations of the sleep–wake cycle are "hypothesized as mechanisms of treatment and include: (1) increases in sleep pressure; (2) synchronization of circadian rhythms; (3) developmental aspects of sleep; and (4) classical and operant conditioning" (p. 1).

Piazza and Fisher based their studies on a successful intervention with a six-year-old girl who had sleep problems and attention deficit hyperactivity disorder using a fading procedure. She exhibited refusal to go to bed, delayed sleep onset, early wakings, and night wakings. The child's grandmother easily implemented the fading procedure, which resulted in an increase in average hours of sleep from 3.5 in baseline to eleven post-treatment. The other sleep-related problems vanished and there were no side effects.

Based on their success with the six-year-old, the researchers undertook the treatment of four nonverbal and profoundly retarded children, aged three, four, thirteen, and nineteen, who were referred primarily for self-injury. Sleep problems were a primary concern and a goal of treatment. Each one exhibited delayed sleep onset, night wakings, and early wakings which had been present for at least one year. When the three-year-old awoke she went into the parents' bed, and the four-year-old got out of bed frequently. Pharmacologic treatment

tried previously had failed. Treatment for all except the three-year-old was initiated while they were inpatients.

During baseline, the children were encouraged to sleep if they wished and
to continue their usual bedtime. Data was collected twenty-four hours a day
every half hour. The child was scored for being in or out of bed or awake or
asleep.

Treatment consisted of first establishing ideal sleep and wake times for each
child and then carefully adhering to them. Fading included adjusting bedtime
by a half hour, based on latency of sleep onset the preceding night. Response
cost involved taking the child from bed and keeping him awake for one hour
if he took longer than fifteen minutes to fall asleep. A multiple baseline-across-
subjects design was used to assess effects of treatment.

As a result, Piazza and Fisher were able to show improvements in the percentage of appropriate sleep after treatment. The four-year-old's sleep increased from an average of 78 percent to 87 percent. The three-year-old went
from an average of 75.6 percent to 89.2 percent after treatment and to 90 percent at one-year follow-up. The nine-year-old increased from 57 percent at the
start to 72 percent after treatment. The thirteen-year-old averaged 74 percent
during baseline, 77 percent in treatment and 86 percent at the one-month follow-up. Similarly, inappropriate sleep and night wakings decreased.

Biological factors contributing to treatment effects were increases in sleep
pressures, synchronizing circadian rhythms with prescribed schedules, and
consideration of the developmental stage of each child. Behavioral procedures
included being placed in bed as a conditioner for the act of lying in bed, which
became a cue for initiating sleep. Fading gradually changed the properties of a
stimulus so that the child did not suspect the change and continued responding as if the original stimulus were present. Finally, negative reinforcement was
also used in allowing the child to avoid removal from bed by decreasing the
latency to sleep onset.

Improvements in treatment techniques were seen in manipulations at bedtime rather than the middle of the night. Also, power struggles over going to
bed were eliminated because a child's going to bed time was tailored to fit his
unique needs. Procedures could regulate sleep so that multiple sleep-related
problems were eliminated.

LEAD POISONING

There are times when children are misjudged by schools as mentally retarded
because they are known to have had experiences or health problems that re-
putedly have certain lingering effects. Lead poisoning is an example of such a
condition, in that children are thought to be retarded if they have eaten lead-
bearing paint.

The myth that all children who ingest lead will become retarded reverts to
reports of early studies when medical treatment was not as effective as it later

came to be (Byers and Lord, 1943; Perlstein and Attala, 1966). Others saw elevated blood levels as related to excessive activity and inattention, impaired fine motor function, or even criminality (de la Burde and Choate, 1972; David, 1974). But these reports did not examine causal factors. Subsequent research has documented good results when lead poisoning is effectively treated medically.

In 1978, Sachs and associates compared forty-seven children treated for lead poisoning with their unaffected siblings next in age. A battery of psychologic tests did not distinguish the patients from their siblings, and physical examinations revealed no residual damage. Again in 1979, they reported results of follow-up studies of 166 lead poisoned patients treated between 1966 and 1972 and twenty-two sibling controls. The mean IQ of the patient cohort was eighty-seven, approximately at the fiftieth percentile for inner-city schoolchildren. Furthermore, no statistically significant relationship was found between maximum blood lead concentration and subsequent intellectual function.

Several entrenched ideas about lead poisoning in children were refuted by the 1979 study. There were no neurological signs after recovery. No symptoms recurred in association with fever or fractures. High IQ scores obtained by the youngest children showed that they were not as vulnerable to brain damage from lead poisoning as was previously thought. Some children who had low IQ scores nevertheless performed well in school.

Sociological data for lead poisoned and control cohorts were similar. Sixty percent of the families received public aid and 55 percent had no father in the home. But twenty-four patients whose parents were home owners scored significantly higher on the Wechsler test, suggesting that socioeconomic factors are more important than lead poisoning as IQ determinants.

5

PROBLEMS IN THE COMMUNITY AFFECTING SCHOOL BEHAVIOR

Public schools face a dilemma. They are established and supported to educate children and young adults. Most of their personnel are trained as teachers, and these teachers have chosen to make education their lifetime profession. But because of the failure of national, state, and local leadership to address major social problems, because governmental bodies have chosen not to deal adequately with them, some communities have turned to their public schools for help with a wide range of problems beyond what could technically be called education. A school social worker or a department of social work in a school system is in a unique position to provide emergency services, help the school administration and school board sort out what is within their province, and confront the community with their responsibilities.

The usual response of school principals to problems that they don't see as rightfully their own is to become frustrated and seek short-term solutions. This is understandable, because they have limited resources and receive little guidance in such matters from their board of education. Principals have sometimes denied the very existence of problems rather than expose their schools to stigma by recognizing them.

But from time to time the media are able to escalate a social problem into the public consciousness, making elected officials in government feel obliged to react. Since money is short, they turn to the public schools to protect, reform, or train the children. However, the problems do not go away, and the schools are left to handling them on a catch-as-catch-can basis, in addition to teaching yet another subject.

This chapter examines some of those problems generated in the surrounding community that directly affect a child's behavior in school. The list is long and growing, from racial segregation and the struggle for civil rights for the handicapped to homelessness, substance abuse, unemployment, gangs and cults, AIDS, inflation, and violation of the law. Discussion here will be limited to those areas in which behavior analysis has generated solutions.

SUBSTANCE ABUSE

Before drug abuse became as widespread as it is today, it was seen as a separate problem from alcohol abuse. The public and publicized view of alcohol addiction was that it was a degenerate, hopeless condition. The alcoholic was relegated to a subhuman status and a life on "skid row." Families with alcoholic members tried to hide their condition or send them away to a sanitorium or anywhere out of their lives. At the same time, alcohol use in a social setting was widely accepted.

But when alcohol became widely used by children of the wealthy and upper classes, alcoholism was correctly placed in the category of substance abuse along with drugs. In fact, it became clear that alcohol is typically used interchangeably or in sequence with drugs. Since most families have an open liquor cabinet for social purposes, alcohol is the easiest substance for children and youths to get. They can remain with it or go on to other things.

Illegal drugs have become a very lucrative worldwide industry, requiring intervention by the federal government. The response of law enforcement officials has been to turn their backs on the problem because the flow of drugs is so overwhelming. Meanwhile, drug use has spread all over society, even into quiet rural communities. Numbers of youths have dropped out of school because of addiction or because they could earn huge, otherwise unattainable sums of money on a regular basis by dealing in drugs.

In addition to drugs being used by students and their families, the school social worker will encounter children who are the victims of their parents' substance abuse. It has taken society a while to recognize the need for viable research and specialized care for these children. Reliable studies of Fetal Alcohol Syndrome are available and will be presented here. However, children's needs detailed in this research still have to be addressed. Heroin and cocaine babies also are being born, but reliable data collection and studies are in their beginning stages.

In extending help to drug and substance abusers, Budziak (1989) has developed guidelines for choosing from among the large number of facilities that offer programs. In making referrals for students who are substance abusers, the behavioral school social worker should ask the following questions:

Does the facility have the resources to make the comprehensive, multidimensional assessments that are needed? These assessments should cover alcohol and drug use, life problems causing the abuse, and life problems caused by the abuse. The school social worker will also want to find out how assessments are made and by whom. Questions should be raised about the training of the assessor in such life-related areas as marital problems, neuropsychological functioning, sexual dysfunction, and parent-child problems.

The behavioral school social worker should also consider whether the assessment procedures are scientifically valid or are untested homemade questionnaires. Is the assessment a narrow, drug-centered assessment that assumes that substance abuse is always the primary problem? Or is there a functional behavioral assessment?

Does the facility differentiate rather than pigeonhole its clientele? Clients must be regarded as unique people and not as a homogeneous group with predictable traits and uniform symptomology. Are the providers rigidly bound to one particular model? Or are they flexible, with an empirical bias? Any labeling of a client as alcoholic or an addict should be questioned.

Does the facility give specific treatment recommendations with an explicit goal? Too many programs advertise twenty-one-day or six-week inpatient cures instead of whatever amount of time it takes to cure the client.

Is the need for differentiated treatment fully understood? Rather than assuming that a specific diagnosis requires a specific treatment, the whole client should be considered and treatment tailored to his unique needs. It should not be assumed that the substance-abusing client has a "primary disease." Other factors in his life should be taken into account, and the abuse viewed in that context.

Is there a thorough adherence/compliance assessment? The likelihood of a client's following through has to be considered. The social worker should raise the question of whether the client is just going through a procedure because the court mandated it, or because there is bona fide, meaningful participation. Is the intervention matched to the client's situation? Or is the provider assuming that treatment is not proceeding well because of the client's denial of his condition or because he is unmotivated? The client should be an active participant in treatment; this should be possible if treatment is on target for him.

Budziak advises the behavioral school social worker to become informed about the field of alcohol and other drug abuse. She should be able to identify drugs in current use and get to know the groups serving alcoholics or substance abusers. She should insist on active case management and open communication with care providers. Finally, the behavioral school social worker should become familiar with a provider's outcome research and be wary of defensive postures.

A number of approaches to treatment, often repeatedly advertised through the media, have developed their own followings. Often a fervor will develop over a particular method, or those who have profited from a particular method will become crusaders for it.

Fortunately, there is a developing body of research (Miller and Heather 1986; Hester and Miller, 1989) dealing with treatment of substance abusers. At the same time, there is continuous support for making treatment of addicts an integral part of any comprehensive program to cure the drug problem, despite the low success rate of treatment programs. More reliable research is needed before it is possible for a school social worker to refer a client to a treatment program with much security.

The next question, then, is whether there is anything a school social worker can do to provide help to children or their families when they are involved with drugs. Budziak offers guidance here. Careful, empirically based evaluations and an accurate match between each client and treatment program are needed. Follow-up plans after the initial intervention also are necessary.

In their careful review of the general state of approaches to treatment of alcohol (where the most work has been done), Hester and Miller (1989) make several points. While a number of treatment methods have been consistently supported by scientific research, none of these methods is in common use in the United States. There is no superior method, and the fundamental need in treatment is still to match the client to the treatment program.

Hester and Miller went on to compare studies of treatment that was inpatient or outpatient, short or long term, and more versus less intensive. They concluded that the effectiveness of treatment did not depend on any of these. Outpatient treatment was clearly cheaper. They concluded that the choices of treatment are not widely known. Therefore, those seeking help can end up in a program that is not best for them. However, the researchers saw an advantage to encouraging a client to make choices of interventions in order to increase the client's commitment, because in the end clients make their own choices anyway.

The school social worker should be aware of the approaches and effects of treatment. The general categories are brief treatment strategies, antidipsotropic medications, aversion therapies, self-control training, self-help groups, relapse prevention, marital and family therapy, social skills training, anxiety and stress management, psychotropic medications, and community reinforcement. When a combination of therapies are needed, they may be offered in tandem or simultaneously.

Miller (1989) sees the individualized treatment of a substance abuser as a complex process from the initial assessment through the maintenance arrangements. This certainly is an area where a social worker should have expertise, and the school social worker is in a favorable position to offer such guidance to pupils and their parents.

Heather (1986) examined the possibility of change in addicts without therapists. He examined self-help manuals and pointed to a range of other materials, such as audiotapes, videotapes and home computers reported in the works of Christenson, Miller, and Muñoz (1978). Data is not conclusive on their effects, but the prospects of using these instead of or in addition to working with a therapist are intriguing.

Behavioral researchers, encouraged by government grants, have pioneered methods for dealing with drug users. Their research has generally focused on either prevention or treatment.

Prevention

In the United States, prevention generally includes cracking down on the sources of drugs, confiscating them, and punishing the pushers, along with educational programs in the school, in the media, and elsewhere. New laws such as those against drunk driving, Sunday liquor store hours, and a higher drinking age have also been tried. But the public schools are consistently turned to for preventive programs.

There have been some creative efforts by the schools, such as the Snowball program, a grassroots movement of high school youth (including junior high), to inhibit the spread of drug usage. The program relies heavily on peer counselling. The snowball effect is seen in the idea that if one person has a positive effect on another, he, in turn, will impact yet a third person.

Operation Snowball was started in Northern Illinois by a group of high school students in the fall of 1977. These youths had just returned from a teenage institute on substance abuse sponsored by the Illinois Alcoholism and Drug Dependence Association. They decided to develop a program to spread the ideals of making responsible decisions about their own behaviors; therefore, choosing alternatives to drug use.

The Operation Snowball participants have influenced others through weekend meetings, day-long workshops, preventive-training programs, and community projects. Adults have served only as advisors. Chapters have spread all over the state. Both students and school faculties have expressed enthusiasm for Operation Snowball. But results have yet to be submitted to empirical research.

In a sociological text, James B. Jacobs (1989) points out that driving and drinking alcoholic beverages are two formidable aspects of life in the United States. Car ownership is a major component of the American dream. "The car is a symbol of social status and personal life-style," Jacobs says (p. xiv). For teenagers it has become a rite of passage into adulthood. Jacobs points out that Americans are not interested in the direct efficiency of mass transportation, and they often go miles out of their way in cars.

Alcohol similarly plays an important role in the social life of Americans. It is a symbol of conviviality and an expected component of any celebration of significance, from beer at ball games to champagne at weddings. A drink, as depicted in advertisements, reduces tension, guilt, anxiety, and frustration and enhances fantasy, sensuality, aggressiveness, self-esteem, and escape from reality.

It is no wonder that Americans have had so many difficulties with drunk driving. Cars and alcoholic beverages represent respected items at the heart of their culture.

Alden (1980) studied a large number of community programs designed to cut down on alcohol abuse. However, research was not adequate to be truly conclusive, and the research that was available was not universally encouraging. Some educational programs have focused on high schools and universities. These succeeded in increasing knowledge about alcohol but were less consistently able to produce attitude or behavior change. In a few studies it was reported that attitudes even became more favorable towards alcohol use.

In studying other educational programs, Alden came to further conclusions. Mass-media campaigns have resulted in little follow-up research. What studies there are tend to show that these programs are more apt to increase awareness than to motivate people to address the problem.

Efforts have been made to improve drinking habits by changing laws. Attempts to restrict the sale of alcoholic beverages to certain hours or locations have decreased the rate of some accidents and arrests but have had little noticeable overall effect. Increasing the price of liquor tends to decrease drinking among teenagers. However, studies of the relationship between traffic accidents and lowered drinking age have conclusively shown that alcohol-related collisions and fatalities have significantly increased.

Attempts to raise the legal drinking age have brought out arguments about whether this will decrease the amounts consumed. Evidence against raising the drinking age points to the easy availability of alcohol and the challenge that raising the drinking age presents to those cut out by the law. The maturity of older users and the greater dangers of alcohol use by teenagers are seen as favoring the law.

School social workers should be vigilant that the school not become a "drug store." Drugs have to be eliminated from the school by school personnel. In the past, while many schools have strictly monitored drugs, others have not, closing their eyes to student drug use and the pushers operating within their buildings.

The school social worker, accepting clients from the school population and sensitive to the community and society, often sees that she is dealing with pupils using or pushing drugs. In order to help these children succeed academically, she must decide to either treat them directly or refer them to competent outside treatment sources. She also has to work with the school administrators to keep drugs out of the schools.

Preventive programs for use by schools have proliferated. Behavioral researchers Rhodes and Jason (1988) trace the programs from those that are merely educational to those that address social skills of the pupils. They observe that some students with good social skills get involved in drugs, necessitating even more sophisticated and comprehensive prevention programs. They advocate taking the influences of the home, school, and community into account as well.

From the programs aimed at substance prevention that they examined, Rhodes and Jason have developed a model educational/preventive program for sixth- through eighth-grade students. Before such a program is initiated, a pretest to determine drug usage is administered to each pupil in the training program. Requirements of this program include:

The person conducting the program establishes herself with the school (a natural assignment for a school social worker). She needs a solid background of knowledge about drugs and their use.

Goals are set and made known to all concerned. Several possible levels of consultation exist: working with the staff to help them implement programs, directly implementing services, or jointly working with the staff and community members in implementing the programs.

Parents give written consent for their children to take part in the program.

Intervention is conducted through weekly forty-five-minute sessions using homework, discussion, and role playing. One session should be held for each of the following topics: introduction, understanding adolescence, skills for life, building self-esteem, communication skills, decision making, illegal substances, identifying pressures to use drugs, resisting peer pressure, overview, and future goals.

Good rapport with the students is established.

Group rules are outlined to facilitate positive interaction among group members.

Role playing and related behavioral methods are used to train students to refuse to take drugs.

Homework must be assigned after each session to further train the students in carrying out a designated behavior. Parents must be asked to assist by checking the pupil's homework. Then they should be sure to offer praise to their offspring for his effort and achievements.

The program uses a post-test after intervention. A data base is used throughout and an evaluation is made of the results, but long-term follow-up is not provided for. It would seem necessary to assess the effectiveness of the method. Also, it is not clear how behaviors learned in the program will be maintained and generalized to the daily lives of the participants. Because this is a newly developed program, results will have to be watched.

Besides the program just described, commercial companies have developed packaged training programs, often using interactive machines, to prevent substance abuse. For example, the International Support Services of Vienna, Virginia, has developed a leader's package that includes a videotape, two audiotapes, participants' workbook, a manager's handbook, a final test, and certificates of completion.

Treatment

Alcohol

Applied behavior analysts have studied alcoholism for some time. They have focused on group therapy or on treatment of individuals. Many early studies focused on aversion therapy (Voegtlin, 1940; Thimann, 1949; Lemere and Voegtlin, 1950; Clancy, Vanderhoof and Campbell, 1967; Raymond, 1964; Hsu, 1965; Liberman, 1968; Farrar, Powell and Martin, 1969; Miller and Hersen, 1972; Wilson, Leaf and Nathan, 1975). Others have worked with maintance medication (Bourne, Alford and Bowcock, 1966; Bigelow, Liebson and Lawrence, 1973). Teaching of behaviors incompatible with addiction has been another area of study (Lazarus, 1965; Cohen, Leibson, Faillace and Allen, 1971; Miller, 1972; Hunt and Azrin, 1973; Stuart, 1971; Sobell and Sobell, 1973).

Some attempts have been made to compare these studies in an effort to establish the most effective method for treating alcoholism. In 1974, Hedberg and Campbell compared four treatment alternatives. They evaluated systematic desensitization, covert sensitization, electric shock, and behavioral family counseling used with forty-nine alcoholics. The mean age was 38.2 and the average subject had been drinking for seventeen years and drank five days a week.

Behavioral family counseling came out the best with 74 percent of the participants meeting their goal and 13 percent of the rest much improved. Thirteen percent were not helped. In the study using systematic desensitization, 67 percent reached their goal and 20 percent met some of their objectives. There was even less success with covert sensitization—40 percent of the clients attained their goals and 27 percent met them partially. Within the electric shock group, four of the twelve group members dropped out before the fourth session, and only one of those who remained reported improvement.

Between 1973 and 1989, Azrin and his associates conducted major comparative studies in alcoholism. These studies began with the recognition that drinking could be controlled when a person was hospitalized, but the real need was for control when he returned home. Therefore, after their patients left the hospital, they worked with three areas of the alcoholic's life: work, family, and social. Within these areas they developed several programs to serve as community reinforcers for remaining sober. A control group was monitored as well.

The community reinforcers included vocational, marital and family, social, and reinforcer-access counseling. Reinforcer access dealt with such things as referrals to agencies providing needed services, as well as obtaining such things as a telephone, newspaper subscriptions, automobile, or television set if the patient did not have them.

Relatives and friends were trained to supply the patient with enjoyable family, marital, and social activities only when he was sober. A non-alcoholic social club was also developed and the patient was encouraged to attend. If a patient became intoxicated during the course of treatment, all of these reinforcers were taken away until he became sober again.

Azrin's patients were visited once or twice a week for the first month after leaving the hospital, then contact was gradually decreased over a period of at least six months. After about six months, the treated group showed significant gains over the control group that had received no post-hospitalization treatment. Those treated spent significantly fewer days unemployed, drinking, or away from home.

In 1975, Azrin made changes in the community reinforcement program to make it more effective and less time-consuming. He studied these results over a two-year period of time. He added a buddy system, a daily report procedure, group counseling, and a social-motivational program component to insure that disulfiram (Antabuse) was self-administered as prescribed. The study included alcoholics serving as matched controls who received only the usual hospital treatment and Antabuse, which presumably was taken as directed by their physicians. Again, the controls showed significantly more days unemployed, drinking, or away from home than did the patients who received the community reinforcement program.

Eventually, Azrin compared three groups which received various treatments. He examined forty-three alcoholics who were randomly assigned to three types of treatment. One used Antabuse, Alcoholics Anonymous, and traditional counseling. The second group used Antabuse, Alcoholics Anonymous, behavioral counseling, job finding, a buddy system and a social-recreational program. The third group received only Antabuse. To make sure the patient did not miss taking it on schedule, he and his significant other were carefully taught ahead of time how to use it. The schedule was then monitored by the patient's significant-other, who was vigilant to see that he took the Antabuse as prescribed.

The six-month follow-up showed that only method three, Antabuse alone, was the one that worked. Neither of the other interventions was as effective. Azrin stressed that this Antabuse treatment would work only if the significant other was able to get the patient to take every single required dose of Antabuse.

Haynes (1973) conducted a community study wherein Antabuse was administered to alcoholics who had a history of frequest arrest for intoxication. Each was given the choice of one year on Antabuse or ninety days in jail. Those who chose Antabuse were required to come to the municipal court once a week to receive it. If they missed more than one or two visits, they were returned to jail without further ado to serve their ninety-day sentence.

Of the 141 alcoholics given the choice, 138 chose Antabuse and three chose jail. By the end of one year, sixty-six of the one-hundred-eight were still using Antabuse, but thirty-five had left town without permission, seventeen had missed treatment and had been sent to prison, fourteen had left the community to take new jobs, three were hospitalized, and three were unaccounted for. The arrest records for those remaining in town showed an average of 3.8 arrests during the year before the experiment. During the year they received Antabuse treatment they had an average of only .3 arrests.

All the above research on alcoholism was carried out with adults, in part because the phenomenon of alcoholic children had not yet come to prominence. In fact, many people have difficulty realizing that children can become addicted to alcohol. But much of the behavioral research is so specific and so carefully described and measured that it should be effective with children and youths as well as adults. Some modification of methods might be necessary.

The few studies of children that have been made tend to be of individuals. However, McMahon and Wells (1989) are able to conclude from them that substance use by adolescents should be treated with parent training combined with social skills training for the youth, focusing on adolescent peer group intervention.

The school social worker may be called on to find help for a child's alcohol abusing parent. However, the school social worker should also be prepared to encounter addicted student alcohol users in the schools she serves—even the elementary schools. Or the pupil could have Fetal Alcohol Syndrome (FAS) or Fetal Alcohol Effects (FAE) because his mother was an alcoholic while he was in utero.

Fetal Alcohol Syndrome or Fetal Alcohol Effects

Rosett and Weiner (1984) define the most common signs of FAS as retarded growth in weight, length, and head circumference both before and after birth. FAS infants are substantially smaller than normal. "Mental retardation, attention deficits, delays in motor development, hyperactivity, and sleep disturbances have been observed in patients with FAS," they report (p. 7). With maturation, behavioral aberrations do not lessen, and the children seem to need interventions for social behavior. In fact, it is now believed that these victims cannot reasonably expect ever to manage living on their own, even in adulthood.

Streissguth and Randels (1988) studied ninety-two patients as adolescents and adults. Fifty-eight were diagnosed as having FAS and thirty-four had FAE. Those with FAS were "significantly more growth deficient on all parameters than those with FAE" (p. 146). The mean IQ with FAS was fifteen points lower than for FAE. However, there were not significant differences in academic learning.

Using the Vineland Adaptive Living Scales (Sparrow, Balla & Cicchetti, 1984), the researchers found there was not significant difference in Adaptive Behavior Quotient or the components, including daily living skills, communication skills or socialization skills. The average adaptive behavior was at the eight-year-old level. From these evaluations it was concluded that a goal of independent living is difficult to envision for the FAS or FAE person. The most frequent maladaptive behavior characteristic was poor concentration and attention, as seen in 77 percent of those examined. Other behaviors of between 50 and 75 percent of the sample included "withdrawal, impulsivity, dependency, teasing and/or bullying, extreme anxiety, and stubbornness and/or sullenness" (p. 148).

Fetal Alcohol Syndrome is now considered a leading cause of mental retardation (Streissguth and Randels, 1988). Although some of these children have IQs in the normal range, they have the most difficult time adjusting to life. Along with mental ability and physical characteristics, there are problems of a social and environmental nature that are unique to these children. Some observers think their most handicapping condition is their poor adaptive behavior.

Indeed, multiple problems are now being noted in the child with FAS or FAE. Recent scientific research has identified these characteristics and the need that these victims have for monitoring for their entire lives. These include specific medical care, early diagnosis (Streissguth and Giunta, 1988), family interventions (Streissguth, 1986), remediation of behavior problems and social skills training, and specialized educational programs.

Schools have not considered that FAS/FAE students might need specialized services that do not yet exist. Often these children go undiagnosed in their early years because they are typically outgoing, lively, and friendly. Also, they often have delayed development. FAE children go undiagnosed even more often than FAS children do.

It takes sophistication on the part of the examiner to recognize characteristic facial features, the presence of growth deficiency, and central nervous system problems that distinguish the FAS baby. As young children, they are also fearless and unresponsive to verbal cautions and therefore hard to handle (Streisguth and LaDue, 1987). Often the hyperactivity belies their lack of intellectual ability.

In studies of alcohol and motherhood partially supported by the U.S. Indian Health Service, Streissguth (1986) concludes that women "may drink as much as they want, but they appear to suffer more serious consequences from consuming less alcohol over a shorter duration than their male counterparts" (p. 1). An added factor not related to men is the in-utero effect on their babies. The most influential reason for alcohol use by women can be found in the customs of their society. The highest ratio of babies with FAS seems to be one in one hundred on some Indian reservations. However, it can vary to one in 750.

Typically, FAS/FAE children leave their mother's care at early ages because continuing alcohol use has made their mothers unable to handle them, perhaps neglectful or abusive. Furthermore, their mother's death rate is exceptionally higher, often turning these children into orphans. The youngsters may be placed in foster or extended family homes, with adoptive parents, or in institutions because of their mothers' disability or death.

Parents caring for them will need help in understanding and relating to their unique characteristics. Typically, unexpected changes occur as they grow older. Help for these families could fall within the realm of the school social worker. Some of this assistance could result in the social worker encouraging the school and the community to provide now-unattainable services.

Other Drugs

There are many behavioral studies of substance abuse, although not as many as of alcoholism. Also, few researchers have used chemical aversion to treat substance abuse (Raymond,1964; Thompson and Rathod, 1968; Liberman, 1969). As with alcoholics, maintenance medications have been used to treat drug abuse. Methadone, most notably, has been used to treat heroin addiction. However, its value has been questioned (O'Donnell, 1965; Kleber, 1970; Conner and Kremen, 1971; Liebson, Bigelow, and Flamer, 1973).

Boudin (1972) successfully used contingency contracting with an amphetamine addict. He modified her behavior in the natural environment. Boudin and Valentine (1972) reported a community-based rehabilitation program for drug addicts, especially those using heroin. They used mainly contingency contracting, along with such behavioral methods as behavior rehearsal, aversion therapy, and systematic desensitization, when needed.

Sherman Yen (1989) has initiated a program for treating cocaine addicts using behavioral methods. His Baltimore County Outpatient Cocaine Abuse Treatment Program began in September 1988. It treats twelve people at a time, with intensive therapy lasting twelve weeks or longer. Acupuncture is used.

Under the program cocaine must be the primary drug used by the clients served. However, they can also be using secondary drugs; more than half of these clients abuse alcohol. Admission to the program is limited to those who have a history of severe addiction or have failed in other drug treatment programs. If an applicant does not meet these criteria, they try to help him find treatment elsewhere.

A participant must sign a behavioral contract specifying the rules and regulations of the program and the consequences for repeated noncompliance. They then must take part in three behavioral/cognitive therapies per week—individual, group, and multifamily group. Individual therapy targets the participants' current problems. The group intervention focuses on education about cocaine and coping strategies to combat its continued use. The multifamily group endeavors to educate family members on cocaine usage and to enlist their participation in the clients' treatment.

Such behavioral techniques as relaxation training, social skills training, and job finding are taught at the Baltimore Cocaine Program. Clients must contact the program daily, either by telephone or in person at program headquarters. Data on client behavior are collected twenty-four hours a day.

Anticipating that an incentive program would be needed to encourage clients to call in daily, Yen and his associates (1989) experimented with a raffle program. Subjects of the experiment included ten males and one female. Data on the calling-in behaviors of these clients were collected for fourteen days of baseline, fourteen days of intervention, and fourteen days of follow-up.

After the first week of data collection, the clients were informed by letter of plans for the raffle. Every time a client called in during the treatment period, he would automatically receive a ticket for a raffle to be held at the office of the Cocaine Abuse Program. On Saturday mornings during client group meetings, all of the tickets were gathered up and three winners were drawn. A participant had to be present to collect his prize. Prizes were gift certificates to local social and cultural events. These rewards were chosen because they would involve the client with his support system. Money was not used because it would have introduced a component of gambling to the program.

Results were encouraging. Nine of the clients increased their calling in during the treatment phase and two did not. Some continued their calling in at the increased rate attained during the raffle procedure, but others did not, a result attributed mainly to individual motivational differences. However, this is a sparse sample and more study is needed for verification.

When clients have successfully completed the program or are not participating, they are discharged. Those who complete the intensive phase of treatment are urged to remain in aftercare for as long as they need it or for at least six months. They are then urged to remain in a group, but daily contact is not required. Post-treatment consists of three- and six-month follow-ups. After six months, about 54 percent of the clients under evaluation either evidenced a degree of success by completing twelve weeks of acute treatment or were discharged as successful.

School social workers will encounter parents of children as well as some pupils themselves who are cocaine abusers. The social worker's potential caseload of cocaine users among the school pupils will be substantially diminished as they drop out of school to push the drug to support their habits. But younger students can be counted on to take the places of those who drop out in some communities. And working with pupils whose parents are on cocaine (and with the parents themselves) provides a wide area for intervention by the school social worker.

EMPLOYMENT

Americans place high value on holding a job. Children look forward to it even when they are in grade school. Many look for ways of earning money well before they reach the legal age of sixteen. Those who succeed in finding jobs tend to be those whose parents are employed, are not of minority status, are ready to engage in illegal acts, or are especially enterprising.

There are some youths who want to work but they have not developed the skills for successful employment. Sporadic federal programs have been offered to meet the problems of unemployed minority youths without job skills. Behavioral researchers have studied job programs developed for youngsters in settings where the market was limited.

Pierce and Risley (1974) experimented with a federal job training program that, unlike most of its predecessors, required that a young employee do more than merely be present to receive his paycheck. The researchers aimed to improve the job performance of a group of part-time workers in a recreation center.

The seven black adolescents (three fourteen-year-old females, three fourteen-year-old males, and one sixteen-year-old male) involved had been told they were on the job to help, teach, and supervise children who played games at the center. But the seven employees studied actually only played games themselves.

To improve the situation, they were given specific job descriptions and a checklist was used to observe their work. Spot checks were made to observe the youths at work. However, this did not provide strong incentive, so the director of the recreation center told them they would be fired if they did not start doing their jobs. This was not productive either. Finally, the youths were told they would be paid for *work time*, not *clock time*. They were then observed for work time and paid accordingly (on percentage of time worked). Finally, work improved.

To address the great difficulties many youthful and adult job hunters face, Azrin and his associates (1975) developed a model job-finding club. This model has been replicated many times since throughout the United States.

The study was made in a town of thirty thousand with a longtime history of above-average unemployment. Participants in the program were recruited through publicity in newspapers, state employment services, personnel departments of large businesses, and word of mouth.

Once recruited, clients were placed in pairs matched by such variables as age, sex, race, education, marital status, number of dependents, salary and position desired, and financial status. Half were then placed in a control group that received no treatment. In the treatment group, twenty-eight males and thirty-two females received at least five sessions of counseling.

Those in the counseling program were required to attend group meetings and to obtain and pursue job leads. While concentrating on finding jobs, subgroups also met daily to get used to following a full workday schedule. Training was given daily on job-seeking behaviors, and encouragement was provided in an effort to motivate the clients in their search. Each group member was a buddy assigned to another member of the group.

Those in the treatment group were expected to dress and groom themselves appropriately, widen their range of positions to be considered, role play job interviews and telephone contacts with potential employers, and listen to taped comments of former clients who now had jobs. Letters were sent to the client's family suggesting how they could help the client get a job.

Azrin and associates made an all-out effort to obtain job leads. Clients shared leads they were not using. Friends and relatives were contacted regularly. Newspaper ads and potential jobs were promptly acted on. Former employers were contacted. Clients placed job-wanted ads in local newspaper classified sections. They prepared resumes, established their own file system for keeping track of jobs, and received some financial or other support for such things as postage, photographs of themselves, or typed letters.

Results of the job-finding club were gratifying. The average job-seeker in the counseling program began a full-time job by the end of fourteen days. It took members of the control group an average of fifty-three days to start jobs. Follow-up studies showed that the counseled group received higher starting salaries, found higher-level jobs, and progressed faster on their jobs than did the members of the control group.

This job-finding model has been replicated by school social workers. The elements of the program can often be used by clients with or without a group setting or without searching full time. Behavioral school social workers have introduced the job club to groups of high school or junior high students who have used the program successfully. Job finding is an appealing purpose for such groups.

School social workers are often faced with helping handicapped youths to find jobs. Often such students have become highly skilled in working hard to achieve what comes easily to most others. They know how to apply themselves diligently to routine, repetitious tasks because these are the skills developed by special education students to learn academics. These skills are usually assets on jobs.

However, some jobs require additional skills for which handicapped youths need extra training. An example can be found in a 1975 study which trained disadvantaged youths to write biographic material (Clark et al.). Four male and four female youths between the ages of fourteen and sixteen were taught how to fill out forms.

Training focused on learning how to fill out four application forms. They were given one application form at a time with a goal of completing each in five minutes. Filling out the forms consisted of supplying only certain types of information. The youths were trained specifically in those areas. During the training they were given fifty tokens for each form filled out completely. They kept practicing on the same forms until they could fill each one out twice without errors.

The trainees came together for two thirty-minute sessions over a period of six weeks. That time was sufficient for them to master the skills of filling out biographic forms.

In a 1989 study, handicapped teenagers were tested for their social-communicative behavior skills (Fromm-Steege et al.). The researchers proposed to document the multiple treatment effects of community-based instruction for four pupils with moderate handicaps aged thirteen to sixteen. Using a multiple-baseline-across-student design for the trained tasks and a multiple probe for the untrained, they showed that acquisition of social-communicative behaviors occurs at a higher rate when training is conducted in a community job setting than in school. They also showed that the students' use of social-communicative behaviors is related to the opportunities they have to display them.

The four adolescents studied could communicate verbally and did not show serious behavior problems. They attended special education classes in a segregated school facility. In the study, each was trained in two dissimilar work tasks one in school and one at a community work site. A task analysis was used in training for specific and related skills.

Results showed that three of the students could perform the work skills at 100 percent of task acquisition regardless of the setting in which they were trained. The fourth needed further training but showed promise for reaching

100 percent. Collateral frequency probes indicated that all students had a greater opportunity to display a variety of social-communicative behaviors in the community setting. Also, they had more learning opportunities in the community than in school. The number of trained skills used in the community was higher (129 vs. sixty-seven) and untrained behaviors showed less (fifty-four vs. twenty-seven).

JUVENILE DELINQUENCY

The school social worker encounters pupils who are involved with the law or have potential for problems in this direction, including those who have been present when others were apprehended and those who have had police-station adjustments for fire setting, petty thievery, curfew violation, robbing parking meters, truancy, disorderly conduct, possession of drugs, or running away. The school social worker is in a strategic position to identify these pupils and help them learn to live within the law.

Some police departments have prevention programs for such youths, whom they see as on the brink of becoming juvenile delinquents. However, police programs have not received the scientific research and evaluation they should. The behavioral school social worker may be able to take some action here.

It is not uncommon for students who are candidates for breaking the law to show several pre-involvement behaviors. These might start with regularly being left alone or unsupervised at home. Such children are rarely involved with positive out-of-home activities such as sports, scouts, artistic endeavors, ethnic or religious programs, or even community-run recreational programs. Instead, they are left free to roam the streets in search of companionship. This is often followed by a downward trend in the student's school performance because he has now found more enticing interests outside home or school.

Unsupervised and unoccupied children often find companionship among young street roamers on their way to becoming juvenile delinquents. The un-initiated learn the excitement of brushing with the law and, reinforced by their peers, go on to increasingly more serious crimes. Sometimes these behaviors receive additional impetus from the media and from paid performers in the movies, video parlors, television programs, or hard-rock concerts, who glorify macho role models. Eventually, they will commit a crime that requires incarceration, or their record of minor crimes will be so long that the authorities will refer them for a court appearance.

Some children will have role models at home for criminal activity, such as parents, uncles, aunts, older siblings, or family friends who have been sent to prison, joined gangs, or died in street fights with other law abusers. Some families are involved in such activities as pushing and using illegal drugs, gang or Mafia activities, robberies, murders, cults, or fraudulent financial enterprises. They play a cat-and-mouse game with law enforcement authorities. Students from such families sometimes become gang members either by choice or intimidation. In fact, all crimes that occur in society are potential reinforcers for delinquent behavior of schoolchildren.

The behavioral school social worker can approach this population in several ways. She can initiate prevention programs for pupils at great risk of becoming juvenile delinquents. Working with the child and the family to get him into constructive activities in out-of-school hours is an effective strategy, but the activities must be carefully chosen to compete with the rewards available from taking part in crime. Once a pupil is involved with the police, the social worker can possibly work with the child's family and the authorities to reverse his behavior by helping them deal with the antecedents and rewards for crime in his environment.

When a student already has a court day, the social worker could go to court to support the child or to help identify viable alternatives to incarceration. If imprisonment occurs, it may be important for her to remain in touch with the pupil and family as well as with the prison authorities to help them deal with the situation.

Once the juvenile has served his term, the school social worker prepares him and the school for his return to school, works with his probation officer, and tries to institute procedures to prevent his return to jail. In addition, the school social worker could try to prevent the student who has been incarcerated from becoming a role model for other boys and girls, especially those at risk.

Unfortunately, the prognosis for potential law breakers is not good. The numbers of those apprehended and incarcerated has been steadily increasing. In 1980, Poulin and associates estimated that in the United States there were an average of 626,223 children and youths who spent time in correctional facilities in any one year during the 1970s. Eighty percent of these were held in juvenile detention centers. The other 20 percent were in jails in small towns without juvenile facilities.

Correctional centers are often located in small towns, where they are run by political appointees for the economic benefit of the locality. Such superintendents are not monitored by higher authorities. Conditions are often deplorable, reflecting the absence of interest in the inmates, including children.

Graziano and Mooney (1984) describe juvenile detention facilities as

liberally laced with severe punishments for minor rule-breaking and even for habit problems such as bedwetting. Shaved heads, starvation diets, solitary confinement, severe whippings, and perversely ingenious forms of inflicting pain and humiliation on young residents appear to be common occurrences. Nowhere else in society is such rampantly brutal authoritarianism allowed—only in youth institutions and only against children (p. 151).

Applied behavior analysts, in sharp contrast, have studied juvenile delinquency at length and developed not merely humane, but effective treatments for them. They have worked in a number of settings, including prisons, residential treatment programs, community settings, and homes of the young-sters. Some of their experiments will be explored here, with emphasis on those carried out in home and community settings. Many can be used as individualized treatment models by the behavioral school social worker on the job.

Alexander and Parsons (1973) studied the impact on recidivism by short-term behavioral interventions with families of delinquents. They engaged in comparative studies of eighty-six families referred by the juvenile court to a family clinic. Of these families, forty-six were assigned to the short-term behavioral family intervention, nineteen went to a client-centered family group program, eleven went to a psychodynamic family program, and ten served as a control group receiving no treatment.

The sample included thirty-eight male and forty-eight female delinquents from thirteen to sixteen years of age. They were referred for running away, being declared ungovernable, habitual truancy, shoplifting, or possession of alcohol, soft drugs, or tobacco.

The short-term behavioral family intervention program used modeling, prompting, shaping, and reinforcing approximations to the target responses. Patterson and Gullion's *Living with Children* (1968) served as a manual for each family. A token economy was used with some families. The goals in treatment centered around developing and improving reciprocity in family interactions.

The client-centered family group program used a warm, empathetic environment where the therapist provided positive regard for the members of the group. The psychodynamic family program focused on the importance of insight as an agent for change. The control group received no treatment but was tested after six weeks, as were all the others.

The outcome measures of all four groups showed that short-term behavioral family intervention was significantly more successful than any of the other groups in developing respect for equality among members and appropriate family interactions. Recidivism rates were 26 percent for the group receiving behavioral intervention, 47 percent for the group in client-centered therapy, 73 percent for those receiving psychodynamic therapy, and 50 percent for the control group.

In 1971, Stuart experimented with behavioral contracting to help families with delinquent members. His work strongly influenced the field. In it he named four assumptions that have to be understood for behavioral contracting: (1) Receipt of positive reinforcements in interpersonal exchanges is a privilege rather than a right. (2) Effective interpersonal agreements are governed by the norm of reciprocity. (3) The value of an interpersonal exchange is a direct function of the range, rate, and magnitude of the positive reinforcements mediated by that exchange. (The return to those participating in the contract will be determined by the amount of positive reinforcement expended.) (4) Rules create freedom in interpersonal exchanges.

Stuart applied these assumptions to the case of Candy, a sixteen-year-old female who had been institutionalized at a psychiatric hospital for alleged promiscuity, exhibitionism, drug abuse, and home truancy. As a condition for taking her back home from the hospital, her parents demanded total control over her, allowing her to leave the house for only two or three hours on a summer day. In response to their demands, Candy began sneaking out of her bedroom at night to visit a local commune, returning home before dawn. After three weeks of this, the parents agreed to a behavioral contract.

At that point, the parents made her a ward of the court. The behavioral contract between Candy and her parents was then initiated. There were two major conditions: (1) It was far more permissive than what her parents had previously demanded, and it was accompanied by a monitoring sheet. (2) In exchange for her new privileges, Candy was made to understand by a court order that if she was found in a commune, the commune members, not Candy, would be prosecuted, for contributing to the delinquency of a minor.

Other specific rules were formulated based on the concept that "in exchange for the privilege of remaining together and preserving some semblance of family integrity . . . all agree to concentrate on positively reinforcing each other's behavior while diminishing the present overemphasis upon the faults of the others" (p. 11). Bonuses and sanctions were carefully spelled out.

Candy responded well to the terms and consequences of the contract, increasing her rate of compliance. As a result, the court dropped the wardship and only the behavioral contract remained. After this, her behavior continued to improve.

Stuart's procedures to achieve effective parent-child interactions include specifying in great detail the privileges as well as the responsibilities of family members. He sees contracting as a process between two people with one allowing privileges to the other in exchange for responsibilities fulfilled by the other. An adolescent's privileges could be use of the family car, spending money, and free time with friends. Responsibilities might be attending school regularly, keeping curfew hours, getting passing grades in school, doing household chores, and keeping parents informed of his whereabouts and expected time of return.

Responsibilities should be kept to a minimum, including only the things that parents really feel strongly about. Likewise, the rewards should be as few as possible and clearly delineated, including exact conditions to be met for getting them. It is important that the rewards be ones that the youth considers worth working for.

Most contracts include a system of keeping track of privileges earned and responsibilities completed, such as Candy's carefully recorded point system. This is most often accomplished with a chart or tokens in a glass jar. The earning of points should be so structured that from zero to whatever number of responsibilities are required can be earned each day. A child who does not complete any requirement on any one day of the program should never be left with no hope of receiving any rewards for the rest of the day, week, or month. He must always have the possibility of earning rewards.

Parents sometimes tell a young person that he is grounded for a week or month or even a year. Or some totally new behavior that the parent thinks of is thrown into the program after the contract is implemented. If such things happen, the youth has no incentive to try, because he has already lost his privileges for a long period of time or the contract is no longer specific.

Stuart's results were positive; they were not only maintained, but they were also improved beyond treatment. The contract generally helped remove responsibilities and privileges from contention. When disagreements occurred, they were tempered by agreement found in the contract. The contract laid the groundwork for more effective interaction among family members, and that was exactly what was needed.

The behavioral school social worker has many opportunities to work with adolescents who, like Candy, are acting out and getting into difficulties with law enforcement authorities because of poor communication with their families. Often these families, doubting the youth's ability to deal with the adult world, are very rigid and punitive with their adolescent offspring.

Behavioral contracting is an effective resource for the school social worker in helping such pupils and families. She can anticipate encountering cases similar to Candy's in the upper elementary grades, in middle schools, and in high schools. However, the technique has even been effectively used with children of younger ages.

In a national study of juvenile detention, Pappenfort and Young (1980) point out that most juvenile delinquency is handled by the police. The police have a number of options open to them for disposing of each case but usually turn the cases away from official processing. Their criteria usually include the severity of the delinquent act, the frequency of the youth's involvement with the law, the community attitude towards juvenile delinquents, and the nature of their interaction with the youth.

Werner and associates (1975) developed an intervention package for juvenile delinquents to use in their encounters with police. They indicated that a juvenile could be charged by a policeman if his behavior at the time of their initial meeting was inappropriate, even if a crime had not been committed. The question has to be raised whether training youths how to impress police favorably when stopped by them would help a guilty youth to avoid charges. However, the program Werner followed and its success are instructive for behavioral school social workers.

An initial study was made in which fifteen policemen and fifteen adolescent delinquents were interviewed to determine what behaviors were apt to influence an officer's opinion. The police officers and the youths agreed on the issues of "the importance of presenting identification promptly, how much effect the juvenile's behavior has on the officer's report, stopping the youth again, detention, and the ultimate decision of the courts" (p. 56). In addition, the policemen thought that looking at the officer, listening attentively, not interrupting him, and letting the officer know that he understands would make favorable impressions.

Six juvenile delinquents in a community group home volunteered as subjects for the experiment. Several groups of police officers and community volunteers also took part in the research at various times. After the initial study, three of the juveniles were taught how to behave when they encountered police, and the other three served as a control group receiving no training. All were given pre- and post-tests in which they role played being stopped by police.

After baseline was established, the experimenters measured and taught four behaviors. These included facial orientation (face turned toward upper torso of the officer), politeness in short answers (respecting policeman's authority by calling him such things as "officer" or "sir"), expression of reform (youth admits he has already been in trouble but says he means to avoid trouble in the future), and expression of understanding and cooperation (youth acknowledges that he understands the officer's concern and will cooperate with him).

The youths were trained in the four responsible behaviors for three weeks each. Each session lasted for one and a half hours. For each behavior they received instructions, including rationale, demonstrations, and practice with feedback. The sessions were videotaped and played back so that the youths could see themselves and comment on each other's behavior.

Werner and associates collected data throughout, and the results of the experiment showed that the three youths who were trained had significantly higher levels of the four behaviors they were trained in than did the control group. In addition, pre- and post-videotapes of the experimental group and the control group were evaluated by five police officers, five parents of delinquents, and five graduate psychology students. All rated the experimental group members much more favorably than the untrained group, who made only slight gains. Such training could be carried out by the behavioral school social worker who wants to help youths who are being picked up by police for rude behavior.

One of the most famous and well-studied behaviorally oriented programs is Achievement Place in Lawrence, Kansas. It has been used by the courts as an alternative to incarceration or probation for twelve- to sixteen-year-olds who have been found guilty. Started in 1967, by 1989 there were 215 group homes throughout the United States replicating the Teaching-Family Model (TFM) of Achievement Place. The homes are certified by the National Teaching-Family Association.

Each home is run by a married couple who have undergone a rigorous yearlong training period followed by continuous on-the-job training. Behavioral methods, modified and refined over the years, are used throughout.

The underlying assumption of the Teaching-Family Model is that delinquent behavior is the product of inadequate social learning experiences. Therefore, the goal of treatment is to develop appropriate behavior patterns. Positive social reinforcement and feedback are used to do this. Practitioners use a multilevel point system, social skills training, academic tutoring, self-care monitoring, prevocational skills teaching, and a home-based reinforcement system to monitor in-school behavior.

Six to eight youths live with one adult couple in the group homes. A self-government system is in place. The average stay for a youth is ten months. Recently, foster homes have been attached to the institutions for transitional training of the youths. Also, home treatment is continued after the youths leave the Teaching-Family institution.

Over the years, extensive evaluations of the in-house procedures of Achievement Place have been made, showing good results in school attendance, academic achievement, and remaining longer in school, with reduced police or court contacts and less recidivism (Fixen et al., 1973).

More recent studies evaluating Teaching-Family Programs have compared them with group homes not using the method (Kirigin et al., 1982; Weinrott et al., 1982). Boys and girls residing in the Teaching-Family Model homes committed fewer offenses than those in the other group homes. The youths earned higher grade point averages and passed more courses in school than did the youths in the other homes.

Weinrott and associates noted that the TFM homes were 22 percent less expensive to run than the others. Also, there was greater satisfaction with the Teaching-Family Model by the adolescent participants, school personnel, the courts, and the police. After the youths left the two types of homes, however, their differences were not as substantial.

III

COMPONENTS OF THE METHOD

6

USEFUL INTERVENTIONS

There is some evidence that the field of social work has been moving towards an empirical orientation. In discussing these trends, William J. Reid (1977) describes them as

outcroppings of a long-term progression toward greater reliance on scientific knowledge and methods in clinical practice—one of the earliest and most persistent goals of the social work profession. The movement has gained momentum with the gradual improvement of clinical research designs and methodologies, advances in data collection and processing hardware, the growth in the number of social workers with doctoral degrees, and the introduction of scientific management methods into social welfare agencies (p. 14).

A distinguishing characteristic of behavior analysis is its reliance on scientific research. Use of a control group, a characteristic of much scientific research, was developed in behavior analysis by R. A. Fisher in the 1930s (Hall, 1971). In this procedure, two groups of matched subjects are studied, but the experimental procedure is used on only one. The other, the control group, is given a placebo or simply not treated.

In some research, two different procedures are compared as they affect two different groups, with a third group serving as controls. Then measurements are taken to see what progress was made. Results demonstrate whether the procedure or treatment was effective; that is, whether treated groups were measurably better off than the control group after a specified length of time.

However, in working with teachers or parents on their own or their child's or student's problems, standard research methods using control groups would be cumbersome if not impossible to apply. One person is the focus of treatment—the one whose particular behavior has resulted in the need for treatment. Scientific method is essential, but a different format is required.

Throughout the 1950s, pioneer studies by M. B. Shapiro in London (1959 and 1961) developed a new approach—single-case design—based on the case-study method that was dominant during the first half of the twentieth century. In the 1960s, J. B. Chassan summarized the pioneer studies and subsequent findings that resulted in a fine-tuned method (Hersen and Barlow, 1976).

Single-case design is used in experimental research by a behavior therapist providing service to individuals. The process became most widely known through applied behavior analysis. The basic tenet of applied behavior analysis is that behavior is learned and retraining is required to change it. Therefore, a person's behavior and his immediate environment that controls his behavior are the focus of treatment. Careful attention is given to defining the behavior and studying what events precipitate it and what consequences result from it.

In carrying out the basic design, a body of experience has been developed in many different areas and with different populations. Children and education have been of great interest to behaviorists, and much directly applicable material is readily available for the school social worker. In this chapter, techniques are explored and questions related to their efficacy that have been raised by those in the field of behavior analysis are examined. The body of knowledge in applied behavior analysis is continually enhanced and modified or fine-tuned by new research. Sidman (1960, 1988) sees such change as an important strength of any research.

To Baer and his associates (1968), *applied* analysis is "not determined by the research procedures used but by the interest which society shows in the problems being studied. In behavioral application, the behavior, stimuli, and/ or organism under study are chosen because of their importance to man and society, rather than their importance to theory" (p. 92).

To behaviorists, a person's *behavior* is composed of physical events that can be precisely measured. Behavior is understood to be pragmatic. The task of a behavior therapist or behavioral school social worker becomes that of changing a client's behavior in precisely specified terms. The question must be raised as to whose behavior is to be changed, and obviously, it is the client's that is sought here. *Analysis* of behavior, to Baer and associates, requires "a believable demonstration of the events that can be responsible for the occurrence or non-occurrence of that behavior. An experimenter has achieved an analysis of a behavior when he can exercise control over it" (p. 93–94).

Applied behavior analysis is not the universal approach for social workers. Jehu and associates (1972) point out that behavioral casework emphasizes contemporary events that control problem behavior rather than "those which led to its acquisition in the first place" (p. 16). But there are still social workers who require a client to think back into his past to find the cause of his current behavior. Once that event from his ancient history is uncovered, he is asked to deal with his thoughts and feelings about what happened. This is seen as therapeutic by the same social workers; current events are merely "symptoms." There is no body of scientific evidence to support such theories.

Applied behavior analysts take the position that human behavior is mainly determined by environment and can therefore be changed by restructuring the environment. However, there are differences in the responses of people to their environment, differences determined by what preceded the behaviors and what consequences followed them. When different consequences are attached to the same stimuli, those stimuli are known as *discriminative stimuli*.

For example, consider the child whose older sister is the only one present when he comes home from school. He sits in front of the television set, ignoring his homework until his mother walks into the house. The television is then turned off, the homework is begun. Doing homework is clearly under the *stimulus control* of his mother.

Applied behavior analysts agree that what can be observed is measurable. But cognition, or what a person remembers or is thinking about, cannot be observed or measured. In this instance applied behavior analysts differ from cognitive behaviorists, who see thought processes and imagery as measurable. Applied behavior analysts find such data unreliable and measure only what can be observed. In fact, *reliability* is checked and rechecked throughout an intervention to insure that behavior change is truly occurring.

A social worker who understands the principles of learning theory can restructure the environment so that the client can develop more acceptable patterns of behavior. In the words of Pinkston and her associates (1982):

Behavior analysis in social work practice reduces the costly errors of subjective inference by determining environmental relationships to behavior change. Adequate analysis requires convincing demonstrations that specified interventions are responsible for behavior change. This demonstration may be explored through replication and control procedures (p. 7).

BASIC COMPONENTS OF APPLIED BEHAVIOR ANALYSIS

Initial Exploration

Contact between social worker and client starts with an *initial exploration* consisting of a thorough and explicit exchange of information as the two try to determine and define the client's areas of concern. William J. Reid (1978) stresses the importance of working only on problems the client acknowledges. These areas have to be specified to the point where a system for recording what occurs can be set up. For example, if weight reduction is sought, the first step is for the client to write down everything he eats for a week or two on a specially designed calendar.

In order to get the most accurate picture of what is supporting a child's particular behavior, the antecedents, behavior, and consequences (sometimes referred to as "ABC") are examined. It is usually found that similar events trigger the behavior, and the direction the behavior takes is supported by what follows after its occurrence. The major determinant of behavior is the consequence (Skinner, 1938).

Antecedents, behavior, and consequences should be charted as the first step in establishing a baseline (Sheldon, 1982). An observer or the student himself may keep a chart of these events as they happen, including the time that the behavior occurs. It is usually observed that the behavior occurs at about the same time every day.

An example is Jesse, who fell asleep in class every day about 1:30. His teacher, convinced that chaos at home prevented him from getting sufficient rest, allowed him to sleep, thereby excusing him from academic work for the rest of the afternoon. But when there was an assembly program or a field trip at the same hour, he typically did not fall asleep.

Analysis of a child's behavior requires taking a careful look at all of the major factors shaping it, no matter how complex. Usually this leads to a decision to proceed with the case. However, health or financial factors that have to be dealt with before social services occur are sometimes discovered.

Targeting The Problem

The school social worker, no matter what her orientation, is regularly called on to give quick preliminary diagnoses of children's problems. That is one of the major services that she renders. She is on the job, always available to a client or those involved with the presenting problem. Her quick, accurate diagnosis, followed by action to deal with the problem, is urgently needed on a regular basis.

A quick diagnosis on the spot requires that the school social worker come up with a tentative definition of the problem in clear language that can be readily understood by parents, children, and school personnel. This is another major component of behavioral therapy. To produce change in a client, treatment goals must first be stated in specific terms. Therefore, behavioral training will equip the school social worker to initiate treatment of a child.

Data must be collected before workable treatment goals are specified. Once collected, the data are examined by both client and social worker, and goals of treatment are determined. These have to be worded in concrete terms, such as "Belinda will lose ten pounds," or "Roger will bring his homework home daily," or "Victoria will speak in class only with the teacher's permission."

There are several ways of collecting data. When practical, the behavioral school social worker can do this herself. However, time is often a factor for the school social worker, and teachers do not always encourage her to sit in the room for long periods of time. If the behavior is of high frequency, spot checks can be made at regular times arranged in advance with the teacher. If, for some reason, a previously trained person other than the social worker (such as a school social work intern) would be less visible in a classroom, data could be collected by that person.

But the data collection might have to be done by other means. Tape recorders, video equipment, one-way screens, and computers are becoming more and more available to schools. They could even go unnoticed, accurately collecting data, if there are no local laws that forbid their use. Or other people in the pupil's environment, such as parents, teachers, other relatives, or peers could be enlisted.

Finally, self-observation by the child himself has been successfully used. The issue of a child's accuracy in self-recording has been raised (Sheldon, 1982). But if a client does not collect data honestly or is not willing to do so, he might not be ready to participate in changing his behavior.

Once data are collected, they have to be organized into a form the client can understand. In some classrooms where applied behavior analysis is used, students keep bar or line graphs on the blackboards or check-off charts on a piece of paper that can then be posted on a bulletin board. Then their classmates, visitors, and teachers can see the progress they are making. This should be done only if the pupil is comfortable with it.

Graphs and charts should be encouraged as much as possible, because they can serve as visible rewards for the child. If the child is sensitive about his progress, the school social worker's office might be a better place to keep the chart or graph. Once initial, or *baseline*, data are charted, targeting the problem to be worked on can begin.

Arkava (1973) suggests a simple procedure for targeting problems. First, the client lists the behaviors he sees as important. Next, he divides the behaviors into those he wants to eliminate and those he would like to develop. Then he ranks them in order of importance. The behavioral school social worker separates the simple behaviors from the complex to help the pupil choose a simple behavior to start with.

If the child wants to work on more than one problem, this can be done simultaneously or one after the other, as mutually agreed upon. It is also possible for a parent, teacher, friend, school administrator, or other person close to the child simultaneously to attempt to change one of the behaviors.

Although clients usually phrase their problems in negative terms, it is important for the behavioral school social worker to phrase the therapy to be undertaken positively. This will set the tone for achieving desirable goals. The client should focus on what *to* do, not on what not to do (Pinkston et al., 1982).

Early on, the school social worker has to determine who will work on the student's problem. It may be the child, the teacher, the parent, another child, or other school personnel. They may work singly or together with the school social worker. It often seems preferable to have certain combinations of individuals working on the target problem. But there is not always a choice; not everyone is willing to participate. When this is the case, the school social worker has to settle for whoever is willing to help.

Sometimes parents or teachers have to be taught skills they do not possess before a targeted problem can be treated. For instance, they might be called on to verbally reinforce a child but not have learned how to do this. Or they may yell at their students a lot and have to be taught to speak softly. Adults who tell a child to do something many times before the child finally does it have to be taught to make their requests the first time as they would have made them the last time. Usually, they have been conveying seriousness in the last request that has not been apparent in the preceding requests.

Arkava (1973) also advises establishing desired results in very specific terms. Then they can be measured, and the social worker and the client will plainly see what has been achieved. He suggests that frequency, duration, and quality of target behaviors be considered. Frequency refers to how often a behavior occurs. Duration involves how long a single episode of a behavior lasts. Quality is harder to determine because it "requires discriminating between acceptable and unacceptable behavior" (p. 19).

Treatment Plans

The behavioral school social worker has many things to consider in developing a treatment plan for a child. She has the advantage of treating the student in the natural environment where the behavior to be improved is occurring. In this environment, three things can happen. Either the school environment that is reinforcing the child's behavior will be changed, the pupil will have to manage to change his behavior in spite of the reinforcement, or neither will change and the problem will persist. The social worker has to explore all three possibilities and make a *functional analysis* and a *contingency analysis* to proceed.

Based on the goals and data, "a technological approach requires careful, clear, and objective descriptions of procedures" (Pinkston et al., 1982, p. 8). The procedures to be followed are spelled out in specific detail. The behavioral school social worker chooses from a number of techniques, such as modeling, role playing, writing down, repetition, and the like, to insure that the client fully understands what intervention is to transpire. Based on understood and agreed-upon procedures, a contract between therapist and client is drawn up and signed. Data collection is continued throughout the intervention and follow-up.

The chosen plan has to be fully and carefully defined so that data can be collected continuously throughout the procedure. It should be possible to determine along the way whether the plan is effective. Should it be found ineffective, adjustments have to be made. This is called *revising the intervention.*

The school social worker has to design treatment plans that will change a child's behavior but also are not so aversive to school personnel that the latter withhold their needed cooperation (Ninness and Glenn, 1988). Even when they accept the plans, there are some teachers who do not really want to improve a child's behavior. These teachers may want to be seen as martyrs having to deal with an impossible child, or they may want to have a "whipping boy" on whom to vent their frustrations. Some teachers, aiming for a child's removal from their class, do not want to try for anything else, even if it might improve the child's behavior.

EXPERIMENTAL DESIGN

Teachers and parents using the procedures of applied behavior analysis can change behaviors in a short time if they do it correctly. Determining accuracy involves measuring and recording behavior. To make measurement possible, systematic intervention procedures must be carried out. Scientific verification in single-case designs comes through one of two procedures, reversal/withdrawal or multiple baseline.

There are four basic steps involved in a *reversal* or ABAB design. First, a baseline (A) is established, followed by the implementing of an intervention condition (B). Next, there is a return to A, or baseline, eliminating the treatment plan for a short period to test its effectiveness. Finally, the treatment plan (B) is returned to in order to establish the new behavior. The AB design can be repeated as many times as the researcher wishes to use it (Hersen and Barlow, 1976). To evaluate the success of the intervention, the data must be studied and a fifth step (C), follow-up studies, conducted.

The basic advantage of the ABAB design is that it shows that the treatment manipulation rather than some coincidental event is changing the child's behavior. Also, it has the technical advantage of helping the behavioral school social worker to control the intervention and reassuring her that she is on the right track.

But the very reversal in ABAB design that is to the practitioner's advantage is sometimes viewed as a detriment to the client. The rationale here is that if a child is doing well because of treatment, why change it? If fire setting or self-destructive behavior is being targeted, the idea of returning the child to this state could be questioned on an ethical basis (Gelfand and Hartman, 1984).

The ABABC technique measures only one behavior at a time. If more than one behavior is to be measured simultaneously, a *multiple-baseline-across-behaviors design* should be used. This is the design most frequently used by applied behavior analysts (Wahler, 1969; Baer and Guess, 1971; Pinkston et al., 1982). For example, a pupil could simultaneously be observed for talking out of turn, leaving the classroom without permission, and being on task.

The multiple-baseline-across-subjects design is used to measure more than one client in a setting. This could be a problem if the clients interact with each other. The design could be effective in such procedures as measuring on-task behavior in a given classroom.

Compared to the ABAB design, the multiple-baseline design has certain advantages. It may be difficult or impossible to revert to the actual conditions of baseline after starting treatment. Also, the child's pain in reverting to the basic condition is avoided. Since multiple-baseline designs involve a long baseline series, they make it easier to observe trends and to prognosticate the future of an intervention.

There are also disadvantages to the multiple-baseline design. In checking a long initial baseline, performance may be disrupted because the behavior is not reinforced; boredom, fatigue, or impatience may be exhibited by the child. To counteract this, temporary rewards for cooperation, game playing, or shorter assessment periods could be used (Cuvo, 1979).

Other disadvantages of multiple-baseline design are the time and effort involved in collecting data on more than one baseline and in stabilizing the initial baseline before initiating treatment. In addition, the compatibility of the behaviors with the planned treatment has to be taken into consideration. With children, developmental tasks are not amenable to treatment design.

There have been some studies employing multiple treatment designs of varying dimensions (Hersen and Barlow, 1976; Kazdin, 1982; Gelfand and Hartman, 1984). Their advantage is that differing treatments can be used and compared. However, they have not been commonly used in research on children. This family of designs has been variously referred to as simultaneous or alternating, multiple schedule, concurrent, and randomized.

REINFORCEMENT

In determining a treatment plan, it is important to be sure that the reinforcement for the new behavior is on target. The school social worker must "recognize that reinforcers are effective in altering behavior only when they are arranged to be contingent upon the emergence of the behavior they are to strengthen" (Arkava, 1973, p. 31).

The Premack Principle (Premack, 1959) was developed as a method for identifying reinforcing events. This puts forth the principle that a response of higher probability can reinforce a response of lower probability. For example, if a parent tells a child that he cannot go out to play until he finishes his homework, finishing homework is being reinforced.

The reverse was also shown to be true. If a child was allowed to go out and play before doing homework, going out to play would be the high probability response. However, the successful application of the Premack Principle depends on the parent's being in control of the child (Ross, 1981). While it has not been conclusively established, it offers guidelines in observing clients.

One reason for the reinforcement procedure's not working could be that goals are initially set too high. Small steps may have to be taken to arrive at longer-term goals, as in the case of a child who does not know how to wash dishes. The parent would have to instruct the child first in scraping the dishes. This would be followed by rinsing them. After that, the sink would have to be cleared to make room for the dishes. This involves a shaping procedure (Bootzin, 1975).

Reinforcement, both positive and negative, is an integral and desired component of behavior analysis. It is used to help clients increase behaviors that will help them get what they need from their environment (Pinkston et al., 1982). This comes naturally to the behavioral school social worker, because social workers have long used social reinforcers, including attention and praise, to increase behaviors that áre the general aim of social work.

Reinforcement is most effective when used with natural consequences. When this is not available, as seen in the history of schools, contrived reinforcers are necessary. In past centuries, pupils were beaten when they did not study, and there are places in the world where this practice persists. In many schools, physical punishment was only gradually replaced by other aversive consequences.

Despite published efforts beginning with Rousseau's and including John Dewey's, educators have failed to motivate students with natural consequences. They have had to resort to contrived ones, such as report cards and suspensions for misbehavior. As a result, "most students study to avoid the consequences of not studying" (Skinner, 1982, p. 4). Skinner sees the early stages of learning to read and write as "too much the product of an advanced culture" to be reinforced naturally (p. 4).

It cannot be assumed that what will motivate one student will motivate another. This must be taken into account when the behavioral school social worker decides on what reinforcements to use in a specific case. One pupil may like to play games, another to draw, a third to read, etc. The social worker must tune into each client separately and determine his unique preferences. The Premack Principle advocates observing a child's behavior to determine what he most likes to do.

Too often teachers will make arbitrary decisions about reinforcing children rather than using natural reinforcers. Ferster (1967) cites the case of a teacher who promises to reward with cookies pupils who put on their coats. He makes the point that teachers (and parents) want children to put coats on because the adults are reinforced by such behavior. Actually, the child would want to put his coat on when he went outside, if it was cold enough. The cold weather would be a natural reinforcer; cookies would not be needed.

There are two main types of reinforcement, positive and negative, both designed to increase desired behavior. Positive reinforcement refers to the presentation of an event following a behavior, while negative reinforcement refers to the withdrawal (or termination or postponement) of an event. They do not mean *good* and *bad*, and should not be confused with pleasing or aversive behavior (Schwartz and Goldiamond, 1975).

The term *positive reinforcement* refers to the frequency of a response followed by a positive reinforcer. It is not the reward that may be used to achieve this result. "If an event follows behavior and the frequency of behavior increases, the event is a positive reinforcer" (Craighead et al., 1976). Skinner (1969) points out that *reward* refers to being given compensation for something, usually because of a prior contract, while *reinforcement* designates simply the strengthening of a response. A teacher's praising a child whenever he does a math problem correctly would be an example of reinforcement.

Bandura (1969) identifies three essential features needed for successful re-inforcement. (1) Reinforcement should be "sufficiently powerful and durable to maintain responsiveness over long periods while complex patterns of behav-ior are being established and strengthened" (p. 225). (2) Reinforcing events should be contingent upon the desired behavior. (3) There should be a reliable procedure for eliciting or inducing the desired response patterns to insure that reinforcers will occur frequently.

Negative reinforcement is also a factor in developing sought change through behavioral interventions. It is commonly considered in behavioral studies (Bandura, 1969; Sheldon, 1982; Wolpe, 1973; Pinkston et al., 1982; Craig-head et al., 1976; Ross, 1981; Michael, 1975; Honig and Straddon, 1977; Schwartz and Goldiamond, 1975). In studies dealing exclusively with negative reinforcement, Brian Iwata (1987) and Bruce Townsley (1989) have raised the question of whether positive reinforcement can be administered without at-tendant negative reinforcement.

Townsley explains that a negative reinforcer is a thing or event that is al-ready present before a behavior occurs. Prior to the behavior's occurring, this thing or event is called an *aversive stimulus*. A situational demand, such as a verbal reprimand, deprivation of a privilege, a loud noise, or a shock, is an aversive stimulus, if the client perceives it to be aversive.

In negative reinforcement, the increase in behavior is a function of escape from, or re-moval of, an aversive stimulus as the consequence of a response. Therefore, a behavior or response has been negatively reinforced if it increases or maintains because of the contingent removal or reduction of a stimulus. (Sulzer-Azaroff and Mayer, 1977, p. 141).

The client may try to remove (escape) or prevent (avoid) an aversive stimulus or negative reinforcer. Escape behavior removes an ongoing aversive stimulus. Avoidance behavior prevents the aversive stimulus from occurring. Avoidance or escape of something unpleasant may be as or even more powerful than trying to achieve something pleasant and harmonious.

If it becomes evident that a student is trying to avoid or escape (negative reinforcement) doing what he has to do to achieve in school, the pupil, school social worker, and teacher will have to face that fact. Plans, even if they are unconventional, will have to be made to get the student on the track of suc-ceeding in his work.

Sheldon (1982) points out that negative reinforcement is a "clumsy term" that gives behavior therapists trouble. Pain and anxiety are the most common negative reinforcers. They result in doing something quickly to remove the cause of stimulation. Sheldon defines a negative reinforcer as "a stimulus which, if *removed* contingent upon a certain response, results in an *increase* in the probability of that response" (p. 54).

Pinkston and associates (1982) define negative reinforcement as "the re-moval of an unwanted consequence following a behavior which increases the future probability of that behavior. That is, the client escapes negative consequences by engaging in specific behaviors" (p. 18). But all reinforcers, negative or positive, increase the targeted behavior. Ross (1981) points out that negative reinforcement strengthens a response and should not be confused with punishment.

Examples of negative reinforcement are the alcoholic who takes a drink to avoid the criticism of his family for imbibing excessively the night before. Another is the mother who yells at her children to get them to stop what they are doing for a moment and repeats the yelling later on. Still another is the motorist who puts coins in a meter to avoid getting a ticket. In fact, all behaviors governed by law are motivated by negative reinforcement to escape fines, court appearances, or imprisonment (Liberman, 1972).

As an example of negative reinforcement, Bruce Townsley (1989), a behavioral school social worker, tells of a teacher who wrote notes to the parents of each child in her class, telling them that the child had not completed a lesson. Each note was put in an envelope. If the child completed the assignment, the note was torn up. If he did not complete it, the note was sent home.

Ayllon and Azrin (1968) offer five points to the behavioral school social worker planning to use reinforcers with clients: (1) Deliver reinforcement immediately after a response. However, if there is "a distinctive and tangible stimulus event (such as tokens, points, or stars on a chart) to bridge any delay" (p. 77), the behavior can be maintained longer. (2) A variety of conditioned reinforcers may be used, including tokens, verbal praise accompanied by smiles or hugs, points, or credits. (3) Use a combination of reinforcers to prevent satiation or in case there are aversive stimuli preventing adaptation. (4) Take into account the uniqueness of individuals in choosing reinforcers. (5) Sample the reinforcer in advance in the setting in which it is to be used.

Gelfand and Hartman (1984) extend this list. They advise administering reinforcers in small units, under an agent's control. The reinforcement should be compatible with the overall treatment program and should be practical.

Because reinforcement can be a powerful force in a person's life, the behavioral school social worker must be conscientious about what it is used for. But it must be something that the client will surely respond to or it will not create the desired change. Reinforcement must be consistently administered in order for agreed-on goals to be achieved.

In a widely cited study by Vance Hall and associates (1968), the effects of teacher attention on study behavior were examined. Believing that some of the problems that arise in the classroom stem from the teacher's behavior, they instructed teachers in the principles of applied behavior analysis and in the effects of social reinforcers on classroom learning in particular. Teacher attention was presented as a key to changing pupils' classroom behavior.

The studies were carried out in two elementary classrooms in the poorest area of Kansas City, Kansas. The principal recommended the teachers to take part, and they, in turn, selected pupils who were disrupters or dawdlers. One or two observers came to the classrooms regularly during the experiment.

The children were observed for their orientation toward an appropriate object or person. At the same time, teachers' verbalizations to the students were recorded, as well as whenever the teacher was within three feet of the student being observed. The observers decided that a period of study was a ten-second time during which no disruptions occurred. Baselines were obtained after two weeks of observation two to four times a week for scheduled thirty-minute periods. These were shared with the teacher, and the fundamentals of social reinforcement were discussed.

Reinforcement sessions followed, when the observer held up small pieces of colored paper which the pupil could not see, to signal the teacher to attend to the child. This consisted of moving to his desk, making some verbal comment, giving him a pat on the shoulder, or something comparable. Weekly after-school sessions were held between experimenters and teachers to discuss the effectiveness of what they were doing. Adjustments in instructions were occasionally made.

When the baseline condition was resumed, it was noted that the teachers paid attention to the students when they were not studying. After this the social reinforcement of study was resumed. When high rates of study were reached again, the teachers were told to reinforce the students without the colored signals. Whenever it was possible after treatment, periodic post-checks were made for the rest of the school year.

Results of the study were gratifying. The use of contingent teacher attention was clearly a quick and effective means of developing desirable classroom behavior. A surprising result was the "degree to which student behavior responds to thoroughly systematic teacher attention" (p. 10).

Whether the experiments could be carried out by teachers in regular school classrooms was unclear. But the teachers were well able to use the technique even with no prior experience with behavioral methods. With a relatively slight adjustment to the usual school environment, the procedures were effective in crowded urban poverty-area classrooms.

PUNISHMENT

The use of aversive measures in behavioral training has been of concern to behaviorists for a long time (Reese, 1966; Skinner, 1968; Bandura, 1969; Dinsmoor, 1970; Ferster et al., 1975; Schwartz and Goldiamond, 1975; Craighead, Kazdin, Mahoney, 1976: Sulzer-Azaroff and Mayer, 1977; Redd et al., 1979; Pinkston et al., 1982). Skinner (1968) sees punishment as a complex system. He writes:

By punishing behavior we wish to suppress, we arrange conditions under which acceptable behavior is strengthened, but the *contingencies do not specify the form of the latter behavior.* When we punish a student who displeases us, we do not specify pleasing behavior (p. 187).

Behaviorists divide punishment into two categories, *punishment by application* and *punishment by removal.* Punishment by application includes being sent to one's room for breaking something, being grounded for coming home late, being spanked for taking something that was someone else's. But they qualify as behavioral punishment only if they decrease the frequency of the response to the antecedent.

If a positive reinforcement can be removed after an unacceptable response, it is punishment by removal. Examples might be having a driver's license revoked for reckless driving, having to stay in after school for getting a low grade, or being grounded for violating curfew.

In an intervention with a child, a behavioral school social worker should not use punishment alone. If this is done, the client will withdraw or become difficult to work with. Punishment is used to decrease the probability of unwanted behavior. The most common forms of punishment used by a behavior therapist are response cost, presentation of an aversive event, time out, and overcorrection.

Response cost refers to the response-contingent withdrawal of specified amounts of reinforcers. It is different from punishment, which presents an aversive stimulus to reduce the rate at which a behavior is emitted. Response cost withdraws a certain number of reinforcers. Fining a person for parking in the wrong place is response cost. Slapping a child for shoplifting is punishment if its contingent application reduces the rate of that behavior.

Aversive event is not a synonym for an unpleasant stimulus. If it occurs after the response and causes the response to decrease in frequency it is an aversive event. Such things as slapping, yelling, spanking, and "putting down" qualify as aversive events. They could help minimize further punishing reactions of family members to each other when this is a goal in treatment.

There have been times when a yell, a shock, or a spank have decreased highly undesirable behavior. However, if considering an aversive event for use in treatment, a school social worker should discuss the matter with the school principal or others in responsible positions in the school. There may be local legal restrictions on particular punishments.

Time Out

Time out has been widely used in and out of schools. Behavioral teachers and clinicians have used the punishment procedure of time out from positive reinforcement in the classroom more than any other method. Craighead et al. (1976) define time out as "contingent removal of the opportunity to earn positive reinforcement" (p. 237). Sometimes the time out is more social isolation than strict time out.

The behavioral approach to time out is to use it sparingly and discontinue it as soon as possible (Schwartz and Goldiamond, 1975). Time out may range from just turning away from an individual to placing him alone in a barren room. It is an aversive technique and should be used in combination with techniques of positive reinforcement for best results.

Mash and Barkley (1989) recommend limiting time out by parents to two problem behaviors, usually involving a command or household rule. Time out should be implemented shortly after the child's noncompliance starts, not when the parents get very upset. The parents should issue a command, wait five seconds, issue a warning, wait five seconds more, then take the child to time out if he has not begun to do as he was told. The child is then told not to leave time out until the parent allows it. He will be ready to leave when he has served one or two minutes for each year of his age, when he has calmed down for a brief period, and when he agrees to obey the command given him. If he does not comply, he will be given a light punishment.

Mash and Barkley advocate using an adaptation of this time-out sequence in public places. This might involve asking the child to stand at an out-of-the-way wall or go outside or to the car until compliance is achieved. An alternative is to delay the procedure until returning home. In that case, taking along a picture of the child in time out and a notebook to write down the fact that he will experience it at home are recommended.

An alternate version of time out involves the mother turning away from the child throwing a tantrum and complimenting the other siblings on something they have done. Then the child is placed in time out for up to three minutes. At that time he is taken out. If he continues to act out, he is returned and remains up to another three minutes. This procedure continues until the child is quiet. Then the parent says something to him about something else that he did well. No mention of the precipitating behavior is made until a time when parent and child are calm. Patterson (1976) advises having the child clean up any mess he may have made during the tantrum.

Skiba and Raison (1989) examined the relationship between time out and academic achievement in an elementary school self-contained program for students labeled severely behaviorally disordered. The classroom was the most restrictive in the whole school district. It was a short-term placement for the students.

Over a period of one school year, eighty-eight pupils who were enrolled in the class for seven to nine months were studied. The sample represented the entire population of the school, except for a program for autistic children elsewhere in the building.

The pupils studied were diagnosed as "emotionally/behaviorally disordered." Eighty-nine percent were males. Fifty of the children studied were not mainstreamed; the other thirty-eight had an hour of mainstreaming a day. Four of the classrooms were primary level, and six were intermediate.

The school used a standard school-wide behavior management plan including classroom token economies, an access-level system like the one used in Achievement Place (starting with rewards after a short interval, periods to earn rewards were gradually lengthened), and a time-out system for disruptive behavior. There were three levels of time out for disruptive or dangerous behavior—in class, out of class, and isolation.

Students sat facing the wall for two minutes for an in-class time out. If the pupil would not comply with that time out, he would be assisted to an out-of-class time out in a special room with open carrels monitored by one or two trained aides. He would stay in the time-out room for one minute for his first out-of-class time out for the day, three minutes for his second, six minutes for his third, and nine minutes for his fourth and succeeding times out. The child was expected to stand with his face to the wall of the carrel with reasonably good posture.

If a child was judged dangerous to himself or others, no matter where his misbehavior occurred, he was put in a monitored, locked seclusion booth for a ten-minute period. If he was disruptive there, he stayed another ten minutes. Upon returning to his class there was no particular attention paid to him, and it was assumed that he could handle himself. He was expected during free time or after school to make up the work he missed.

All out-of-class time out was logged carefully and continuously by computer. There were no records kept for in-class time out. The computer data on out-of-class time out were compared with Skiba and Raison's observations. Careful data were also kept and examined on truancies, suspensions, and absences. Curriculum-based data were kept in fall, winter, and spring each academic year and were standardized district-wide.

Results showed that students averaged six to eight times out and a little more than one isolation time out per month. Most spent an average of less than ten minutes in time out each day they were there. The majority of students used the time-out room on an average of one to two times a week, but 18.2 percent were sent there more than 100 times a year. The mainstreamed pupils spent more time in time out than those not mainstreamed.

The average amount of time spent in time out per year was eleven hours, or two days. In addition, students lost an average of 11.41 days a year due to absences, truancy, or suspensions. None of the measures of time out related in any significant way to academic achievement.

The students studied were the most disruptive in the district. The low levels of time typically spent in time out make it unclear how much the positive programming contributed to the above result. Two of the students, however, spent more than six thousand minutes, or twenty instructional days, in time out. It was not possible to study the effects of this on academic achievement. In spite of limitations of the study, Skiba and Raison concluded that time out did not pose a threat to the instruction of the student. The positive reinforcement was a possible factor in improving results.

White and Bailey (1989) developed a time-out system to control disruptive behaviors of elementary physical education students on the school playground. They worked with two classes: a regular fourth grade of thirty pupils and an alternative-education class of fourth- and fifth-grade boys with severe behavior problems. Disruptive behaviors were seen as the result of lack of consequences for inappropriate behavior. Most of these behaviors were aggressive and defiant (noncompliance, aggression, and throwing objects) and often prevented the teacher from completing the lesson.

To establish consequences for inappropriate behaviors, White and Bailey chose a time-out procedure known as "Sit and Watch" that had previously been used with preschoolers. It was like other times out used in the school but with two differences. The time out was limited to three minutes, and the students monitored their own time out with an hourglass egg timer.

A multiple baseline using Sit and Watch was used in each class. The teacher of the alternative-education class had been using a behavioral checklist. While the baseline was being established, the misbehaving child was told what he had done, sent to Sit and Watch for three minutes, then returned to the class activity. He used the timer to monitor his time. If a child was sent to Sit and Watch more than once in a class period, he lost free or computer time.

The decrease in disruptive behaviors was immediate and dramatic with Sit and Watch. During a ten-minute observation period, the mean number of disruptive behaviors in the alternative class started at 219 and decreased to 98.5 after the teacher used the behavioral checklist. With Sit and Watch, the mean number decreased to 4.6 in ten minutes. The mean number of disruptive behaviors in the regular class during baseline was 53.6; it decreased to 3.7 with Sit and Watch.

Dougherty, Friedman, and Pinkston (1982) studied time out used with response-cost procedures with children in a special education classroom where there had been problems with a time-out program. The goal of the intervention was "to develop a less restrictive punishment program with an improved or equivalent level of effectiveness" to be accepted by staff and implemented in the facility (p. 322).

The program was monitored by a social worker consultant who supervised the teachers' data collection and observed teachers and pupils herself. Spot checks were used to test reliability of teacher observations. The researchers found a private school class of thirteen boys from ten to fourteen years old. All had been "tuitioned out" of public school for aggression against teachers or other children or for "hyperactivity."

A point system for completing assignments and evaluating attitudes during assignments was put in place for the entire school. Points were also given intermittently for other positive behaviors, such as ignoring teasing or getting down to work quickly. Rewards were time in a "free room" equipped with such items as a snack shop, pool and Ping-Pong tables, television, and other recreational equipment.

Time out and fines were given for inappropriate language or locale, aggression, distractions, noncompliance, damage to property, stealing, or violation of smoking rules. Time out was three minutes in a non-isolated corner of the classroom. Refusal to take time out in the classroom could result in a five-minute time out in the hall or the loss of free-room privileges for the day. Or refusing could result in warnings for inappropriate behavior (reminder status) if they had gone four days without refusal of time out or leaving school. Fines were subtracted from points earned.

Results of the study showed that response cost (fines) functioned as well as time out. As a result, the school adopted the response-cost system instead of time out, which they had considered overly restrictive. The use of research methods as an integral element of social work consultation proved valuable here in making operational decisions.

Ethical issues have been raised about time out. In fact, there have been laws passed and lawsuits around this issue (*Morales v. Turman, Wyatt v. Stickney, Horacek v. Exon, New York Association for Retarded Children v. Carey*). The courts and the public have regarded it as solitary confinement. They fear that institutional staff could lock up a person for days on end with no connection to a treatment plan.

This is far removed from the behavioral use, which makes it contingent on the occurrence of previously determined undesirable behavior. Also, it usually lasts one to five minutes and never more than fifteen. It is used only as part of a larger intervention and only if it is observed as productive in reducing undesirable behavior (Budd and Baer, 1976; Redd et al., 1979).

Sulzer-Azaroff and Mayer (1977) list a number of safeguards to observe in using time out in schools.

1. Call the place where the child goes the "quiet place" instead of the "time-out room."

2. Be sure the place is equipped with adequate lighting and a carpet.

3. Remove dangerous objects from the place, including anything that can be swallowed, thrown, or torn off the walls or that has sharp corners.

4. Be sure the child can be observed, and set a timer to insure his removal after the prescribed time elapses.

5. Only use the quiet place after more benign and positive measures have failed.

6. Get the informed consent of the pupil, parent, guardian, advocate, and administrators in the school before using time out. A school social worker must be familiar with current politics and laws that may restrict its use.

7. Before visitors see the room, tell them about it and its safeguards. Show and interpret for them baselines and intervention data that indicate the effectiveness of the procedure.

Flooding and Implosion

Behavior therapists have considered and sometimes used flooding or implosion (Bandura, 1969; Wolpe, 1973; O'Leary and Wilson, 1975; Schwartz and Goldiamond, 1975; Craighead et al., 1976; Mash and Barkley, 1989). Flooding consists of massive exposure of a person to something he fears. In implosion, the client imagines exposure to the feared object.

Behavioral school social workers have used these techniques to help a student cope with the name calling he receives from other students, the idea being that if he hears a bad name enough he will ignore it in the future. Thus, a school social worker would sit with the child while the insult is repeatedly mentioned. This continues until he can listen to it without reacting.

While there have been successes reported, Schwartz and Goldiamond warn against use of these techniques. They point out that "while repeated exposure may produce extinction of fear in some people, many (if not most) people react extremely negatively when presented abruptly with a feared object" (1975, p. 243). It is possible that flooding and implosion will inflict pain on a client, which could worsen his behavior. Also, once exposed to such techniques, a client may not return for further treatment.

GENERALIZATION OR GENERALITY

From the beginning, the school social worker should consider ways of maintaining the behavior achieved through treatment. If natural reinforcers or reinforcers in the environment have been used, maintenance should be possible. Otherwise, reinforcers or the person to provide the follow-up reinforcers will have to be integrated into the treatment plan before it is terminated. After treatment, there should be a spot check at regular intervals for at least a year by the behavioral school social worker or someone working with her who is trained in behavior analysis.

The question of generality or generalization (the terms are used interchangeably) of the new behavior to other settings has been raised. Generality cannot be expected to occur automatically. It must be programmed and should be an integral part of treatment. Drawing from the research of Kazdin (1977) on token economies and the review of the literature by Stokes and Baer (1977), Pinkston and associates (1982) have prepared a comprehensive plan for insuring that changed behavior will generalize from the treatment setting to the natural setting.

Several suggestions are made by Pinkston and associates for insuring that generality will work and that the clients' newly learned behaviors will be applied in other situations. There must be an ongoing plan for generality from the initial interview through termination. Generality must be monitored and addressed during assessment, intervention, and termination of therapy; any unplanned generality also requires monitoring and addressing.

Another important consideration is the "law of extinction," which teaches that if a behavior is not reinforced after treatment, it will not continue (Ayllon and Azrin, 1968). The behavioral school social worker has to integrate a plan for maintenance, generalization, and follow-up of the new behavior. Because she is changing in-school behaviors with their continuance in school as the goal, continuation after treatment should be an easier task for her than it would be for the therapist who has to bring the behavior from one type of environment to another.

Pigott and associates (1987) devised a plan to develop a more pragmatic generalization technology. They determined that this could be done by tracking at an early stage the behaviors that were being maintained in the natural environment. This would allow a more accurate evaluation during and after treatment of the effects of treatment. An example might be a child who reads avidly at home yet underachieves in school. The home environment maintained the avid reading already. Achievement in school would be a goal in treatment.

The instrument they researched and recommend for sorting out behaviors already maintained by the natural environment is a scatterplot analysis. The scatterplot would compare treatment and nontreatment behaviors starting with baseline and continuing throughout the intervention.

The scatterplot would (1) assess the amount of baseline and post-baseline covariation between behaviors, (2) determine whether the observed generalized effect was due to a preexisting covariation between behaviors, and (3) assess whether there is a significant change in strength of the relationship between the behaviors as a function of the intervention. They found it crucial to determine whether the generalization was due primarily to preexisting covariation (baseline) between these behaviors or was a unique function of the intervention.

During the assessment stage there are several crucial areas in which the behavioral school social worker needs to make correct choices. These include selecting target behaviors likely to be maintained in the natural environment, determining availability and scheduling of reinforcement, planning for client self-management, removing cues that lead to undesirable behavior, and involving significant others in supporting client-change efforts.

During intervention, concern with generality or generalization is considered at every step. Strategies include extending stimulus conditions, scheduling intermittent reinforcement, strengthening out-of-session behaviors, and training basic behavior analysis skills for future problems.

Termination should be a period in which to plan maintenance of the new behaviors acquired during treatment. Included in this plan should be instruction by the therapist teaching the client how to control new behaviors, substitution of the new program for the old one, enhancement of generality while terminating, modification of termination and maintenance contingencies, and generality occurring spontaneously without prior planning. Finally, generalization should be evaluated as the direct intervention would be.

TOKEN ECONOMY

There are many teachers who see "token economy" as synonymous with "behavior mod." This could imply anything from sending home a smiley or sad face to keeping data on a child's on-task behavior, followed by increasing it with differential reinforcement. Token economies have been widely studied and used by behaviorists (Ayllon and Azrin, 1968; Patterson, 1968). They are an integral component when behaviorists study children in the school setting (Carter, 1972; Homme et al., 1973; Sulzer-Azaroff and Mayer, 1977; Ninness and Glenn, 1988).

The behavioral school social worker has many uses for token economies. When putting one in place, she should be careful to consider how behavior changed by the method will be maintained. Rewards integral to the environment will be the easiest to maintain. It is also important to be sure conditions for receiving rewards are carefully spelled out, known to all parties involved, and adhered to throughout.

In introducing token economies in school, the behavioral school social worker assesses the degree of sophistication of the adults she is dealing with. She should not be seduced by their claiming prior knowledge and experience. A delicate situation may exist if those teachers do not really know how to use the method and have to be taught by the school social worker.

SOCIAL SKILLS TRAINING

The school social worker encounters children who have been labeled as behavior problems simply because they lack the social skills to adjust to the middle-class standards of school personnel. This may be caused by low rates of reinforcement in the child's environment attributable to a lack of necessary response repertoires (Pinkston et al., 1982). These may be related to a person's language or the acceptable style in his social environment.

Social skills have been described as the ability to practice behaviors that are positively or negatively enforced and "not to emit behaviors that are punished or extinguished by others" (Libit and Lewinsohn, 1973, p. 304). Goldsmith and McFall (1975) define social skills training as useful for any "specific skill deficit in the individual's repertoire" due to faulty training, lack of experience, or biological dysfunction that can be overcome or partially compensated for through "appropriate training in more skill response alternatives" (p. 51).

Because social skills training emphasizes developing and facilitating prosocial behavior, problem behaviors are seen as deficits in social skills. The types of skills taught will vary with each client. Such coaching techniques as prior instruction on how to initiate social interaction and how to play specific games, peer pairing, behavioral rehearsal, film viewing, modeling, shaping, prompting, role playing, and feedback are used.

Assertiveness training is sometimes used in conjunction with social skills training. Wolpe (1973) has defined assertive behavior as "the proper expression of any emotion other than anxiety towards another person" (p. 81). According to Liberman (1972), "Assertiveness training is a valuable therapeutic tool for patients with difficulties in expressing justified resentment and anger or for patients who are passive and withdrawn in interpersonal situations" (p. 157).

It is an educational method used to teach clients specifically how to state exactly what they think—but in an effective way—as a deterrent when they are approached aggressively. Behavior rehearsal is an integral part of assertiveness training. It includes such techniques as modeling, role playing, shaping, operant reinforcement, feedback, and rehearsal.

Assertiveness training teaches the client to speak and present himself in a favorable social light: "Its purpose is to teach people how to stand up for themselves without being aggressive. Since social workers, more than other professional groups, deal with the weak, the powerless, and the put-upon, this technique has particular relevance for us" (Sheldon, 1982, p. 188).

Weist and Ollendick (1989) conducted a study to determine whether assertive behaviors in children are actually related to interpersonal efficacy. They were further concerned about whether assertiveness training of children is really on target because therapists usually use "subjective validational methodologies" (p. 1).

For their study, they selected fifteen popular boys and fifteen rejected boys in a regular classroom. These boys were chosen through a standard classroom sociometric procedure which they saw as an adequate measure of social skills. The researchers assumed that popular boys would show higher levels of traditional assertive behaviors than the rejected boys, if assertive behavior is an important, meaningful social skill. To further insure the validity of what they would be doing, they trained child prompters to an effective level of performance, to prompt during the role-play assessment to "improve the validity of the procedure" (p. 2).

To determine the status of each boy, they were randomly assessed on a standardized test for five minutes each before a videocamera. The videotape was then saved for eventual data analysis. The taped behaviors were carefully examined by the researchers to select behaviors that popular and rejected boys engaged in. They then determined traditionally observed behaviors. From these, several behaviors were charted for study.

The traditional behaviors to be studied were eye contact, smiles, praise, noncompliance, intonation, and response duration (number of words the subject emitted). The behaviors observed in videotapes were orientation, grammar, negative statements, context-inappropriate behavior, verbal repertoire, and energy level.

The popular boys showed significantly higher levels in two of the six traditional behaviors (smiles and speech intonation) while five of six behaviors observed on videotapes were displayed differently between the two groups (more body orientation, elaborated speech, and energy among rejected boys; fewer grammatical speech errors and less context-inappropriate behavior among popular boys).

Weist and Ollendick concluded that behaviorists researching assertiveness behaviors should empirically validate behavioral targets before intervention and use systematically observed (on videotapes) alternative behavior targets. They believe they showed that had they observed only traditional behaviors, they would have had significantly different and less effective results.

Richards (1989) has developed guidelines for conducting assertiveness training groups. She recommends that group members be of the same age and meet in a quiet room where there will be no interruptions. There should be eighteen to twenty sessions, each lasting about forty-five minutes to an hour. The group leader (school social worker) should meet with the students individually before the group starts to inform them of the details of meeting as well as what they can expect to accomplish. In this pregroup interview, as with any behavioral intervention, initial exploration of the child's problems should be addressed.

During the first group session, the school social worker should help students distinguish between effective communication and behavior that is negative, ineffective, too passive, or too aggressive. Pictures, videotapes, movies, or other visual aids could be used to improve understanding. Thereafter, at the start of each session, time should be taken for the pupils to discuss good or bad experiences associated with communication.

Richards suggests that the school social worker do the following throughout the assertiveness training:

Use short role plays, because shy students are less threatened by fewer words and other students do not become bored.

Involve parents when possible to help group members practice and generalize their skills.

Do not permit any one student to monopolize any part of the session.

Try to involve shy, passive pupils by shaping through role playing and social reinforcement (praise).

Be careful not to demean a group member when he makes an error that has to be corrected.

Lavish students with praise when they demonstrate good communication.

Oden (1983) evaluated the effects of social skills training designed to enhance children's relationships. She examined five studies that used "coaching" methods designed to "enhance the peer acceptance of children with low peer status" (p. 76). Control groups and sociometric testing were used throughout. In addition to the preparatory coaching, a variety of techniques were taught to the children for use in future planned interactions with other children.

Oden's comparative studies revealed that simply putting low-status children with peer partners to play games resulted in no gains and even some declines. But when they were taught how to play games in advance and then paired with peers, gains were made by the low-status children.

In a similar study, children who were peer paired and coached showed gains that continued, as reported in follow-up studies, several weeks later. In generalizing the effect to the classroom, it appeared that having some peers from the child's own class was helpful in all cases. However, a child who was severely rejected by his class probably would do better with students from another classroom and just a few from his own.

Oden indicates that reviews and comparisons with other studies were not conclusive. Feedback and instruction to the low-status pupils by peers seemed to have potential. Also, placing socially isolated students with well-accepted peers who were a year younger was productive at the preschool level.

Oden indicate that the value of modeling in this situation requires more research with isolated or rejected children. Answers are needed on the value of using "demonstrations, live or filmed, compared to other social exchanges that depend more on coordinated activity and communication with a particular individual" (p. 81). Rejected children may not know what are basically acceptable behaviors in a given social situation. These will have to be taught before they can be practiced. Modeling could be used with coaching to teach such social skills and procedures as starting a conversation, sharing and taking turns, and approaching a group.

Weinrott, Corson, and Wilchesky (1979) used social skills training with withdrawn children but added the dimension of training teachers to intervene. They used twenty-five teacher-pupil pairs from regular grades one to three in seventeen different schools. The teachers identified the children, and their judgments were verified by follow-up observations. All of the children were thought to be in need of professional intervention because they rarely or never volunteered in class or initiated conversations with peers. They seemed to be daydreaming most of the time.

Twenty of the children and their teachers were placed in a treatment group, and the remaining five pairs served as a control group. After six and a half weeks of baseline condition, the teacher training began. In weekly sessions, the teachers were taught increasingly more complex interventions, including contingent attention, modeling, role play, point systems, and group contingencies.

Trained observers made classroom observations through all phases of the study, including baseline, ten weeks of intervention, and more than five weeks of follow-up. The children were watched for frequency of self-stimulation, looking around the room, appropriate peer interaction, volunteering, and addressing the teacher.

By the end of the treatment period, the treated children equaled their normal peers. The control group made no gains. There was no objective data, but other school personnel reported improved behavior on the part of treated children outside the classroom.

Teacher intervention, in the studies of Weinrott and associates, became increasingly more elaborate as time went on. After the treatment period ended, the teachers continued to use the interventions as long as they thought the targeted children needed them. During the first five weeks of the program, targeted children were treated individually with contingent teacher attention and role-playing sessions outside the class.

During the last five weeks, the other children in the class became involved with group contingencies and the reinforcement of peers for starting interactions with the withdrawn classmates. The most pronounced change in the targeted group occurred during the last five weeks.

Jones and associates (1989), of Project 12-Ways at Southern Illinois University, reported on their use of social skills training with a thirteen-year-old white male who had scoliosis and had had two major corrective spinal surgeries. His family of four had been referred to the project because of child neglect. He was reported and then observed as verbally aggressive, noncompliant, and having poor social and academic skills.

The parents of the thirteen-year-old were poor role models. The father had been unemployed since a vocational accident, and the mother was alcoholic. The father abused the mother physically and sexually. The ten-year-old sister had chronic enuresis.

Two assessments were developed, targeting social skills initiation and play behaviors. Based on these, remediation steps were developed to teach the client, one by one, behaviors he could use in initiating an interaction with another person. The behaviors involved approaching another person, maintaining eye contact, using a neutral tone of voice, stating the person's name, and asking him to play a game. Discriminative behaviors were included to deal with rejection in a suitable manner.

Play behaviors were targeted by Project 12-Ways staff as the social skills were. Appropriate play behaviors included such things as how to make a request, positive verbal behavior, and appropriate voice quality. Inappropriate behaviors consisted of threatening, criticizing, and name calling.

Three procedures were used. During the first, the trainer coached the boy on the targeted behaviors. During the second, two staff members modeled each social-skills behavior that had appeared on a task analysis at the start of the intervention, in addition to the play behaviors. During the third procedure, confederates (mother, sister, project worker, or friend) role played with the subject to provide opportunities to test skills. Toward the end, staff members provided verbal praise when indicated.

The boy said he enjoyed the game playing; it may have been reinforcing in itself. Data was collected throughout. Both social skills and play behavior were measured as significantly improved. After the intervention, the boy was randomly observed and continuing improved behavior was reported.

SYSTEMATIC DESENSITIZATION

Systematic desensitization, or counterconditioning, has its roots in the animal research of Wolpe (1973). A pioneer of behavior therapy, Wolpe based his theory on deep relaxation therapy (sometimes using hypnosis or medication) and substitution of non-anxiety-producing experiences for anxiety-producing ones. Methods used, such as gradual verbal imagery, slowly increasing talk about the fear, and exposure to the feared object, have been widely practiced to reduce fears and phobias.

After massive research on the method and some good results, Wolpe supports cognitive therapy. But operant behaviorists have criticized systematic desensitization in terms of the reliability of the research, given that the client's imagery has to be measured. This is not a method for the behavioral school social worker to use because a specially equipped private office is often a basic requirement, and whether referral should be made to a specialist is questionable. But the method shows promise, and the behavioral social worker should watch for future research on its reliability.

INTERACTIVE MACHINES

Because immediate feedback is seen as essential for effective teaching (Skinner, 1968; Sulzer-Azaroff and Mayer, 1977; Vargas, 1977) various methods, devices, and machines have been used to accomplish it. Recently, sophisticated machines have been developed for data collection, testing, and providing information to those who want to learn or who need behavior changes (Woll, 1989).

In the 1920s, Sidney L. Pressy designed several teaching machines to test intelligence and knowledge. These were used after the pupil had received some instruction. They were important because the student could be involved in using them, in contrast to the audio/visual aids, which were just beginning to be developed. Pressy's machines did not succeed because educators were not ready for them, and psychologists had not yet come to grips with learning theory.

In the 1950s, Skinner experimented with teaching machines and developed interest in them (Skinner, 1968). A pupil using a teaching machine read the information presented, answered test questions, found out whether his answer was correct, and immediately checked his answer for accuracy. Machine programs in spelling and mathematics were easily developed, as were college courses. Teachers could prepare their own material for use in the machine.

Skinner's machines offered the advantage of directly involving students in monitoring their own rate of progress in a subject. Other advantages of the machines included the potential for home study. Also, use of the machines reduced the practice of punishment techniques used widely by teachers to motivate their pupils. Many questions were raised about machines. Teachers feared they would be used to replace teachers in the classroom, although Skinner did not see this as an outcome. Instead, he saw them as efficiently reinforcing the teaching and helping manage the classroom.

Meanwhile, a plethora of gadgets has been developed to help the classroom teacher. These are primarily designed to offer a student immediate feedback after testing his knowledge or to record behavior. Kitchen timers, pocket parking-meter reminders, signals set on prerecorded cassette tapes, and lights cued to an electrical timer have been used to alert an observer to record behavior. A chemical process used with a magic marker has been employed for immediate feedback in supplying pupils with correct answers (Vargas, 1977).

Automated films and videotapes have also been used to record data. Ethical and legal concerns should be taken into account before procedures for recording data are implemented (Sulzer-Azaroff and Mayer, 1977).

Bass (1987) used computerized interactive videotapes to train observers to use a ten-second partial-interval observational recording system. They viewed videotapes and scored response occurrences on a computer keyboard. Incorrect scoring resulted in immediate computerized feedback and rescoring. Average accuracy rates across all target behaviors were consistently above 90 percent.

With the advent of the personal computer, all kinds of new learning opportunities are available in the classroom. Computers are gradually appearing in schools. Interactive electronic networks have been initiated to improve the educational systems of the country (Woll, 1989).

In order to keep pace with the advances in technology needed by schools and industries, Woll has proposed computer-based instructional systems, interactive training systems, and electronic data networks. In fact, he sees these as necessary for competitive survival.

Woll proposes that an industrial and educational electronic service be made available to industry and schools much as electrical power service is now delivered. The users could contribute to the data base as well as take data from different networks.

A national educational network would distribute educational curriculum packages and testing services to the schools for a central database. Classroom teachers would manage electronic classrooms and order, from the central database, courseware to be downloaded to local memory with which each individual school would interact. This could then provide fully individualized instruction and learning to each student (p. 2).

Other advantages would be current, continually revised curricula, standardized course format, new enhancements easily added as technology improves, better statistical base for evaluation of student progress, ability to track changes in subject matter, skill, and knowledge requirements, and a better understanding of procedures by which pupils learn.

The White House Task Force on Innovative Learning has proposed developing such systems (Messeir, 1989). It points out that there are innovative public and private schools and corporate training programs using the cutting-edge technologies, plus major breakthroughs in brain/mind research and recent research on optimal conditions for learning. State-of-the-art learning methods and software could link human intelligence and artificial intelligence, increasing enjoyment and interest in learning, accelerating learning, improving attendance, decreasing retentions in grades, referring fewer students for special education, enhancing motivation, and reducing delinquency and antisocial behavior.

Such a system could ultimately produce a self-regenerating work force, a new ethos of lifelong learning throughout society, heightened competitiveness and worker productivity, and less dependency on government. Using a greater array of learning approaches and technological tools, it would reach a broader spectrum of individuals and be more cost effective than learning programs that end up retraining and remediating as well, according to the task force.

RELAXATION THERAPY

Behavioral school social workers sometimes use relaxation therapy to help a child become more comfortable. Relaxation therapy has been used outside the school for a number of problems, including alcoholism, asthma, migraine headaches, seizures, and tics (Davidson and Davidson, 1980). It has often been used with systematic desensitization procedures (Wolpe, 1958; Davison, 1968; Graziano and Kean, 1968; Bandura et al., 1969; Ross, 1981).

Azrin and Nunn (1977) recommend relaxation techniques combined with other customized alternative procedures in treating eye squinting, hair pulling, hand or foot tapping, head shaking, nail biting, posture control, stuttering, teeth grinding, tics, and hand trembling. Weil and Goldfried (1973) reported on the exclusive use of relaxation therapy in treating an eleven-year-old girl for insomnia. Mash and Barkley (1989) cite use of relaxation techniques with children suffering from abuse, chronic diarrhea, and eating disorders.

A wide variety of relaxation therapies has been used and advocated, including:

hypnotic relaxation, autogenic training, biofeedback, various forms of meditation, and perhaps the most frequently used of all, such disparate behavior as engaging in regular prayer, listening to music, jogging, deep breathing, having a good meal, practicing Eastern martial disciplines, watching television, bowling, taking a cruise, having sexual relations, or lying on a beach. (Lehrer and Woolfolk, 1985, p. 95).

But only three have been researched by behavior analysts: progressive relaxation, autonomic therapy, and behavioral relaxation training.

Jacobson (1938) used progressive relaxation to treat medical and psychological problems related to tension. Progressive relaxation training has been the most frequent method used in the United States (Bootzin, 1975). It aims to identify the muscle group causing tension and then to systematically relax those muscles. The client learns to relax one muscle at a time, a task that can take months.

Progressive relaxation also has been used with systematic desensitization, which relies heavily on the power of suggestion. This is known as autonomic therapy. It is thought to be a quick method. Tapes are used to monitor it.

The many different techniques used by relaxation therapists have been a bar to empirical study. Lehrer and Woolfolk (1985) made a comprehensive literature review in which they concluded that "progressive relaxation has greater muscular effects and autogenic training greater autonomic effects" (pp. 100–101).

Poppen (1988) advocates Behavioral Relaxation Training (BRT), which can be measured on a Behavioral Relaxation Scale. He views research on other methods as unreliable. Unlike other methods, the BRT has been standardized and is "an observational procedure providing a reliable, valid, quantified measure of the motoric aspects of relaxation" (p. 46).

BRT studies the relationships between antecedents, behaviors, and consequences of the client. The BRT procedures are carefully spelled out as to actions and timeframes. After clients are carefully trained by the behavior therapist, they are expected to practice the procedures regularly throughout the day and at home between sessions.

Pre- and post-tests are used, and the client is observed during application of procedures. He is also provided with feedback. Although formal research on this procedure has established "immediate physiologic results" (p. 69), Poppen suggests that more research is needed.

7

PARENT TRAINING

Some schools provide services beyond classroom education of children, such as parent training courses given or arranged by the school social worker. But others discourage parents from participating in the child's formal education or from bringing home problems into the school. Therefore, the school social worker's functions with parents will differ from school to school. School social workers could work individually with one or both parents, hold prescheduled group treatment training series, and teach behavioral parent training to parents who then become trainers of other parents.

Work with families has long been a given in social casework. It has been natural, therefore, that school social workers would see their function as working with the families of the children referred to them. However, in order to truly serve the child in a school setting, parameters must be established on how much work should continue with parents. It is the position of this author that any home issues directly affecting a presenting problem that she is called on to address are valid concerns of the school social worker.

Data has not been forthcoming on specific parameters set by school social workers on work with parents. However, a study by Kurtz and Barth (1989) did attempt to measure the amount of school social worker time spent in work with families and to describe the direction of concerns. It was found that school social workers throughout the nation spend a third of their time working with parents. Most often they become involved providing short-term services to low-income and single parents.

Parent training has been widely studied and used by behaviorists, resulting in an extensive body of literature and further research in this area (Hawkins et al., 1964; Ryback and Staats, 1970; Herbert et al., 1973; Pinkston et al., 1982; Patterson, 1976; Pinkston et al., 1981 and 1982; Hall, 1982; Dangel and Polster, 1984 and 1988; Graziano and Mooney, 1984). However, for parents who suffer from socioeconomic disadvantage, insularity, and a large number of day-to-day aversive stimuli, parent training should be a major—but not the only—component of therapy. Other debilitating factors in their lives must also be dealt with (Lutzker et al., 1982; Dumas and Wahler, 1983).

The parent training method uses parents as therapists who administer treatment in the home. The behavioral school social worker's major role here involves training the parent by arranging for data collection, setting up a program related to a targeted goal, monitoring results, making changes as necessary, evaluating the procedure regularly, and conducting follow-up studies.

Using parents as observers has the advantage of sharpening their skills in pinpointing behaviors, and of providing a large sample of behavioral data at low cost. But there are also numerous disadvantages to the use of parent observations, such as the possibility that parents will react to their awareness of what the treatment effect is expected to be by skewing the data in that direction (experimental demand).

Several studies have raised questions regarding the validity of parent reports. Patterson (1973) cites a study in which a group of parents receiving a placebo treatment reported positive changes in a global rating scale, while data collected by independent observers indicated that rates of deviant behavior had increased.

In their review of outcome measures used in parent training, Atkeson and Forehand (1978) note that parent reports on specific problems and more global (therapist generated) parent questionnaires are in agreement with each other more often than either source is in agreement with data collected by independent observers. When parent observation data is analyzed separately from global reports, however, the results have agreed with data collected by independent observers in 78 percent of fourteen out of eighteen studies. This indicates that parent observation data is a reliable measure of problem change.

Behavioral parent training has been described in the literature since 1964. It has been given in group and individual settings and has become increasingly popular. Literature delineating the method has been developed for parents and is used to accompany parent training programs or as resource books (Becker, 1971; Hall, 1971; Patterson, 1976). Books directed at parents have been so popular that they have been revised periodically.

Guidebooks for professionals have been written by Dangel and Polster (1988) and Marilyn C. Hall (1982). Parent training has become an integral part of intervention programs by behaviorists working with families in need of an alternative to out-of-home placement of their children (Ginsburg, 1989).

Parent training is currently one of the major therapies for the treatment of children. Dangel and Polster (1988) find parent training as most suitable for three- to twelve-year-old children. They have worked with three thousand families in the last fifteen years; parents receiving training have represented all races, nationalities, ethnicities, educational backgrounds, and socioeconomic levels. Also, they have treated a wide variety of differently structured families and child behavior problems. Their videotaped parent training programs are used in thirty-four states and three countries.

The weekly treatment hour of traditional therapy does not allow the therapist to observe the actual behavioral problem (truancy, aggression, neglect of homework). Data as to the generalization of treatment effects into the child's natural environment are limited to retrospective reports by parents untrained in behavioral observation skills. Behaviorists assume that memory is not a reliable measure of behavior, but that planned, consistent, and checked observation is.

Similarly, traditional and behavioral therapists differ on the source of inappropriate behavior. The traditional therapist sees behavior as the result of developmental stages that a person has internalized. The client is supposed to develop insight about such matters during the course of treatment and then struggle with himself to make changes. Since he is only dealing with himself and talking about it to his therapist, an office or clinic is a satisfactory location for treatment.

Behaviorists, on the other hand, assume that maladaptive behavior is maintained by the child's current natural environment, primarily by the kinds of interactions that occur between parent and child. Therefore, the development of appropriate behavior in a clinic or lab setting may be extinguished at home. In order to insure maintenance and generalization of changed behavior after treatment, there must be an integral plan throughout a behavioral intervention. This often involves work within the home environment.

Training parents in observation skills and behavior modification techniques increases the amount of data available to the therapist and alters the parental contingencies maintaining the behavior. The focus of parent involvement has gradually shifted from enlisting parental aid in solving discrete behavior problems to changing the parent-child interactional system (Berkowitz and Graziano, 1972).

In family systems theory, a rule refers to regularities in interaction, either actual or potential (Reid, 1978). A metarule governs a whole class of interactions. Reid points out that the parent-child conflict can be viewed as a descriptive metarule in which coercive and often ineffectual parental authority is challenged by the child. In parent training this metarule is changed to the effective exercise of parental authority characterized by reciprocal exchange through contingency contracting.

BEHAVIORAL STUDIES

Berkowitz and Graziano (1972) reviewed thirty-four studies of parent training, fifteen of which involved parents of aggressive children. Most of the studies reported positive results. Although many of the studies did not have rigorous experimental designs, four used reversal designs, and two series of studies used control groups.

Patterson (1973) and Patterson and Reid (1973) have done a great deal of work in this area. In a pilot study and two replication studies, Patterson trained the parents of aggressive children in behavioral techniques. The subjects in the replication studies consisted of a series of consecutive referrals for extremely aggressive behavior.

Substantial changes in the rates of deviant behavior occurred. For example, in one study nine of eleven families showed decreases of 30 percent or more in the rate of targeted deviant child behavior. Intervention procedures consisted of training parents to observe and record data on deviant child behaviors, reinforce appropriate behavior, and withhold reinforcement from targeted deviant behaviors.

Noncompliance, or refusal to obey parental requests, was also a frequent presenting problem among the families of aggressive children. In one of Patterson's samples, all eleven sets of parents chose noncompliance as a target problem.

In reviewing several studies, Forehand (1977) found that noncompliance is frequently perceived by parents as their child's most significant behavior problem. Behavioral interventions increased compliance in a clinic setting. Studies in which parents were trained in the clinic to use behavioral principles at home had mixed results. But when parent training occurred in the home setting, all studies reviewed found training in differential attention with time out to be effective in increasing compliance.

In 1970, Vance Hall and associates used teachers and parents as researchers in a study of multiple-baseline designs for measuring the effects of punishment and systematic reinforcement at home and at school. Three different interventions were studied. These included a fifth-grade teacher measuring tardiness; a high school French teacher recording quiz grades; and a mother studying the clarinet practice, Campfire project work, and reading of her ten-year-old daughter.

Hall used three basic types of multiple-baseline techniques: across situations, across individuals, and across behaviors. In one, baselines of two or more behaviors, one after the other, were recorded, "causality being demonstrated if the behaviors change successively at the point where experimental procedures were applied and not before" (p. 253). The second design involved measuring the concurrent behavior of several individuals in the same situation, followed by successively applying experimental procedures to the behavior of one after another of the individuals. The third multiple baseline measured "the same behavior of a single individual concurrently in different stimulus situations" (p. 253).

In this study all three methods were found to be workable. Also, the teachers and parents used were effective in their therapist roles. The subjects were under careful instructional control through the whole experimental study. When a new procedure was introduced, "there was an immediate change in behavior directly related to the announced change in condition" (p. 254).

A study reported in 1970 by Ryback and Staats used parents as therapy technicians in treating learning disabled children using the SMART procedures and token-reinforcer system. SMART is a complex reading training program based on that used by the Science Research Associates Reading Laboratory. The procedures insure that the child with learning disabilities will be continually motivated throughout the training program.

Every day, the pupil is given colored tokens in amounts based on his successful reading behaviors. At stated intervals, achievements of the child are measured on standardized tests. As a consequence of the SMART approach, the reading rates of the four children studied by Ryback and Staats accelerated, even though the material read became increasingly harder as they went along. The program was extended to an average of 51.25 hours for each pupil taking part in the experiment.

Neisworth and Moore (1972) made use of a parent as therapist with an asthmatic child. While they recognized that asthma is a medical problem, they showed that its manifestations can be changed with behavioral interventions. The mother in the case was anxious about her son's asthma and kept cautioning him about it. She gave him a great deal of sympathy and attention at bedtime when his wheezing attacks occurred.

To treat him, the parents of the asthmatic boy agreed to put him to bed on time with no more attention until morning. They did this affectionately but definitely. The intervention allowed the child to buy his lunch at school instead of packing it if he had coughed less the night before. As a result, his attacks diminished significantly and remained at a low level during eleven months of follow-up.

Studies have been conducted to determine whether parent training techniques can be employed with mentally retarded parents. Good results have been achieved if a slower pace is used (Budd and Greenspan, 1984). Arthur Sontag (1988) reports success in teaching a profoundly retarded nonverbal child of retarded parents to understand the meaning of "no." This was done using extensive repetition and training the parents to use the same response to inappropriate behavior.

Feldman and associates (1989) used picture books with illiterate retarded parents. Eight such mothers, whose children were judged by child protective services at risk for being neglected because of parent incompetency, were trained. In this study, the trainers used a different picture book for every skill being taught.

The trainer showed the picture books to the mothers one at a time, allowing each one a week to practice each skill. Then the trainer returned and observed the mother while she went through the skill "without instruction, prompting, or assistance from the trainer" (p. 2). When one skill was mastered, they went on to another. Results showed that a majority of the mothers improved their parenting skills with picture books and no further training.

Bakken and associates (1989) experimented with five mildly retarded parents who were being followed by child protective services. They wanted to determine if child-parent interactions could be improved by clinical instruction and then generalized to the home. Assessment by observations in the home showed no significant generalization to the home. However, when the same parent training was given in the home and followed by rewards, it did result in improved child-parent interactions. This would seem to favor the use of parent training on an individual basis for retarded parents at home but not in group settings.

PARENT TRAINING GROUPS

Not only have parents been used as therapists with their children working one-on-one with a professional behavior therapist, but behavioral parent training has also been extended through group training and structured courses for parents. One group program, Regional Intervention Program (RIP), serves parents of two- to four-year-olds. It has been replicated in various settings nationwide. It uses parents "as primary therapists for their own children, as trainers of fellow parents, and as implementors of the service delivery system's daily operations" (Timm, 1988, p. 146).

Some parents are so confined by their parenting and breadwinning roles that the school social worker can help simply by arranging baby-sitting to allow the parent to get out of the house and for errands and recreation. Respite programs have been developed in the home and hospital for such relief for parents of developmentally disabled children. For the in-home program, a social agency assigns a qualified person to the home to relieve the parent for a specified time. In the hospital respite program, a handicapped person is taken into a special section of the hospital for an agreed-upon time to free the parent. Other parents need such breaks, too.

In parent group training, the conducting school social worker presents general principles of behavior analysis and therapy to the parents at the outset. Each parent is interviewed before the training begins. In the interviews, parents are exposed to behavioral methods and informed about what to expect from the training. Some initial exploration is made of what the parent wants from it, as well. Details such as time, place, and duration of group meetings are also included. In addition, the school social worker should get a commitment from the parent to take part in the group.

In the first session, parents are trained in data collection and are asked to begin keeping data immediately. In succeeding sessions, on the basis of data collected and exploration of problems in the group, each parent targets a behavior of his child that he wishes to change. Then an individual plan for each parent to follow is developed and carried out under supervision of the school social worker.

Throughout the training process, parents in the group are encouraged to share their thinking, progress, results, and expected plans with the other members of the group. Thus the group becomes a means of expanding the perspective of each parent as well as offering support for each participant in his enterprise.

Such parent training groups are usually conducted at times most convenient to the parents and meet for weekly sessions of approximately one and a half hours. Of course, the services of the school social worker are offered without charge. One parent training group found a volunteer pair of grandparents who enjoyed caring for a group of youngsters gratis while the parents were in session.

When parent training groups are offered after school hours at the parents' request, some have included baby-sitting services for a fee shared by the parents and going directly to the baby-sitter. Since mostly younger pupils (less than twelve years of age) are targeted in parent training, it has been effective to use responsible upper-grade students to baby-sit.

If the behavioral school social worker is conducting a group series or teaching a course, she has to organize and arrange it in advance. She may decide to use another behavior therapist whom she imports to the school setting or to be the therapist herself. Or she and another therapist may decide to co-lead the group. Parent training could be carried on during or after school hours.

When group parent training is planned, the school social worker will have to recruit participants, make arrangements for space, decide if baby-sitting is necessary, and determine the best time and place for the group to meet. She will have to explain all these details, as well as the approach and content of the parent training group, to each parent. She should include here a statement of realistic expectations from the group experience.

PARENT TRAINING COURSES

Courses in behavioral parent training have been conducted. Notable among these is the Responsive Parenting Program worked out by Marilyn C. Hall and the staff of the Responsive Parenting Institute in Overland Park, Kansas. A parent manual designed as a workbook to accompany the course has been developed (Hall, 1976 and 1982).

The course begins with procedures to define and measure behavioral parent interventions. This is followed by methods of computing reliability, graphing, and research design. Next, major concepts and procedures are taught. Consequences to decrease inappropriate behavior follow. Then what to do about specific behaviors is taught. Finally, generalization and maintenance of new behaviors learned in treatment are considered.

Hall's course has reduced the content to what she terms The Four-Step Model In Teaching Behavior. The first step is to define the parent's concern, the second is to decide on an appropriate method to measure the behavior. Step three is designed to intervene through the systematic use of contingencies. In step four, efforts to improve behavior are evaluated.

Kathleen Westling (1986), a school social worker at LaGrange Area Department of Special Education (LADSE), has developed a parent training program known as *Supportive Home Teaching*. It is designed to strengthen the parent-school relationship for those involved in special education.

Along with *Parents As Effective Partners*, its companion course, *Supportive Home Teaching* has designed methods for professionals to respond to parents' needs for support, specific skills, and information. LADSE has recognized parents as their child's "first teacher," and they have emphasized that parents are full members of their child's special education multidisciplinary team. Between 1978 and 1984, twenty-four courses have been taught, and 544 parents completed the courses. Others attended the courses but did not finish them.

Westling's program has several features. It provides for co-leadership of the course by a parent and a professional team member. Courses are clearly sponsored by the school and held in school buildings. They are skill-based and include teaching of specific skills needed by parents in dealing with their offspring. Also, parents participating in the course become a support system for each other.

To insure success of the *Supportive Home Teaching* course, the school social worker advises getting administrative approval first. This did happen at LADSE, where Dr. Howard P. Blackman, executive director, negotiated with the school board for adoption of a policy for the school district that supported applied behavior analysis. When the parent training courses were initiated, not only were the philosophy, content, and costs of the program discussed with him in advance, but the benefits to the school district were presented. (See chapter 8 on settings).

Benefits were seen in clarifying matters about which parents were troubled, giving them a school contact to whom to express their concerns, and thus avoiding future problems. Westling also advises that after the course is initiated, it is important to keep the administration informed about the attendance, parent responses, results achieved, and any other matters that develop.

The LADSE school social worker encourages seeking teacher support for the parent training course. This is needed to recruit parents and spark interest in the training among teachers. Eventually, the same teachers are used to colead courses with a parent who completed it. A carefully spelled-out procedure involving the teacher is followed to set up the course.

TRAINING PARENTS INDIVIDUALLY OR IN PAIRS

In conducting parent training, there are several areas in which the school social worker might have to deal with sensitive matters. Basically, these will be a parent's own behaviors that he needs to change in his handling of his children, beginning with the parent's attitude. The attitude needed first is agreement that improvements can take place.

Change is sometimes threatening to parents, and it requires consistently hard work to alter their handling of a child. Even one targeted problem could require that their very way of life (the child's environment) be adjusted. Parents have been known to make all sorts of excuses not to change, even when their child's behavior is causing them much pain (Patterson, 1982).

One of the excuses some parents make for not attempting parent training relates to previous exposure to the psychodynamic method. That approach is based on the cognitive assumption that if a person has insight into what he is doing, he will then correct it. B. F. Skinner is not a cognitive psychologist because "we need to change our behavior and we can only do so by changing our physical and social environments" (Skinner and Epstein 1982, p. 189).

Psychodynamically oriented social workers have sometimes countered that what one observes is only a symptom of a deeper illness, and if taken away, another symptom will appear. This has not been proved and in fact has been refuted many times. The studies of Baker (1969) and Ayllon and associates (1970) prove the validity of the behavioral approach by treating observable behavior that is not replaced by another "symptom" when it is removed.

In introducing behavioral parent training to the parent of a child referred to her, the school social worker might encounter a parent who states that his child has a deeper illness and any attempt to improve her behavior will not work. The case of six-year-old Louise is an example. The girl was referred to the school social worker because she cried often in school; she said it was because she missed her mother. She was living with her father because her mother was an alcoholic, and a divorce was in progress.

Father complained that Louise would not mind him. As part of the divorce proceedings, Louise had been examined by a court psychiatrist who told the father that she had a fundamental psychiatric problem, namely, that she was rebellious and oppositional.

The father went on to insist that he could not comb Louise's hair because she would not keep still. This he attributed to her basic problem of being rebellious and oppositional. He saw her condition as permanent and one he never could change. Nor did he really want to.

It is often the knee-jerk reaction of school personnel and parents to assume that if a child has done something of which they disapprove, the solution will come if the child can state the underlying cause. This, of course, will not be possible. Failing to get the child to explain why he did something, school personnel will then turn to the parents to explain. This will also be impossible. It has even happened that a teacher will then decide that the parent is remiss because he could not explain his child's behavior.

Behavior therapy looks for explanations of a person's behavior in what occurred just prior to the behavior and in the consequences immediately following the behavior. All of this can be seen and documented. Data collected on initiating a behavioral intervention usually reveals an antecedent triggering the behavior and a consequence that supports it. As more data is collected, a pattern of repeating the same antecedent and consequence comes to light.

Once a parent has agreed that he can change his child's behavior with behavioral parent training, there are other areas that require adjustment. He will have to make peace with the idea that data must be kept throughout the entire intervention, so the school social worker must help him develop a data collection system that requires a minimum of record keeping. A simple check mark on a page or placing a token in a glass jar might be in this category. Also, having another person in the home to check reliability could serve as a reminder to the parent to keep the data.

Once data has been kept, it becomes the task of the school social worker and the parent to work together on targeting the problem they wish to eliminate. If there is more than one problem, they can be worked on simultaneously or consecutively. The school social worker must develop the skill of cutting through all of the generalities and ramblings of a parent to get down to what specifically is the problem behavior. Just defining a problem as a behavior will be helpful. The target problem must be stated clearly. It might be "Louise will stand still while having her hair combed," or "Victor will put his completed homework in his book bag as soon as he finishes it."

Next, a treatment plan that the parent agrees to has to be developed. This will take considerable specification and modeling. It can never be assumed that a client understands exactly what he is agreeing to unless it is made very clear in advance and he can accurately describe it in his own words. Every method that the school social worker can use should be employed here, including such things as behavioral rehearsal, role playing, repetition, writing things down, and having the parent feed back what he has learned.

"The modeling and rehearsal technique gives the client the opportunity to first observe another person exhibiting the desired behavior and then enables the client to practice the desired behavior before trying it outside the interview" (Pinkston et al., 1982a, p. 32). The school social worker should use as many of these techniques as are needed until she is satisfied that the client understands exactly what will transpire. Pinkston and her associates emphasize further that feedback enhances the rehearsal and should always be included in positive reinforcement. In addition, fading out should be used once the targeted behavior is established.

Follow-through is important for both the parents and the school social worker. There should be regular meetings between the two set for a specified time (for example, meeting once a week for thirty minutes over a period of two months). By the end of this time, the parent should have reached the targeted goal. In some cases, it will be necessary to curtail or extend treatment time. At the end of the course of treatment, it is important to continue with plans for maintenance, generalization, and follow-up checks.

PARENT EDUCATION PROGRAM

Pinkston and associates (1982a) conducted in-home parent training for children referred by their school social worker as showing behavior problems in school. During initial clinic interviews, a standardized description of behavior principles was given to parents. Modeling, behavior rehearsal, and manuals were used next to teach the parent management skills. A copy of Becker's *Parents Are Teachers* (1971) was given to each parent.

Differential attention (parent showing approval of good behavior and ignoring bad behavior) and contingency contracts were the treatment procedures for each child. Two punishment techniques, time out and overcorrection, were used sparingly. To insure this, parents agreed in writing to use no more than a limited amount of time out.

After agreeing to participate, parents were sent questionnaires covering the child's strengths, consequences used for positive and negative behaviors, relationships with siblings and peers, household chores assigned, and school-related behavior. Next, they attended a thorough orientation to the behavioral educational approach to intervention, and this session was videotaped in the clinical media laboratory. Target behaviors were then defined.

The researchers collected data recordings and baselines daily. In the home, fifteen minutes at the dinner time were audiotaped a few days a week. An observer then visited the home to check reliability and revise targeted behaviors.

After two or three weeks of baseline data, a parent training session was scheduled. After this, the home intervention system was set up, including modeling and rehearsing of all anticipated parent participations. Then, through home visits, feedback and reliability checks were employed. The final step was a termination procedure and a two- or three-month follow-up.

The studies (Pinkston et al., 1982a) did show that parents could alter aggressive behavior in their children by contingency contracting. Parents learned that they could benefit quickly from a brief investment of their time and the social worker's time. Parents demonstrated that they could act as agents of change for their child's behavior. Importantly, it was shown that "there is an alternative to excluding children from normal interaction with their families" (p. 260).

School social workers have replicated this model for use and reuse. In several cases, Susan Drager and Patricia Hanrahan, behavioral school social work interns of the author, were the therapists. They reported on their procedures and findings in the Parent Education Program (1979) directed by Elsie Pinkston at the University of Chicago School of Social Service Administration. The program was carried out in conjunction with the author.

Drager and Hanrahan used parent training as an approach to the treatment of aggression in children. This training, as a treatment approach, targeted two aspects of the child's adjustment: modifying the parent-child interactional system and improving the child's behavior in school and at home (Berkowitz and Graziano, 1972). To accomplish these goals, the therapists worked in a variety of settings and times.

In Drager and Hanrahan's interventions, parents were trained in the use of differential attention, contingency contracting with an in-home token economy, time out, and overcorrection. The hypothesis was that this training should increase parental attention to prosocial behaviors and decrease parental attention to deviant behaviors. The training techniques used to teach parents behavior modification skills are closely related to procedures implemented by parents to change their child's behavior.

Instructions

Parents were presented with a standardized explanation of behavioral principles, such as reinforcement, punishment, extinction, and shaping behavior, during the training session. Examples of these principles were given to them, based on the parent's child management problems.

Parents were asked to give their own examples of home-based behaviors to illustrate their understanding of behavioral principles. Instructions were also given when the practitioner demonstrated specific child behavior-change procedures. After the training session the parents were given a standardized set of instructions in behavior principles and behavior changing procedures.

Modeling

Modeling was used because of its usefulness in teaching a wide variety of behavioral skills (Bandura, 1969). The modeling procedure is a set of activities designed to increase the observers' probability of imitating behavior. These activities include pointing out behavior to be imitated, modifying situational conditions to facilitate imitation, teaching observation and imitation skills, reinforcement, and behavior rehearsal (Rose, 1972).

The modeling served two purposes: the parent observed the procedure applied correctly with the child, and the child became aware of the procedures that should be used contingent on specific behaviors. The practitioner presented verbal praise and positive feedback following parental rehearsal of the modeled behaviors. Modeling was used in both clinic and home settings.

Behavioral Rehearsal

According to Bandura (1971), to effect maximum behavior change, modeling should be followed by behavioral rehearsal of the modeled responses. Behavior rehearsal appears to stabilize and strengthen acquired skills (Bandura, 1969; McFall and Marston, 1970). Modeling and behavior rehearsal have many advantages. First, the entire chain of behavior can be demonstrated and the client can then imitate it one step at a time. Another advantage is the availability of the model to verbalize her thought processes in terms of appropriate self-statements. When the client imitates the model, the self-verbalizations may gradually be faded until they are understood. The role playing involved in behavior rehearsal is important in that it allows the client to practice the behaviors. Finally, behavior rehearsal conditions a total behavioral response, not just a verbal response. Training and modeling have led subjects to gather more information in dealing with problems, while behavior rehearsal and role playing along with instruction and feedback have proven successful in training parent-child pairs in conflict negotiation skills (Kifer et al., 1974).

Manuals

Parent training manuals have been used with parents to assist in training and in learning behavioral principles (Patterson, 1971; Becker, 1971; Patterson and Guillion, 1968). Drager and Hanrahan asked parents to use Becker's book as a reference to increase their knowledge of behavioral principles and their application in treatment.

Treatment Procedures

Treatment procedures used in the Parent Education Program include differential attention, time out, overcorrection, and contingency contracting using a token economy. Home notes and a home-based reinforcement system are used to intervene with problems occurring in the school setting. Training occurs initially in the clinic, then is followed by training in the home setting. Treatment is short-term, lasting about three months.

Differential Attention

Parental attention to deviant behavior maintains that behavior (Wahler et al., 1965). Differential attention consists of reinforcement through attention to appropriate behaviors and ignoring undesirable behaviors. Parents are trained to use social and nonsocial reinforcers for behaviors they wish to increase and to ignore behaviors they wish to decrease. Differential attention is used with other treatment procedures. The use of differential attention often involves shifting the usual pattern of parental attention, which is attending to deviant behavior and ignoring appropriate behavior.

In reviewing a number of studies of parental attention patterns, Patterson (1973) found that one fourth to one third of the child's coercive behavior received positive reinforcement. Wahler and associates (1965) trained parents in two families to use differential attention to increase cooperative behavior and to decrease excessive dependency. In a third family, differential attention was not effective until accompanied by a time-out procedure.

It is important to note, however, that Herbert and his associates (1973) report that training parents to use differential attention had adverse effects on child behavior. In contradiction to previous research, four of six children increased their deviant behavior when it was ignored. The increase remained stable and did not follow an extinction curve. One child showed no change. A sixth child showed some improvement that did not occur again in a second experimental condition when differential attention was reinstated. The use of differential attention, therefore, should be carefully monitored.

Time Out

Time out, as previously noted, is a punishment procedure in which the child is removed from access to reinforcement for a brief period of time. Wahler (1969a) hypothesized that differential reinforcement is ineffective when parental attention is not reinforcing to the child. He found that the time-out procedure, when coupled with differential reinforcement, increased the reinforcement value of parental attention and decreased deviant child behaviors.

Forehand and Atkeson (1977) found that a time-out duration of four minutes was more effective in increasing compliance than ten seconds or one minute. Research reported by Patterson (1973) indicates that three minutes in time out was as effective as thirty. In the Parent Education Program, parents are instructed to limit time out to three minutes per occasion. This is specified in a written contract signed by parents and practitioner. The procedure is demonstrated with the child; a time-out area is chosen and the contingencies for its application are made clear.

Overcorrection

Overcorrection is a mild punishment procedure that involves the repetition of positive behaviors after the performance of incompatible or inappropriate behaviors. It is similar to time out because it temporarily interrupts offensive behavior and uses a set period of time (one to five minutes) to train alternate appropriate behaviors.

Overcorrection was considered but not used by Drager and Hanrahan because of the time involved to implement the techniques and the program guidelines, which stressed using positive reinforcement, ignoring, contingency contracting, and token systems before punishment procedures were introduced.

Contingency Contracting

The contingency contract (Homme et al., 1973) between parent and child is useful for making expectations and contingencies explicit. A contract delineates each person's rights, privileges, and responsibilities. It pinpoints behaviors to be accelerated or decelerated, determines back-up reinforcers, and points out gains and losses (Patterson, 1973).

During the training session, the child's wishes and reward list are incorporated into the reinforcement menu of the contingency contract. Rewards are negotiated with the parents. Access to rewards is built into the contract between parent and child. Included are daily rewards such as television, playing outside, and bike riding, and weekly rewards such as attending a movie, baseball game, or other special event.

Alterations in the contract are made to shape behavior or to substitute and strengthen rewarding events. Parents alter contingencies in person or by telephone with the practitioner. Contracts can be most effective when conducted at a family meeting session. Parents were taught certain contracting rules.

1. Sit down with the child.
2. Select one behavior and define it in observable terms.
3. Describe all the important aspects of the behavior, such as how often it should be done, by what specific time it should be completed, where it should be done, and who will demonstrate and teach the behavior to the child.
4. Agree on a reinforcer to be given for performing the behavior.
5. Decide who will determine whether the behavior was completed as previously defined.
6. Write down all of the above information in a contract format similar to the contract written in the training session.
7. Both parents and child should agree to and sign the contract.

Other guidelines are offered:

Give the payoff (reward) for performing the contracted behavior immediately.

Call for and reward small approximations in initial contracts.

Reward frequently with small amounts.

Have the contract call for and reward accomplishments rather than obedience.

Reward the performance only after it occurs. This is Grandma's Law—first your vegetables, then your dessert. Promises to perform should not be rewarded.

Make the contract clear, honest, and fair.

State the terms of the contract in positive terms—what should be accomplished, not what should be stopped.

Use contracting systematically and consistently, and follow through to maintain the effectiveness of the program.

Modify the contract when necessary.

Put the contract in writing to eliminate future disagreements over what terms mean.

Home Point System

The home point system frequently employed with children and their parents is reviewed by Gambrill (1977). Such a token program aims both to increase the reinforcing potential of parent approval by pairing it with back-up reinforcers from the reinforcement menu and to aid the parent in consistent use of verbal praise. Tokens used to shape behavior have the advantage of a standardized exchange value.

Token programs are often employed with aggressive children because these children are not as responsive to adult social reinforcers and tend to increase coercive behaviors when parents try to punish them. Pairing parental praise with points and back-up rewards should enhance the reinforcement value of positive parental attention. The point system is used with the contingency contract and is written down so that behaviors and resulting benefits or costs are clearly understood by all participants.

Home Notes

When problems occur in the school setting, notes to the home are used as a communication system between home and school. Appropriate behavior in school is rewarded at home as part of the token economy. There are several reasons why home-based rather than teacher reinforcement is used.

In their review of the research on home notes, Rzepnicki and Bremer (1977) found that children do not find reinforcers available in the classroom as attractive as those available at home. Also, two out of five teachers in one study could not to be trained in the appropriate use of teacher attention as a reinforcer. Home notes with back-up reinforcers have been used successfully with a predelinquent population including some aggressive adolescents. The procedure has been used successfully to increase academic performance and decrease classroom disruption with adolescents from an Achievement Place group home (Wolf et al., 1976).

Short-Term Treatment

There are several sources of empirical evidence cited by Reid and Epstein (1972) in support of short-term treatment. Reid and Shyne (1969) found that by several measures of problem change, short-term treatment was more effective than long-term treatment. Several studies indicate that the average number of treatment interviews per client was about five or six visits, regardless of whether or not long-term treatment was planned.

Parent training programs have frequently demonstrated treatment effects within a short period (Patterson and Reid, 1973). Because of the empirical support for short-term treatment, the guidelines of the Parent Education Program suggested a three-month treatment contract.

Home Visits

In the Parent Education Program, the initial interview and training session for parents beginning treatment took place in a clinic. This was followed by home visits to review treatment principles and modify the behavioral program as needed. There is evidence that success in effecting behavior change is greatly increased by moving into the client's natural environment. Research reviewed by Forehand and Atkeson (1977) showed that decreases in noncompliance in the home can best be improved by training parents in the home and that generalization or generality from clinic to home setting for reduction of noncompliance is poor.

Communication between parent and child is an important process by which parents teach children and children teach parents how to get what they want from each other. To facilitate communication of expectations to their child, parents should present a united front. Decisions in child management should be made jointly, with follow-through and consistency practiced by both parents. Without this, reliable child behaviors cannot be expected.

8

SCHOOL-RELATED SETTINGS FAVORING BEHAVIOR ANALYSIS

Basic to any behavioral program are the ongoing research and training available, usually at universities. At least one "off-campus" source, initiated by the University of Kansas at Lawrence, the Juniper Gardens Children's Project (JGCP), has been developed and maintained for the purpose of designing programs to intervene in the health and education of the community's children. Many of the references in this book have been taken from the publications of its personnel. They have had a continuous, close relationship with the University of Kansas at Lawrence.

The JGCP began in 1964 when a group of civic leaders, local civil rights advocates, University of Kansas faculty members, research scientists from the University of Kansas Bureau of Child Research, and others formed a working group to establish a research project within an economically depressed inner-city area in Kansas City, Kansas. It is administered through the University of Kansas Institute for Life Span Studies and the Bureau of Child Research.

JGCP identifies significant problems in human development and then seeks ways of dealing with them through principles of applied behavior analysis. The work is carefully documented so that findings can be applied to similar problems in other urban settings. Concerns of local citizens, both social and educational, are addressed. JGCP is supported by state and federal funds and contributions from interested citizens and organizations. Its federal funds are obtained through competitive grant peer review.

While JGCP's work keeps changing to deal with current demands, a brief review of some of its accomplishments is instructive. Among these are behavioral assessments, school-based educational interventions, early childhood educational interventions, language research, computer applications, and graduate and postdoctoral education.

JGCP has developed several programs that have been adopted around the world. It was their staff that developed classwide peer tutoring into a near-perfect tool for educators. They have studied this method from several angles. For example, they have worked on the application and evaluation of the classwide peer tutoring model for teaching and mainstreaming learning disabled and mildly handicapped students in reading and comprehension skills classes in the general classroom. This involved developing and implementing an administrative procedure to increase the system-wide maintenance of the reading component of the program. They focus on regular classrooms into which learning disabled students have been integrated.

But peer tutoring has been developed and researched for every type of classroom, a school, and a school district (Delquadri et al., 1986; Adams et al., 1987). It was initiated because observation research (Hall et al., 1982; Greenwood et al., 1985; Stanley & Greenwood, 1983) showed that "children were not actively engaged by the curriculum or the teacher's lesson" (Delquadri et. al., 1986, p. 535). The basic component of peer tutoring is the opportunity to respond or practice.

It has been applied to all classroom academic areas and all populations, special education or regular. Even autistic students have responded well. Peer tutoring offers advantages to teachers because it requires no extra teaching time. Every child can be helped because half are paired with a tutor and they exchange positions, the tutor becoming the tutee. As tutor, they must teach and listen in ways that those just in the role of student do not enjoy. In addition, a team approach including a point system is used.

JGCP is also developing the ecobehavioral approach, which deals with all systems in a person's environment to address the problems of needy children (Ginsburg, 1989). This approach has so far been applied to assessment of effective teaching procedures in the middle school and of education and treatment programs for autistic and developmentally disabled students.

JGCP has produced three computerized behavioral assessment systems that are widely used in classroom-based research projects at Juniper Gardens and at university and public school programs nationwide. They include the Code for Instructional Structure and Student Academic Response (CISSAR), Code for Instructional Structure and Student Academic Response—MainStream Version (MSCISSAR), and Ecobehavioral System for the Complex Assessment of Preschool Environments (ESCAPE).

CISSAR quantifies students' academic response time in relation to specific classroom instructional variables, including ecological factors, teacher behaviors, and student responses. It is designed for the regular classroom. MSCISSAR is similar to CISSAR but is sensitive to variables of students with special needs. ESCAPE measures instructional effectiveness of preschool programs.

The three assessment systems take advantage of the most advanced computer technology. JGCP staff have developed advanced classroom data collection programs for use with small lap-top computers. They also created software to support these programs, with such features as interobserver agreement, conditional and unconditional probability analysis, and sequential analysis.

The accomplishments of JGCP are impressive. In twenty-five years staff members have published approximately 380 articles about work completed.

They have presented hundreds of workshops around the nation on the research and instructional techniques they have developed. About seventy-four hundred children have received training, education, or health services at the JGCP site, and more than three thousand parents and teachers have received training there in child management and behavioral teaching techniques developed at JGCP.

One hundred twenty-nine students received master's or doctoral degrees as a result of research conducted and academic instruction given by staff members. In addition, university students from all over the United States, Canada, Mexico, Panama, Australia, New Zealand, England, and Israel have come to JGCP for part of their training. More than 150 residents of the community have been trained, and six are permanent professional staff helping to operate the project.

JGCP attributes its success and recognition to three factors. First, members address problems of practical importance. Second, they carefully employ the scientific principles of applied behavior analysis to different problems in different environments. Careful data collection and evaluation are used in the design of effective behavioral intervention procedures. Third, there is well-planned follow-up and development of programs and materials that can be replicated. These programs are then effective in other inner-city environments.

EXAMPLES OF BEHAVIOR ANALYSIS ADOPTED AS THE PREFERRED METHOD

Nichols Middle School

Carmen Marcy, Ph.D., the principal of Nichols Middle School in Evanston, Illinois, a suburb of Chicago, has training and experience in running a school where behavior analysis is the method of choice. She has provided leadership in instituting the method and behavioral training for her faculty. In some instances, she has been able to recruit personnel who have some background in applied behavior analysis. The school social worker, Arthur Sontag, is behaviorally oriented. Academics are taught through Programmed Instruction.

Every aspect of Nichols School reflects its behavioral philosophy. A carefully detailed behavioral code has been developed for the children and faculty. This is distributed in printed form at the beginning of each school year in a handbook for parents and students. Ongoing changes or modifications are recorded, and the updated copy is always available in the school office. The handbook contains information on the goals and philosophy of the school, school organization and routines, and the behavior management plan, including school rules and rewards available for meeting specified criteria.

The behavioral guidelines for the school can be found in the Nichols school-wide behavior management program. Based on behavior management techniques, which take up seven pages in the handbook, its stated purpose is "to give students a structure in which they can learn productive, self-disciplined behavior" (p. 19).

The program rests on the assumption that every child can, and is expected to live up to a set of behaviors that is good for the student, his peers, teachers, parents, and community. Nichols' teachers believe that their students want to reach the highest level of self-discipline. They also believe that good behavior is a necessary precursor to academic achievement. (p. 19)

The school rules on specific behaviors are detailed. To achieve these, positive consequences are seen as an integral component. Teachers are encouraged to put up discrete and unobstrusive signs to remind themselves to praise and reinforce improved behavior. Such signs might say: "Catch them being good," "Praise," "Don't wait for misbehavior," "Reward improvement," "Be specific," "Tell Joe what he did right," "When you praise Jim, describe what he did well," and "Praise Mary." Teachers are also encouraged to use a variety of activities and tangible reinforcers to increase rule-following behavior. Use of potentially reinforcing events or objects should be contingent upon desired behavior.

A student of the week is named in each homeroom, and there is a schoolwide monthly good citizenship award. Infractions of school rules are listed with the consequences detailed. For students who are "chronic" or "habitual" offenders of school rules, there are two plans of action. Such pupils will be served in either or both of the following ways:

First, teachers, administrators, and support staff will identify those students who continually violate established school or class rules. Up to thirty students from the entire school population are placed on the guidance counselor's caseload.

Second, a permanent behavior management team meets on a regular basis in order to design an individualized plan to improve the rule-following behavior of these chronic offenders. The behavior management team includes a guidance counselor as chairperson and an administrator, psychologist, social worker, and at least two teachers who are familiar with the student.

The team doubles as behavior managers. At their meetings, they discuss individual children and schedule special education staffings. As behavior management advocates, selected teachers meet with small groups of children needing help. The advocates try to work with the misbehaving children as they are referred. Requests from community service programs are channeled to the behavior management team.

If the problems appear to stem from family, community, or other sources outside school, the student is referred to the school social worker. The school social worker also coordinates special education in the building. For many children, changing classes is stressful. Therefore, the pupils are allowed to come to the school social worker when they are angry or frustrated.

A long list of rewards is offered school-wide. Ongoing help, such as after-school homework services by teachers, is offered daily so that each child achieves academically. A plethora of extra programs and activities is provided. The teaching faculty is divided into grade-level general studies teams. Each team member is also a homeroom teacher who has to know and coordinate all aspects of the pupil's program According to the handbook, the homeroom teacher:

(a) insures that new students are oriented to all aspects of their program at Nichols School;

(b) coordinates data-based placement decisions for each homeroom student;

(c) engineers all aspects of each student's individualized program;

(d) meets daily with other members of the grade-level team;

(e) monitors student progress;

(f) knows what works regarding discipline for each homeroom student;

(g) insures that report card data is timely and accurate;

(h) communicates with parents on a regular basis (suggested minimum: four times per year). (p. 12)

Each day there is a 10:30 study period for those who are late to school and not caught up. This "second-period study" is open only to those students who are not caught up.

In such a setting, Mr. Sontag, the school social worker's functions are clear. He is available for pupils and parents who need attention. He works closely with "Earn and Learn," a behaviorally oriented program that operates in the Evanston schools (see below). The Nichols school social worker has made Earn and Learn the core of his program. Individual contracts are signed with each student who receives this service. He then meets once a week in a group with the school social worker. As many groups as needed are formed.

Teachers submit daily reports to the school social worker on whether the child is on time and prepared with materials, completes classwork, completes homework and turns it in on time, behaves appropriately by not talking or playing out of turn, and does not argue with teachers. These behaviors are scored on a point system. If a child completes all his work, achieving at least 80 percent accuracy on all homework and classroom assignments and behaving in an acceptable manner, thus completing 90 percent of the goals on the daily point sheet, he will be treated to pizza on the last school day of each month.

Some children see the answer to their misbehaviors as changing the teacher's behavior. They are encouraged to do this, the rationale being that they will have to change their own behavior to get the teacher to treat them differently. On the other hand, there is always the possibility, even in a behaviorally oriented school, that there is a teacher who encourages misbehavior in her pupils by criticizing them more often than offering them praise for good behavior.

At Nichols, children join a group behavior club (related to Earn and Learn) through a variety of referrals—from teachers, parents, or the children themselves. The teacher of learning disabled students is an advocate for the program. The school social worker conducts the groups.

Earn and Learn

The Earn and Learn program was started in 1971 at the initiation of Don Ferguson, the Evanston High School Board president and head of a major manufacturing plant in the suburb. As he saw it, students were dropping out of high school lacking not only skills but also "appropriate work values." His company gave a $10,000 grant to the school board to get a program under way to address this problem. A task force was appointed by the school board to study the matter and help determine what sort of program was needed.

The task force pointed out that the children at risk could be distinguished in the first and second grades. These children were characterized by disruptiveness that resulted in suspensions from school. They recommended an incentive program to help the children succeed immediately in school and later on in life. They were interested in the future workers' getting to work on time daily or calling if they would be late or absent.

The program was open to Evanston middle school students (sixth through eighth grades) and high school freshmen. Participants in the program were to remain for at least two years, preferably through the first year of high school. This age group of students was considered pliable and capable of change for the better. A behavioral mode was established as a goal for the new program, and staff people were originally hired with this goal in mind.

The program has openings for fifty participants. Usually, 200 students are referred. Every spring, eighty of these are accepted. Each one signs a contract. A child is directed to the program by anyone who thinks the child would benefit from it. Referrals have been made by school personnel, parents, pupils themselves, and community members.

After a child is referred, he comes with his parent for an intake interview with the program director. A serious commitment and parental participation are essential. This intake procedure has to be evaluated in terms of whether it really insures that the neediest students will be served. Lack of parental involvement and lack of seriousness in the child eliminate those not able to meet these prerequisites.

Each day of the academic year, participants attend an after-school workshop in the program's own school building. Beginning the day after signing a contract to participate, the student brings a form to each class he attends in his regular school. The pupils are paid for their work. If they lose their cards, they have to work a whole day free. If they receive a mark of zero, money is subtracted from their earnings.

In the August following their entry into the program in the spring, all participants go to a twelve-day summer camp with the staff. This is the major training ground for participation in the program. Each child is required to pay a fee to cover costs. If the parents cannot afford it, the child may earn the money in the workshop program. After camp, each child is given a membership in the local YMCA for a nominal charge.

Another important summer program is the summer school which is held for children graduating from elementary and entering high school. Part of this experience is a camp weekend with a teacher from the high school. The aim is to get the students off to a smooth start in high school.

The Earn and Learn program is funded through various sources. The program takes in a substantial amount of business every year from the job contracts with industries for the workshop. This pays the children's wages and finances some of the programs. Some programs require fees from the participants. Twenty percent of the funding comes from foundations, corporations, and government agencies. The school district pays the bills and Earn and Learn pays the district back as they collect the money.

One of the special programs is a social worker for three days a week. Another is a homework lab. The homework lab helps the pupils do their assignments. In addition, the staff try to identify any learning problems among the children. Then parents and schools are notified about possible school problems. For a while, Earn and Learn had a basketball program for students who had a good day in school. To participate, they had to have their daily cards signed and in order.

The pupils stay at least two years in the Earn and Learn program. They can remain in it for four years if they start in grade six. If a child moves or does not attend camp, he is out of the program. The program usually loses only two or three children from June to September.

The pupils are transported to the Earn and Learn building from school and returned home at five o'clock. Each ride costs a child a small amount of change unless he has work slips for good performance. Students can also use the slips for other benefits. Field trips can be paid for only with such slips. Bonuses are given for good attendance. Students can earn several dollars a month by perfect attendance. They earn pay raises for good school and work performances. If they stay in the program, pay raises are given after every quarter in the program. A participant can earn a substantial sum of money in a year through bonuses.

Data are collected regularly on a computer. The participants are followed through high school and compared with those children who did not get into the Earn and Learn program because they were not judged reliable. The data reveal that if students get through Earn and Learn in their freshman year, they have a 90 percent chance of finishing high school on time. Another 5 percent make it in a longer time. Since those served are already the reliable ones, it may be argued that they would have finished high school even without the Earn and Learn program. How they would have fared if the pupils judged not reliable had had the program has to be asked.

A program such as Earn and Learn can be started anywhere that work projects, such as mailings or even small-parts assembly, can be generated. If one faculty member can be freed to make contacts and get community support, such a project could be established. It might even be considered for rural areas, where seeds might be packaged for a farm cooperative (Macnab, 1979).

The Chicago Catholic Archdiocese Schools

The Chicago Catholic Archdiocese school system provides a tutorial services program for children who transfer schools frequently. After seven years of studying the problems of these children, Professor Leonard Jason of DePaul University initiated the project in 1985 with grants from the National Institute of Mental Health. The program has been administered by David Betts, a behaviorally trained social worker. One purpose of the project was to introduce a model that could be replicated in all elementary schools.

Indeed, change of classrooms or of schools seems to have become a common factor in the lives of school children in this highly mobile society. Too often, such changes have been encouraged by school personnel who feel overwhelmed by the social problems presented daily by some of their students and welcome the prospect of saying good-bye to them. Thus even within a school or school system children are subjected to many changes. Often, transfer students are referred to the school social worker because of problems related to their constant moving.

Children move about their own school building so often that there is no stigma involved should a child need special help. He may be in a "walking-reading" program or getting specialized assistance from special education, the speech pathologist, or the school social worker. Every year the entire class moves on to a new grade and new teacher.

Some children leave the school for special education classes in another school. Others are bused to another school to enhance integration. In the upper grades and high school, students move from class to class, individually or as a group, throughout the day. Some elementary students are programmed to high school or special school programs for an honors class or two. Other children move from a kindergarten through fifth- or sixth-grade school to an intermediate or junior-high school for three years. Eighth graders in big cities now are offered an overwhelming choice of high schools to attend.

All of the above are programmed changes. Then there are unscheduled changes by families or schools. Some are related to the lack of affordable housing; many families save money for their next apartment by not paying rent for three months, allowing themselves to be evicted, and using the unpaid rent money to move. They see this as preferable to living in a poor neighborhood or substandard housing.

Other reasons for families to move are related to job changes, divorce, separation, or illness. The child may have to live part of the week or month in one home and the rest in another. Indeed, a child may change his living quarters on an almost daily basis when his parents are divorced and have joint custody. Other children live with their grandparents during the work week and their parents on the weekend so that their parents can hold down jobs. Some families are evicted because their behavior is disturbing to neighbors. The reasons go on and on. The child who lives in the same house and goes to the same school from kindergarten through grade eight is the exception in most urban school districts.

With the transfer program, the archdiocese schools offered the parents a choice. Some felt their children were not safe in a public school. Or they wanted the child to receive a Catholic education. Some thought they would get a better quality education there. Others chose a parochial school because it was closer to home.

For children who attend the schools of the Catholic Archdiocese of Chicago the factor of cost is involved. These are private schools charging tuition. This means, of course, that should a family be experiencing a financial crunch, they may have to transfer their offspring to public school to make ends meet. This is sometimes very difficult for families who consider a religious education important. Some will take the children out of Catholic school in harder times and return them when income increases.

In an effort to minimize the effect of changes that create gaps in children's education, Jason and his associates (1989a) developed tutoring programs that have been shown to boost academic achievement and ease the transition into new schools. They targeted high-risk groups of transfer students having multiple risk factors, such as life stressors, academic problems, and low socioeconomic status.

Selection of Participants

The project's original plan was to work with ten schools as experimental settings, with ten more serving as a control group. Three hundred pupils were tested. Of these, 120 were identified as high risk and in need of tutoring. This group was divided in half—sixty to be tutored and the others to serve as controls. The twenty schools were paired by racial makeup and economic levels. One of each pair received the program.

Guidelines were established to identify high-risk transfer students in the third, fourth, and fifth grades. (First and second graders were not considered high risk yet, and it is hard to test such young pupils accurately.) The students selected came to the Catholic schools from other parochial schools, local public schools, or other schools in the United States or other countries.

At the start of every school year, each child who had transferred was tested for academic skills and self-concept. In addition, the parents were interviewed by phone to find out the distance of the move to the present school, the child's grades in the previous year, the socioeconomic status of the family, and any negative events occurring in the student's life during the past twelve months, such as divorce of parents, death in the immediate family, or a parent's loss of employment.

All new students in the school were given parent permission forms for their parents to sign before participating in the project. Then they were given the Wide Range Achievement Test and the Pierce-Harris Self-Concept Test for one hour. This was followed by an hour of orientation covering school rules and special activities and including a discussion of what it feels like to be a new student in a school. The schools paired each program participant with a buddy of the same age, sex, and class to guide the new transfer student during the first few months of school and to be a friend.

The Interventions

Outgoing undergraduate students at DePaul with above-average academic records were hired as tutors by the project and trained in direct instruction teaching techniques. After this, they worked fifty minutes twice a week with each high-risk transfer student. The children were taken out of their regular classes and tutored in mathematics, reading, spelling, and phonics during the school day. Tutors worked closely with the teachers and gave weekly feedback on how their students were doing. Occasionally, social skills and behavioral programs were introduced. Most schools had one tutor, but larger schools had two.

Results were studied in terms of self-concept and academic criteria. The same tests as were given at the start of the school year were readministered at the end of the year. School records, such as grades and absences, were used. Also, sociometric tests were given to the entire class to identify students who were good workers, well liked, or withdrawn. At that time, the teachers also filled out a reporting form on each transfer student.

During the second year, the project staff increased their work with parents. They had had limited results the first year with twice-a-week tutoring and thought that parent involvement could make a difference. An initial one-hour parent meeting was held. During this hour, the project staff talked with the parents about the children and testing results. After this the tutors' supervisors (graduate students in psychology) went into the homes. Some of this work was shared by the social worker in charge of the program.

The first part of the in-home interview was devoted to getting to know the parent. After this, an effort was made to get the parent or another family member involved with the child's learning. The involved member would be trained to tutor the transfer student at home during the school year and continue to help the student after the program was finished. If a member of the family was not available, the program directors went to the community to find someone who could fill this job. Through this system, an effort was made to maintain the acquired study habits beyond the intervention of the tutors.

Twice a week, level-appropriate cards from the Science Research Association (SRA) reading program were brought home by the children. The home tutor listened to the child's reading and corrected any mistakes. After the story, the exercises were worked on together. The project maintained contacts with the home throughout and parents gave oral reports to the staff every two weeks.

The project worked on more than academics. There were no social workers in the archdiocese schools, so tutors were trained to carry out social work functions. They introduced reinforcement programs to get the child more organized. Also, they worked with the pupils on how to make friends and avoid being picked on. They worked on turning in homework when it was a problem.

The tutors had caseloads of four to six students. They worked three and a half hours per child per week. The staff for the project consisted of four graduate assistants, eighteen part-time tutors, and a one-third-time investigator. Two hours were required for actual tutoring, and one and a half hours were used in meetings with supervisors, teachers, and parents, and in general preparation.

Behavioral interventions, such as reinforce or reinforce and prompt, were followed throughout. To assure uniformity and high standards, supervisors observed tutors as they worked in the schools. Together they aimed to help each child have weekly success with classroom assignments.

Results

The program got off to a late start its first year due to a delay in receiving federal funds. Initially, each child was to remain in the program for one year. Because of the late start, results were poor the first year: grades did not improve. However, participant satisfaction was high. Teachers, principals, students, and tutors all liked the project.

They were on target in the selection of students to participate. It should be noted that they did not have many students from the very lowest socioeconomic strata because parents had to pay tuition for a child to attend the parochial school. A few children moved during the school year. But at the end of the year, 35 percent of the high-risk students had not transferred again.

Parents agreed to a child's being in the program at the start of the year, but they were not involved during the first year. During the second year, when there was consistent effort to involve parents, one-third did not cooperate. Another third gave a little help. Characteristically, they worked a few months and then dropped out. From the remaining third, they had good results. Overall, fifty-five out of the sixty parents in the group receiving services were more or less in direct contact with the project staff.

Originally, the transfer student project was designed as a two-year intervention plus a one-year follow-up. But researchers were learning so much in the intervention and parent involvement was so encouraging that they applied for another grant and were funded for two more years. There were major differences between the first and second years; the researchers had clearer goals and a trained staff in the second year.

Tutors were supervised by graduate students, a few of whom dropped out. A bond between the tutor and child was encouraged. The tutors were trained to be friends of the pupils, and the children, many of whom were from one-parent families, thrived on the attention.

If the parents were willing, the tutor went into the home to watch the parent work with the child on work related to his school and to give feedback. Most parents were willing to let the tutors in. Others preferred to go to school to demonstrate what they could do. Successful attempts were made to get parents to be volunteer tutors.

The control group did not make as much progress as did the group serviced. No work was done with the school administrators to institute progress in the high-risk pupils. Also, there was no intervention with the classroom teacher's performance. These were identified as target populations for future interventions.

LAGRANGE AREA DEPARTMENT OF SPECIAL EDUCATION (LADSE)

LADSE is a joint agreement cooperative to provide special education services in sixteen school districts in the western suburbs of Chicago. The districts include fifty-five schools, four of which are high schools. With the endorsement of Dr. Howard Blackman, the executive director, this agency has adopted applied behavior analysis as its method of choice for educational and treatment interventions with the children in its charge.

Personnel who have training in applied behavior analysis are sought and employed. Ten school social workers are hired by LADSE in addition to the school social workers employed by each of the sixteen member districts. While the primary focus of LADSE is on students in special education, some of their interventions involve both special education and regular students, such as when they return special education students from self-contained classes to regular education classes.

All children in LADSE attend special education programs within the LADSE school districts. The LADSE social workers provide services to them there. The district social workers are informed of the work of the LADSE social workers with a particular child, but the district workers are not necessarily directly involved with these children. All of these specialized professionals get together from time to time, but the regular school social workers tend not to be behaviorally oriented.

In the spring of 1978, four LADSE school social workers went to the University of Kansas at Lawrence to receive training in applied behavior analysis. After that, Vance and Marilyn Hall of the University of Kansas faculty came to LADSE to teach parent training.

In 1983, LADSE received a grant from the United States Department of Education, Office of Special Education, Department of Personnel Preparation, to develop two training courses for parents (Westling, 1986): "to recruit and train both professionals and parents as co-leaders; to evaluate the effectiveness and generalizability of the programs; to provide a written curriculum, training materials, methods of implementation and consultation to local educational agencies interested in establishing similar programs" (p. 3). Since then LADSE has initiated and followed through on many projects.

Parent training has been a continuous service offered by the LADSE social workers. They have four or five courses going at any time. Also, they have their own manual (Westling, 1986) for a course for co-leaders that describes procedures in detail. For a fuller description of this program, see chapter 7 on parent training.

A strong LADSE behavioral component is carried out by two full-time "mainstream instructors." These individuals often provide service to students found ineligible for special education. The mainstream instructors also serve in the schools as peer consultants and trainers for teachers in their own classrooms.

Other programs carried out at LADSE include social skills interventions employed by all of the school social workers. Delquadri and associates' (1983) spelling game and tutoring program are used regularly. The Pre-Referral Intervention Support Model (PRISM) encourages school teams to develop interventions prior to case-study evaluations. LADSE prefers that each team have a leader for each intervention.

Bruce Townsley (1989), a school social worker who works at LADSE, has singled out negative reinforcement in behavioral interventions in the school environment for extensive study and has developed training materials for school personnel on the subject. He has prepared worksheets and videotapes to present this concept. This approach helps those working with students to recognize the escape and avoidance behavior they encounter in the children (see chapter 6 on interventions).

Nederhouser and Labak (1988) of the LADSE staff developed a buddy system that has been used successfully in the programs for students with behavior disorders and developmental delay. They conducted a study with six students of fourth, fifth, and sixth grades enrolled in a self-contained classroom (target peers). A pool of behaviorally trained non-special education fourth, fifth, and sixth graders became buddies to these target peers.

The Attitudes Toward Disabled Persons scale (ATDP–Form O) was used to measure results. "Target peers were successfully integrated into twelve new learning settings.... And the recognition associated with performing as a buddy contributed to a self-perpetuating buddy pool totalling forty-seven at project conclusion" (p. 1). Another benefit of the buddy system was the interaction of parents of buddies with parents of target peers.

Nederhouser, a teacher, and Labak, a school social worker, used a number of behavioral techniques to create an environment in the school that would improve acceptance of the handicapped children. Thirty-nine fourth-, fifth-, and sixth-grade typical education students from regular classrooms were trained as buddies to work directly with the target peers. Another group of eighty-three students in the same regular classrooms were not formally trained as buddies but had intermittent contact with the target peers.

LADSE has developed and employed a number of assessment instruments. For example, one was used to conduct preplacement assessments of selected settings for integration and to monitor performance progress or regression in integrated sessions. Reinforcing certificates were given as indicated to buddies, target peers, and receptive building personnel. Forms were developed to be used for feedback by the receiving teacher and the buddies. A daily log of all activities was kept.

Behavioral strategies were also used with school personnel to improve their acceptance of school-wide integration. The principal was identified as an "indispensable, multi-level reinforcer" (p. 5). He supported, explained, and publicized the program at every turn. The coordinating teacher established her professional credibility before the project was undertaken. She then assessed the school environment for suitability and accessibility, specific settings, teacher attitudes, and available buddies.

Next, the building staff and the parents of both the buddies and the target peers were oriented to the program. This was followed up by individual visits by the coordinating teacher with each teacher in the setting. In addition, target peers were integrated into the learning settings one at a time.

The buddies were trained in shaping skills. School personnel observed and gave feedback on their performances. Also, targeted students were oriented and placed into the new settings within twenty-four hours. Intermittent observations were conducted throughout by the coordinating teacher or project staff. The program was assessed and reinforced at every step.

The possibility of an all-out approach by school personnel to achieve a desired change in school environment presents a challenge to the school social worker initiating such projects. The school board's endorsement of applied behavior analysis as a desirable policy was certainly an integral factor in allowing Nederhouser and Labak to conduct their integration program.

There are many more models of behavioral services developed by LADSE personnel. For example, Labak used a number of these to conduct simultaneous treatments for a seriously nonfunctioning handicapped child. Regina, age six, a profoundly mentally impaired girl, is a case in point. She had been displaying self-abusive, physically destructive, and noncompliant behaviors at home and to a lesser extent in school.

During the school year, Regina's parents placed her in a residential facility because they could no longer tolerate her home behavior. After one month of her presence there, the facility refused to keep her any longer and she was returned to LADSE. At that time, her parents became more cooperative with the school in their efforts to improve Regina's behavior.

Data taken for sixty days showed that Regina engaged in noncompliance, verbal aggression, tantrum-like behaviors, physical aggression, and property destruction. These behaviors indicated a history of learned dysfunctional behavior and messages which had been misunderstood or overlooked.

Parents had reinforced or strengthened Regina's behavior inadvertently. For example, when she refused to ambulate they insisted she do so. When she refused to do something, they eventually did it for her. While eating, she was given attention only when she threw things, and was thereby negatively reinforced. However, in-school observers found that she responded successfully to consistently employed differential reinforcement programs.

With behavioral programming in school, Regina's problematic behaviors were eliminated or significantly reduced. On the basis of this success, a behavioral parent training program was undertaken by Labak and the social work intern he supervised. Techniques included descriptive praise and reinforcement using differential reinforcement of other behaviors (DRO), a behaviorally based communication system, facilitating skills (clear directions and structured interactions), mechanics underlying the prudent use of cost contingencies, and a contractual agreement with Labak, the intern, and the community agency that provided respite services from time to time.

Along with the parent training, behavioral programs for Regina were undertaken in school. One program involved getting her to communicate her preference for either solid food or a beverage by touching the appropriate picture. This was undertaken for the enhancement of communication during meals.

Another intervention involved her sitting quietly at her desk with a "quiet mouth" (not screaming or making noncommunicative noises) and with "appropriate hands" (not pinching, hitting, or otherwise making undesirable physical contact). For compliance with "quiet mouth" or "appropriate hands," she would be given tangible reinforcers.

If she did scream, cry, or make noise, reinforcers would be removed and she would be placed in a vacant chair reserved for this purpose. Regina would also have the option of touching a card with her picture on it; doing so would return her to her desk, where she could resume suitable behavior. Once at her desk, reinforcers would be reintroduced. A similar pattern would be followed if she did not have "appropriate hands." Data were kept on the duration of on-condition behaviors and the resultant consequences.

Regina also took part in an integration program developed by the social work intern to establish friendships and further attitudes of acceptance and familiarity between students in the second-grade classroom and the students in her primary class. Games were used for this interaction. Two students from the primary grades were grouped with two second-grade students for board or card games lasting twenty to twenty-five minutes each. A management system was used to shape desired behaviors, and reinforcement opportunities were made available on an immediate or intermittent basis.

Dr. Blackman, the executive director, also facilitated a number of other specific behavioral interventions at LADSE. Some of those carried out by Labak will be found in the Appendix of this book.

BOONE ELEMENTARY SCHOOL

Boone School is a kindergarten through eighth-grade Chicago public school. Its principal, Anastasia P. Graven, is firmly in charge, and her goal is an atmosphere that will enhance humanitarian values. In behavioral terms, she aims to maintain a positive, rewarding environment. In such a place, children are automatically rewarded for good behavior, while poor behavior is discouraged.

The environment of Boone has been encouraging to its behaviorally oriented school social worker, the author of this book. There the social worker is seen as a specialist in children with behavior problems. These students must learn to adapt to a positive reinforcing environment. Therefore, if a pupil surfaces who is having some adjustment problem, the principal consults the school social worker. Together they determine the source of the child's misbehavior. Then their diagnosis is translated into an action plan. The principal and school social worker agree that each child must be helped to reach his greatest potential academically and that the student's social skills are an integral part of this process.

Because the child sometimes needs services from several sources, the school social worker could be working with school personnel; the psychologist, nurse, truant officer, speech pathologist, teacher, or school counselor. Other times, the pupil's home or a community resource will have to be involved. As an integral part of the school, the school social worker at Boone is as free as any other faculty member to use the resources of the school.

Students encounter many types of impediments to success in school, despite the nurturing atmosphere at Boone. Sometimes a pupil's misbehavior develops out of some educational lag acquired through coming from a foreign culture, frequently accompanied by changes of schools, home problems, juvenile delinquency, poor attendance, or learning disabilities. The social worker has to look into these areas to try to find the source of the student's malfunctioning. If tutoring or special education are indicated, the proper resource person in the school has to be made aware of that child's need for services.

Occasionally, a teacher (usually a new one) will take a punitive attitude toward a child. Or there could be a personality clash. Or the teacher may see her job as dealing with academics, not with other problems. If the teacher appears to be the problem, methods for improving her performance with the student are considered, and the school social worker joins the principal in working to reach this goal.

If the pupil's problems appear to be primarily rooted in the home or community, the school social worker will have to look into these. The child could be left alone at home after school hours for extended periods of time because parents are working or because the quality of parenting is poor. The school social worker might then want to refer the parent to the local park program or some other suitable after-school activity so the child is monitored until there is an adult at home to supervise him. Or there may be a neglectful situation at home that has to be reported to the state department of children and family services. In neglect cases, collaboration with the truant officer is often indicated.

Boone's school social worker has been involved with changing unacceptable behavior of students. She has developed a group program for boys who have a record of fighting frequently. This has involved self-monitoring and reporting at weekly meetings to the school social worker and peer group members. A new member might be referred to the group by his teacher, an administrator, or another group member.

Each child keeps a chart that he fills out daily, indicating any fights he has taken part in at home or in school. These charts are posted side by side, one for each member of the group, in the school counselor's office where each child comes daily. In addition, each child makes a verbal report at the group meeting; other group participants verify what the child relates and make suggestions for the future should a fight have occurred. Verbal praise is given to the pupils who have excellent or improved records for the week—and most of them do. Occasionally, at meeting time, the members treat themselves to a pizza party for their successes.

The Boone School social worker is well integrated into the faculty. A team spirit is encouraged by all who work there. This includes the administrators, engineers, lunchroom workers, teachers, clerical staff, crossing guards, and itinerant personnel. A warm, caring approach is sought, and all school personnel are positively rewarded for this. Reinforcement comes from one's colleagues and, not infrequently, from the pupils themselves and their parents.

The positive reinforcement starts with the school principal at Boone. Mrs. Graven sees the school as an extended family or community. All information channels through her, and she is equally interested in what every child and faculty member is doing. When indicated, she meets with and counsels students and parents. She conducts weekly meetings with all teachers in teams and stays abreast of their concerns. She is particularly sensitive to workers who are coping with difficult personal or professional problems and offers them support and whatever help she can provide. In addition, she is quick to recognize and celebrate their achievements.

The humanities program at Boone School accents the caring approach. It teaches the children to know and develop humane qualities. Two teachers are assigned to teach humanities classes to the entire school and to counsel children about their personal needs. Often the school social worker receives referrals from these teachers, and work is carried on in concert or separately.

In addition to studies in the humanities, the program provides the school's diverse student population with multiethnic and multicultural experiences that enrich their understanding and appreciation of various backgrounds. Chicago children from all types of backgrounds are encouraged to attend Boone through this humanities program. They are bused between home and school without charge. The diversity of students thus achieved enhances the humanities program.

REGULAR EDUCATION TEACHER CONSULTANT PROGRAM (RETC)

This is a program developed by the Northwest Suburban Special Education Organization (NSSEO) in the northwest suburbs of Chicago. It is carried out under Pamela K. Gillet, department editor and superintendent, Northwest Suburban Special Education Organization, Mt. Prospect, Illinois. There are two full-time regular education teacher consultants, Nancy Buechin McGill and Liz Robinson. Although they are employees of a special education district servicing fourteen school districts, their work is mainly with regular education teachers.

The purpose of the RETC program is to prepare teachers for "moving regular education and special education into a seamless curriculum" (McGill and Robinson, 1989, p. 71). It is designed specifically to teach regular education teachers to work with children with mild handicaps who are mainstreamed into their regular education classes. Or it could be for the transition of a special education child who is being mainstreamed. In other instances, they work with a problem class or group of children therein. The program has been in effect since 1985. The framework involves teaching one teacher from every school, who then becomes a peer teacher in her own school.

The peer teachers are taught behavior analytic techniques. The basic text is *Modifying Classroom Behavior* (Buckley and Walker, 1978). This text covers how behaviors are learned, why behaviors continue to be performed (maintained), how behaviors can be eliminated, measuring behavior, and modifying classroom behavior. In addition, the peer teachers receive training in academic interventions for slow learners, students with learning disabilities, gifted students, and other students with special needs.

After completing training with the regular education peer consultant, each peer teacher is expected to be able to do the following:

1. Collaborate with other teachers, developing appropriate behavior or academic modifications as needed.

2. Assist in collecting and recording student performance.

3. Demonstrate instructional or behavioral techniques or programs.

4. Follow up and evaluate classroom programs implemented.

5. Increase reading of professional journals containing research on effective teaching techniques and consultation skills.

All behavioral and academic techniques included are "data based and applicable in regular, heterogeneous classrooms. Participants are also trained in various observation, data-recording, and data-reporting techniques" (McGill and Robinson, 1989, p. 72). Activities go along with everything taught. Such already-marketed interventions as Delquadri and associates' Spelling Game (1983) and Barrish and associates' Good Behavior Game (1969) are used.

The teachers who take part in the initial training by the regular education teacher consultants are volunteers recommended by the principal. Thirteen or fourteen teachers are selected for every training course. The fourteen three-hour learning sessions are intensive. The teachers get release time, and NSSEO reimburses the schools for the substitutes needed. This gives the teachers a changed role. School districts that want exclusive training pay for it.

At the training course, the teachers have one practice session with one of the regular education consultants, who observes them and discusses what happened. They may have to practice until they achieve reliability. The peer teachers practice the skills taught in the training course in their own classrooms before working with the other teachers. Standards are kept high and the participants are given certificates as reinforcement.

Before the project was initiated, the teachers indicated that they were tired of in-service meetings. They wanted someone to come into their classrooms to assist. Therefore, collaboration, rather than being an expert with the teachers, is stressed in the training course for peer teachers. However, the peer teachers are encouraged to work with a teacher wanting to implement techniques or programs a peer consultant is familiar with to expand the teaching skills of both teachers. Basically, peer teachers are told to find out what the problem is before doing anything with the teachers back in their schools. These become very intensive interventions.

The trained teachers go back and consult on academic and behavior problems. They are encouraged to come to the teachers as friends. The teachers may want the peer consultant to demonstrate or just to consult with them. Many like to have feedback. After peer teachers are back in their schools, if they want more training for observation and consultation skills, the regular education teacher consultant provides it.

Data are kept throughout the program, and there is a 100 percent return rate on forms to be filled out. Pre- and post-tests are given to the peer teachers. The tests try to determine their knowledge and comfort level. They are asked such questions as whether they know about behavioral direct instruction techniques and behavioral principles.

A short principal evaluation sheet is kept. The principals meet regularly with the regular education teacher consultants. They tell the classroom teachers not to refer a child for a case-study evaluation for special education until they have tried interventions under the guidance of the peer teachers. The number of children referred for case-study evaluations has dropped significantly since this program was introduced.

PARTNERS IN MINISTRY

Partners in Ministry is an after-school program for "latchkey children" run by the Reverend Kim DeLong for the Chicago Baptist Association of the American Baptist Churches. It is located in an impoverished city neighborhood that had formerly been middle class. It offers a model for badly needed after-school programs. Starting with a rented apartment that tried to emulate a home environment for the ten children aged five to twelve who were served there, it grew to include several other needed components in two years.

The parent-clients all work, and most are single parents. The after-school program is in session for the children until six o'clock. From six to seven, the parents drop in to pick up the children and talk to the staff. From this, a parents' group developed that has come to include other parents in the community. Half are parents of children in the program and half are others.

This group meets weekly to help each other with personal problems, socialize, and address community problems. Efforts are made to maintain a positive environment. Meetings start on a positive note, such as friendship, love, peace, justice, or women's rights. If there are community problems, action is taken to solve them. Individual concerns are addressed. Nutritious snacks are served. The group's treasurer collects the dues, some of which have been used for outings for the adults. Every meeting ends with a joke, and all walk out laughing.

Also, a group for ten girls from thirteen to seventeen years old has developed and meets weekly. They are concerned with issues of drugs, teen pregnancy, AIDS, suicide, crime, and education. Another major interest is job finding. Since the school system has not helped with this, a program preparing teenagers for jobs is being considered by the Partners in Ministry.

In addition, the program director meets once a month with each child's schoolteacher. These meetings focus on in-school problems, homework, and reinforcement of school programs. When indicated, a parent is invited to the meeting. Most of the children are behind in their academics. So every day the program participants set aside a time for homework, with tutoring available as needed.

Behavioral techniques are used throughout. The after-school program for latchkey children is instructive here. Reports to parents focus on things the child does well for the day. If there is a serious problem, the child is present when it is revealed to the parent. A solution is determined at this meeting. A typical solution might involve not viewing television until homework is completed.

At the program's apartment, every child has his daily chart posted on the wall. The charts address use of appropriate language, treating others with respect, and doing chores. As soon as a child completes five days (not necessarily consecutive) of achieving all three goals, he is rewarded by being excused from a day of chores. Most children attain the goals consistently.

There is a bead system to encourage working out interpersonal problems. Each child has an empty bottle; when kindness is shown to a peer or a conflict has been avoided, a bead is placed in the jar. Rewards are individualized. Stickers are given for encouraging another child. If a participant breaks something or makes a mess, he remains after hours to clean it up.

One youngster was continuously seeking attention by being bad. It was agreed that instead of being bad, he would receive one minute of positive attention from the group any time he felt the need for it. There has only been one fistfight in the two years of the program's operation.

Every parent and volunteer in the program is taught behavioral techniques for dealing with the children at home. For example, the program enlisted the help of the mother of an overweight girl. Both mother and child went on a diet together and reached their goals.

An effort is made to generalize learning in the program to the homes. The daily meetings and phone calls to parents are part of this. The personalized parent training is another factor. Besides this, every day a problem is posed to the children. The children are asked, for example, what would you do if your mother promised to meet you at two o'clock to attend a movie and she did not show up until six? The typical reaction of the children is to retaliate with violence. At this point, more appropriate reactions are taught through such behavioral rehearsal techniques as modeling and role playing.

APPENDIX: CASES OF A BEHAVIORAL SCHOOL SOCIAL WORKER

The interventions reported on here were carried out by Robert A. Labak at the LaGrange Area Department of Special Education (LADSE), LaGrange, Illinois. A team approach is often used at LADSE to develop a program for a child, to specify methods for carrying it out, and to assess it throughout. This has the advantage of controlling the child's environment and dealing with him consistently around behaviors to be changed. When a team approach was used, those involved in working with a particular child were called together. These might be the school psychologist, the student's teacher, the school nurse, the speech pathologist, an administrator, an occupational therapist, a student teacher or social work intern, and teacher aides.

The cases described here represent a sample of the types of behavioral interventions with which a school social worker could be involved. Because special education personnel have been quick to adopt applied behavior analysis, it is not surprising that most of these interventions were carried out with children enrolled in special education classes. Nonetheless, many of the procedures reported on here could be used with students in regular classrooms. The amount of teamwork and general acceptance of such procedures vary from school to school.

In the variety of cases discussed here, only relevant information distinguishing the school social worker's participation is provided. In every case the name of the pupil has been changed to maintain anonymity.

A Motivational Program to Generate Greater Independent Seatwork and Performance in Groups for a Student with a Moderate Mental Impairment.

The mother of John Pell, a moderately mentally impaired boy with chronic seizure disorders, had requested a motivational program for her son.

The objective in working with John was to increase his work productivity. To do this, motivational techniques aimed at greater independent seatwork and performance in groups were established at a LADSE team meeting. The team also made assessments to revise or augment their efforts throughout the treatment.

The team began by generating a list of effective reinforcers (materials and activities for which team members had observed John demonstrating a liking or preference) to shape those behaviors linked with increases in work productivity. These rewards were used in addition to continuous verbal praise and stars (see below) for academic behaviors such as focusing on his paper, using his pencil appropriately, and asking for assistance on a reasonable schedule.

The team agreed to use a token system (stars displayed on a laminated five-box scale) to motivate John while engaged in independent seatwork activities. All classroom personnel were asked to reward John with a statement of praise and a star for instances when he displayed desirable work habits. Whenever five stars were earned, a staff member would immediately give them to him.

The team encouraged John to taste new foods at snack time by using natural reinforcing events such as "Games Are Us" (an integrative recreational activity which typically began at 10:45 a.m. and included four regular second-grade students). Snack time immediately preceded "Games Are Us." At the same time, other students also could receive various rewards for tasting new foods.

The team worked with John's mother to establish regular meal times for him. This involved the team's encouraging him to eat at lunchtime in school and the mother's setting regular mealtimes at home instead of continuing to feed John on demand.

Behavioral Strategies Recommended to a Parent to Assist Her in Addressing Her Daughter's Troubling, Home-Based Behavior.

Mrs. Gray, mother of Stacy, requested immediate assistance from the child's teacher and other student support team members for help with some of her daughter's recent home-based behaviors, such as outbursts of aggressive behavior directed at the mother. The school social worker and classroom teacher visited Mrs. Gray to discuss Stacy's troubling behaviors. The teacher had asked social work team member Labak, to represent the support team.

Using behavior management principles that have been successful at school in shaping desirable behaviors and reducing severe noncompliant behaviors, the following guidelines were adopted for the mother to use with Stacy at home:

Give no more than two directions at a time to Stacy such as, "Go into the kitchen and sit down for dinner." Stacy had become frustrated, irritated and angry when confused by multistep directions. Obtain Stacy's undivided attention before delivering directions (eye contact and awareness), then deliver the directions simply and clearly.

Give signs of approval (verbal praise and simple rewards) immediately and regularly when Stacy complies with directions. This reaction was adopted to teach Stacy that "wanted" behavior carries expected payoffs. Furthermore, she had been noted to strive for positive attention from adults and other children. Also, shaping desired behaviors would prevent resorting to punishments, because Stacy could not act "bad" if she chose to be "good."

Remain calm yet assertive when Stacy refuses to follow a direction or to cease exhibiting an unwanted behavior. Specifically, keep voice and body messages calm, because Stacy had been observed to challenge a direction at school, apparently in an attempt to get adults to overreact. Mother was advised not to let Stacy get her to do anything she would not otherwise choose to do.

Keep physically away from Stacy and do not give her attention when she is physically violent. Wait for her to calm herself. Mother was allowed one or two comments while Stacy was tantruming, such as, "Stacy, let's not think right now about what Joe did. When you're quiet, I'll come over and help you with the game."

Mother was urged to use the recommended procedures consistently because consistency would be comforting to Stacy. Also, mother was advised to keep a keen eye for opportunities to praise or reward Stacy when she did follow directions, capitalizing on teaching opportunites when things were quiet and going well. This would also keep Stacy from feeling that others were being treated more fairly than she was. Above all, mother was advised to keep her emotions down and her mind clear because she could not be effective if both she and Stacy were out of control.

Mother was assigned as reading material "Catching your Child Being Good" and "Cheering for the Good Things" from Elizabeth Crary's *Without Spanking or Spoiling: A Practical Approach to Toddler and Preschool Guidance* (1979). She was also given information adapted from Martin Kosloff's *A Program For Families of Children With Learning and Behavior Problems* (1979).

A Program to Help a Boy Diagnosed as Emotionally Disordered to Develop Age-Appropriate Play/Interpersonal Skills.

The student support team determined to help Bruce Ramos enhance his social/adaptive skills around the school by supervising his interactive performances during recess, on the playground, and in other less structured situations. He was seen as needing direct-instruction opportunities emphasizing a high frequency of behavior rehearsal and constructive post-performance feedback to overcome identified skill deficiencies including initiating, conversational, and concrete play skills as well as concept and stratagem weaknesses and emotional responses. For example, he was not skilled in board games or competitive sports.

The following procedures were recommended to those who would be coaching Bruce in the goals sought:

Vary the settings, such as the classroom, playground, or gymnasium, in which instruction is given in play and interpersonal skills. This will increase chances of generalizing his improved behavior.

Review the mechanics of games and performance expectations for participating students before beginning any training procedures with Bruce. Assuming that Bruce's current play/interpersonal skills were underdeveloped, it was vital to simulate the subskills required for recreational activities. This could require practicing skills involved in games ahead of time. For example, in using a question-based variation of "Go To The Head of the Class," the following instructions would be given: "First, we need to throw the dice to determine who will proceed first. Once we have identified who goes first, I will read the first question to him. If he gives me the correct answer, he can then throw the dice and advance his player that number of desks."

Demonstrate to Bruce the skill involved in an activity when he works or plays with another boy who is more skilled. This might be true in a basketball game, for example. It would be good if Bruce could observe several examples of the correct way to perform ahead of time. A verbal review could also be part of the modeling for him. This procedure will help the therapist be sure that Bruce has an accurate understanding ahead of the game.

Instruct Bruce in simple skills and games at first. Since he has poor athletic skills, he will need a great deal of practice before attempting anything as complex as a game.

Employ sound teaching strategies when working on interpersonal skills with Bruce and any other boys:

Keep directions to him simply worded and clear. Instructors should be sure to have the attention of everyone in the group that Bruce is going to participate in. One or more other boys could be called on to repeat instructions in the middle of the explanation session. If everyone knows the rules and expectations, the activity should be more rewarding.

Keep the praise rate high and specific by making descriptive comments on desirable behaviors. For example, say, "Bruce, I like the way you walked right over to the side of the hoop after you took your foul shot. You're now in perfect position to take the rebound from Tom's shot."

Ignore disruptive comments or unwanted behaviors whenever possible. (Attention to them could strengthen them. Noticing the positives helps keep the instructor in control of the group.)

Select and group boys for Bruce to play with on the playground on the basis of where he is in his skills development. If he has mastered a skill, it would be good to introduce students who will be impressed by his success. If he is not so well developed in an activity, introduce pupils who are more tolerant and receptive to working with him.

Monitor Bruce's free play on the playground, directing him to situations in which he is almost sure to have success.

The school social worker saw these directions as preliminary to weekly meetings with Bruce's support person to make needed changes or additions.

An Impromptu Program to Remediate Out-of-Seat and Running/Pinching/ Grabbing Behaviors of a Profoundly Mentally Impaired Boy.

Tony is a six-year-old boy who is impulsive and has trouble staying in chairs. Social worker Labak developed a program to shape and increase Tony's "sitting behavior." Instances of either sitting normally in his chair or being in contact with the chair (even if he was leaning over and his upper body touched the floor) would earn him a reward as follows:

Present one toy to him when he meets the sitting definition.

Introduce a new toy whenever he appears disinterested in the toy he has.

Introduce a new toy if Tony remains in contact with his chair while retrieving a toy he has dropped and then returns to sitting position with it in hand.

Praise him verbally from time to time with such phrases as "Good sitting, Tony," when he is sitting well.

Wait for him to resume sitting position if he has thrown a toy away and then introduce a new toy to him. Do not retrieve the thrown toy.

To decrease Tony's running and pinching/grabbing, the social worker provided the following program:

Remove a toy from him if he has one in his possession when he runs or pinches.

Place him in the closest time-out location immediately to avert attention to him.

Tell him why he is in time out when he arrives at the time-out location.

Remove Tony from time out after he shows he can sit calmly for a few seconds.

After he returns to his regular seat and remains there a few seconds, give him one of his favorite toys.

Management Strategies for Two Students in a Self-Contained Program for Moderately Mentally Impaired Students.

Labak presented the following program for treatment of Jeff Williams during instances of noncompliance:

Direct Jeff to return to task using a simple, verbal direction.

If his noncompliance continues, ignore it to allow Jeff time to redirect himself.

After several seconds give him another direction, with the warning that noncompliance means a return to his desk.

If he is still noncompliant, send him back to his desk.

Generally, to prevent instances of noncompliance and promote desirable behaviors, the staff will provide Jeff with attention when he is exhibiting desired behaviors;

provide Jeff with tokens contingent on observed good behavior;

use a "Good Behavior Badge" as an immediate reward to Jeff for additional management leverage.

To decrease Mark Miller's talk-outs (songs), staff will use planned ignoring consisting of

no eye contact;

no talking;

keeping physically away from Mark when practical.

It is imperative that the staff consistently use planned ignoring regardless of the temptation to react with attention to escalations in talking out of turn. It is an all-or-nothing procedure. If ignoring is not possible, the program needs to be completely discontinued and a new replacement program developed.

Contract to Enhance a Seven-Year-Old Boy's Direction-Following Skills.

The following is a copy of the contract drawn up between Andre and his teacher, Ms. King. It is a typical contract, easy to understand and apply.

CONTRACT
Following Directions with an 'OK' and a Smile

I, Ms. King, will give Andre ten (10) minutes of free time on days when Andre follows direction (with an "OK" and a smile) with 1 or 0 pouts.

I, Ms. King, will keep a record of times when Andre pouts after a direction. I will record these pouts and refusals to work on a square piece of paper placed on Andre's desk.

We, the undersigned parties, agree to this contract:

Ms. King, Teacher: _____

Andre Young, Student: _____

Dates earned free time: _____

A Program to Promote Weight Loss in a Ten-Year-Old Boy.

Steve Short, the pupil involved, had gained three pounds since his last weigh-in. According to Steve, he indulged the day before at his grandmother's house because it was his birthday. This brought his weight to 208 pounds. He began the school weight-loss intervention at 210 pounds. During ten weeks of the program, he had gone down to 205 pounds, but his final weight was 208.

The school social worker, teachers, and nurse had tried to enlist the cooperation of Mrs. Short, Steve's mother, in taking him to Weight Watchers or a doctor or using the materials supplied her by the schoool nurse. No response could be elicited from Mrs. Short. However, the school social worker decided to continue Steve's school program with periodic contacts with his mother and reinforcements made available to Steve for weight loss or maintenance.

The results with Steve are in line with general findings for weight reduction treatment (Marcus, 1985). The average weight loss by any type of therapy is about twelve pounds, but the average client is more than fifty pounds overweight before treatment. Ross (1981) points out the need for both parent and medical cooperation in working with obese children.

Sample Communication Sheets for a Parent, Secondary to an Individualized In-Class Behavior Program.

TO: (mother)
FROM: (teacher)   Date:_____

                        (Circle the level of performance)*

Work Completion:

                                              GOOD   FAIR   POOR

(Comment) _____
_____

Compliance with Teacher Direction(s):

                                              GOOD   FAIR   POOR

(Comment): _____
_____

Respectfulness to Teacher:

                                              GOOD   FAIR   POOR

(Comment): _____
_____

*If Steve is rated "Fair" or "Poor" in a given category, please provide an explanatory comment.   RAL:jk, 10/88.

In addition to the above form, the parents were sent weekly notes such as the one that follows.

Dear Parent(s):

The social/interpersonal skill taught to your child this week was:

ANSWERING

Definition: *Answering means to talk back nicely when someone talks to you*

Expansion: *Answering is what you do right after someone talks to you. People like it when*
you have something to say back. When someone talks to you, you should stop,
look at the person, and say something back.

When someone asks you what your name is, you should answer. When someone
asks you to sit by them at lunch, you should answer. When someone asks you to
play a game at recess, you should answer.

Please try to set time aside each day to briefly practice this critical social skill with your
child.

A Momentary Time Sampling Recording Instrument and Its Application for Assessing a Student's Adjustment and Developing Interventions as Warranted.

A form for use in behavioral planning was copyrighted in 1983 by Nancy
Buechin and her associates at LADSE. It is for observational planning and
provides for ten-second observations of client and peers. Off-task, talking,
out-of-seat, wrong assignment, throwing, and other behaviors are included as
behaviors to observe. Observations are made on this form by the school social
worker when a child enters a LADSE program. In addition, a child's participation in his reading group and his seatwork are examined. The school social
worker summarizes and records findings and then discusses them with the
classroom teacher.

A similar from, given here, was developed by the school social worker and
the speech therapist working together to record observations of a child requiring social skills training. The component behaviors observed were turn
taking, eye contact, direction following, and "good" speech.

Social Skills Training

Turn Taking _____

Eye Contact _____

Direction Following _____

"Good" Speech _____

Turn Taking Code: 1 Exhibits "waiting," i.e., hands to self, quiet mouth, eyes tracking person/activity

2 Demonstrates knowledge of whose turn it is

Eye Contact Code: Y Focuses on person/interaction/activity that is occurring/
dominant

YWPA Yes, but with physical assist

YWVA Yes, but with minimal verbal assist

Direction Following Code: Y3 Followed a three (3) step direction

Y2 Followed a two (2) step direction

Y1 Followed a one (1) step direction
YIW with assistance
"Good" Speech Code: Y Eye contact and appropriate volume
E Eye contact (alone)
V Appropriate volume (alone)
YY Yes, demonstrated the ability to answer a "yes" question
(E/V)
YN Yes, demonstrated the ability to answer a "no" question
(E/V)
1/20/88
RAL: In date dictated 1/20/88

Mahoney & Labak - Continuing Social/Leisure Training Activities

A Social/Developmental Study Using Behaviorally Based Notations/Perceptions/Strategies.

Labak's social/developmental study first records identifying data. This is followed by the reason for assessment, pertinent sources of information, and cultural factors vitally affecting the child's adjustment. Next there are observations of the family and an overview of the child's educational history. This is followed by a lengthy report regarding the child's social/adaptive skills in the classroom and community.

Social skills are assessed from an applied behavior analysis perspective. After a summary statement about the pupil's general overall adjustment, successful behavioral interventions are described in detail. These can include comments on his interactions with his educational peers. Behavioral concerns warranting continued or new behavioral interventions are identified and addressed. In summary, the student's strengths and weaknesses in response to treatment are put forth.

The functioning of the family is invariably considered in any social/developmental study. A general summary of the family's interaction patterns is provided, with behavioral concerns explored. Behavioral concerns occurring in the home are compared with the student's behavior in school and assessed in terms of what the school has been able to accomplish in relation to home behaviors. The response of family members to suggested behavioral interventions is recorded.

Entry Assessment
(Sample)

Date:

Student's Name: Alexander Kelly   *File No.:*

Date of Birth: *Res. Dist./School:*

Address: *Current Placement:*

Report completed by: Robert Labak, M.S.S.W.

Purpose of Report: To obtain some preliminary assessment information from which possibly to generate programmatic interventions and goals for Alexander Kelly.

Observation Results: An admittedly brief, preliminary observation of Alex was conducted; the primary intent of this formal observation was to collect data on his on-task behaviors and prioritize a list of behaviors in need of corrective intervention. This observation began at 9:42 a.m. when Alex was working at his desk on an assigned seatwork paper. Using a momentary 10-second interval time system, discrete observations were made of Alex and another boy, selected to obtain comparative on-task information. Alex was on task (effectively applying himself to task and refraining from talking out and other distractible behaviors) 66 percent of the time. Forty percent of observational time focused on Alex performing independently at his seat, and 60 percent focused on his performing in a direct-instruction reading group.

Alex's off-task behaviors while working at his desk included frequently talking out to other students and out-of-seat or poorly-seated behavior, increasing his susceptibility to distraction. While working at his desk (twelve observation frames), Alex talked out three times and was found out of seat on three other occasions. It should be noted that these off-task behaviors, although obviously preempting work time, did not stop Alex from doing quality and timely work. During Alex's participation in his reading group, he was similarly observed being productive yet concurrently talking out. In fifteen observational frames, he talked out on eight occasions. The teacher's behavioral skills of coupling planned ignoring and descriptive verbal reinforcement to students demonstrating quiet on-task behavior kept the negative distracting effects of Alex's talking out to a minimum. From seatwork examined and confirmation by an aide, it appeared that Alex did submit quality work within the prescribed time frame. Overall, his talking out and out-of-seat behavior appeared to be mild though frequent.

Since he is new to his primary school placement, it is likely that Alex will need some time to adjust to the established classroom rules. However, it is suggested that his teacher use a "star system," clear and regular communication of classroom rules, and consequences for compliance and noncompliance. The school social worker will discuss possible approaches to these behavioral concerns with her.

Social/Developmental Study
(Sample)

Date:

Student: Stacy Gray   *File No.:*

Birthdate:

Address:

Phone No.:   *Dist./School of Res.:*

                                                                Current Placement:

Report completed by: Robert A. Labak, M.S.S.W.

Reason for Assessment: Files indicated that Stacy was due for a three-year reevaluation. The student support team at her school identified the need to update its records, particularly her social/developmental progress. A series of emerging behavioral concerns reportedly occurring within her home emphasized the need for such a study at this time.

Sources of Information: Information in this update was obtained on a recent visit to the Gray home, from Stacy's teacher, and from the school social worker's observations and interactions with her over the past school year. Historical information was obtained by review of her records.

Cultural Factors: Cultural factors do not notably affect Stacy's academic and behavioral profile.

Family Information:

    Legal Guardian(s): Sara Gray, mother and single parent

    Father: Divorced and absent from the home.

    Mother: Sara Gray

    Occupation: Professional house cleaner, self-employed

Sibling(s):	Harold	Richard	Robert
	Age:	Age:	Age:

    Stacy lives with her mother and brothers without other family members.

Educational History: (List)

School year	School	Teacher

Medical History: See "Medical/Health" portion of Annual Review/Reevaluation Document

Social/Adaptive Skills (Classroom and Community-based Observations):

    Stacy was observed in a variety of learning situations over the past school year. Within the classroom, she has varied work habits. These range from working independently for sustained time periods to making undue requests for assistance or teacher attention.

    When Stacy exhibits attention-seeking behaviors, such as invoking "whines" and premature hand raising for assistance, it helps to inform her that "whines" and unnecessary requests will not be honored. On the other hand, carefully completed or attempted work will be regularly honored and suitably praised. Given her need, stemming from family dynamics, for regular attention and reassurance, Stacy can be best shaped by planned and consistent use of concrete, motivational strategies. Powerful inducements are stars, timely verbal acknowledgement, running errands for the teacher, and free-time privileges for compliance to direction or work demands.

During the last two years, Stacy's overall behavior and academic/social skills have improved at school and in the community. Most of her social/adaptive gains stem from integrative opportunities at school. She has increased her more age-appropriate, useful language, and coping behaviors. These gains were achieved by spending more time with typical education peers in the lunchroom, music class, home room, assemblies, and special events in the school. These experiences have given her honest, immediate, and remedial feedback invaluable in reducing Stacy's "actress-like" episodes of obstinacy and feigned victimization. "Telling it like it is" by most of the other children is a strong shaping influence on Stacy.

This student still has mild behaviors that her teacher and support personnel monitor and address regularly. These include talking out, mimicking taunts, initiating negative remarks towards peers, and throwing brief but sometimes severe tantrums when reprimanded or denied requests. Reverse times out related to the classroom's assertive discipline program have been effective in reducing the frequency and duration of her unwanted behaviors.

In play/leisure situations, Stacy gets along well with peers and actively seeks play partners. She is becoming increasingly skilled at adjusting her behavior to be accepted in group situations. Also, she shows regard for the property of others. However, at times she will argue and push her classmates to communicate her displeasure, which can be eliminated by directing her to stop. Instances of manipulation noted in the past have become less frequent; instead, healthy, cooperative play has become more common.

In total, Stacy's need for attention and approval is her greatest strength and weakness. She is an absolutely lovely and pleasant girl to be around when she chooses to obtain approval by socially appropriate means. On the other hand, she can be difficult and intractable when set on having her own way despite the resistance this will bring. In spite of all this, she is liked by her classmates, has a commendable social approach and engagement skills, and can share enough with others to be sought after as a play partner.

Family Functioning: As a single parent, Mrs. Gray carries demanding responsibilities. She maintains a busy schedule as a self-employed professional house cleaner and as the parent of four. Not having an available network of friends from whom she can request assistance and respite, Mrs. Gray has little personal life. She is active in her church, but it is not clear whether they offer her any practical, day-to-day assistance.

During a home visit by the classroom teacher and school social worker requested by Mrs. Gray to discuss Stacy's behavior, she described the family dynamics. Mother had become concerned about some of Stacy's occasional violent and aggressive outbursts. They would be aimed at a door or directly at Mrs. Gray, whose hair might be pulled. The social worker and teacher responded by describing a number of behaviorally based in-school strategies used successfully in preventing or mitigating such attention-seeking outbursts. As a result of these interventions, Stacy does not have as many outbursts in school, where consequences are understood and immediately introduced. Skills reviewed with Mrs. Gray were discriminative reinforcement ("If. . . . then" contingencies) and precise, simply worded directions.

Mrs. Gray is currently seeking help in managing her daughter and sons. She has had an intake interview at Haywood Hospital and is waiting for an appointment for family therapy. She should be congratulated for her ability to view her family situation objectively and seek necessary professional help in the school and the community. The motivation for Stacy's outbursts appears to be attention seeking but other interpersonal issues among her brothers and mother undoubtedly make her feel she is not receiving enough quality time from her mother. Given Stacy's observed excessive need for attention and approval at school, it is hard to presume that her emotional needs are being overlooked. Rather, Mrs. Gray needs instruction in how to distribute her time and attention so she conveys clear behavioral expectations accompanied by earned rewards to her children.

A Relaxation Drill for a Boy with Moderate Mental Impairment who Exhibits Behaviors Reflecting Acute Stress when Exposed to Disruptions in his Daily Routine.

These are the steps in a highly routinized relaxation drill used when Mike Kelly communicated displeasure and discomfort through verbal and physical tantrums. It was considered important to emphasize smoothly working through each step in the drill as follows:

Have Mike rehearse the drill's activities before applying them in a situation where he is in significant distress.

Tell Mike to assume the "start" position—hands open and flush on the top of his desk with his upper body erect and close to the desk.

Model and perform the step, standing facing him with hands positioned similarly to his but not necessarily on the desk. This should insure that Mike learns and regularly performs at a level of mastery.

Instruct him to begin counting very slowly to five. With each number spoken, Mike is gradually to form his fingers into a clenched fist by the count of three and have the fist fully relaxed and returned to the palms-down state by five.

Instruct Mike to count in a relaxed quiet voice. Breathing can be substituted for speaking here as long as the physical routine is unaltered.

Have Mike continue the drill until you and he agree that he has resumed a calm state. To assess this he should be asked periodically, "Mike? Are you relaxed now?" while observing his body language.

Praise him in a soothing voice as he works through the drill and the conclusion of the drill.

Have Mike repeat the drill at least four times.

Have Mike perform this drill at a predictible location such as his desk. The drill may be used when he is outside of his classroom, but the steps should remain the same.

It is imperative to repeatedly rehearse all steps in the drill with Mike before using it while he is in a state of emotional stress.

Integration/Social Skill Enhancement Program for a Primary Age Boy with Autism.

The school social worker wrote a friendly encouraging letter to Herman's mother describing a new second-grade group for "special play and learning activity." The group was in fact organized to help Herman. Having been given prior notice of the group, mother had contributed assorted "goodies," and the letter recognized that the treats encouraged the group members.

The above examples are asampling of sorts of individual cases the behavioral school social worker may encounter. The amount of teamwork and general acceptance of such procedures vary from school to school.

Social Skills Training Groups

Student group programs provide the behavioral school social worker with an opportunity to help solve individual and group problems as well as provide training in social skills. Usually, such groups meet somewhere else in the school than in the regular classroom. Labak has offered social skills training and illustrative reports that follow.

These groups usually included no more than six members. They met for half-hour sessions for ten weeks. Frequent reinforcement was an integral component. Teachers and parents were given reports of the group's activities and asked to recognize progress that a student made in the social skill currently being concentrated on in the group meetings. Teachers were asked to write a note to the group leaders if a group member showed positive instances of any of the skills taught in the group. These would be used to reinforce the pupil in the group setting.

Peer Relations Group

A six-member group called a peer relations group, related to language development, was conducted for regular and special education students. Weekly meetings of the group were held. The stated purposes were:

To discuss the importance of making many friends.

To encourage students to identify reasons why they should include many people in their circles of friends; and

To assign a "friendship-making task."

The students were asked to write a list of their close friends from school, home, or wherever. This was followed by a discussion of the reasons why it might be important to enlarge one's circle of friends. The following ideas were elicited:

In case your other friend(s) get sick.

In case your other friend(s) get mad at you.

In case your friend(s) move.

Because the left-out person might feel badly.

So you have more people to play with.

Next, the students were given an assignment sheet and told to try to play with different children that week. Whenever a student played with someone other than his previously identified close friends, he was to write the new person's name on the list and briefly describe what they did together. Group members were told that an incomplete or lost sheet meant no time to play "Uno" the next week.

Two group members had very good days. Two others got off to a bad start, although one of these "shaped up" quickly. A fifth member was continuously disruptive and lost his privilege of playing "Uno."

A report to parents of group members working in the area of getting along concentrated on using polite words. This was defined as saying words and terms like "please," "thank you," "I'm sorry," and "excuse me" at the right time.

Expansion on this definition included "Using polite words means you are being kind to other people. You are telling people how you feel in a nice way. When someone does something nice for you and you say 'thank-you,' you are letting him know at the right time that you like what he did."

More specifically, the pupils were told "If you are out on the playground and you bump into someone by mistake, polite words to use would be 'excuse me' or 'I'm sorry.' " Or "If you needed to borrow a pencil from your neighbor you would say, 'Please may I borrow a pencil?' After he gave it to you, you would say 'Thank-you.' "

Parents were asked to try to set time aside each day to briefly practice this skill with their children.

Another written report to their teachers summarized the group's progress so far and gave the agenda for the next two meetings. Purposes of the group were listed as (1) to establish a positive working relationship with students, (2) to pursue further problem identification, and (3) to collect general personal and family data on the students involved.

The summary of group dynamics to date explained that throughout the introductory session, all students freely volunteered information, usually responding appropriately to management directions and appearing comfortable with the other children and the adults. Since the members seemed responsive to simple verbal management, it was decided not to develop a formal management system at this time. However, it was noted that a time-out procedure might be needed to help one member limit frequent interruptions or sharing of irrelevant information.

During the forty minutes of group discussion, the three group purposes were accomplished. Based on the information received from the students, the topics for at least the next two sessions were decided: "What is a friend?" "How do I make a friend?" and "What hurts or destroys friendships?"

Teachers were told further that skills training using items from the school's *SBS Social Skills* curriculum would be provided to these students. Behaviors which undermine friendships, such as teasing, bossiness, intolerance and aggression, would be discussed.

Suggestions for future sessions included:

Individualized programs to encourage each student to demonstrate the skills taught in the sessions. Before any individualized programs are implemented, teachers (and perhaps parents) will be contacted and in-serviced on how they can be of assistance.

If time and practicality permit, a session on promoting self-esteem in children will be targeted.

Before the pupils "graduate" from this peer-relations program, they will be required to demonstrate mastery of the skills taught. How mastery will be measured has not yet been determined.

This plan was followed by a later communication which posed the questions "What is a friend?" "How can you tell?." At this point the group decided its specific purposes were:

to develop a practical definition of a "friend";

to generate a list of characteristics of a friend; and

to personalize their view of "friendship" by asking the students about their own experiences in making and maintaining friendships.

A full description of events of this session was provided to the teachers in this memo. It covered the setting up of a behavior checklist system which could lead to a one-minute time-out cost. Also, it was noted that the members of the group were comfortable with each other and the group size (five members) was optimal.

In terms of content on the targeted purposes, responses from group members were forthcoming. They were able to list eleven characteristics of friends. Each was elaborately discussed. Positive consequences associated with demonstrating "friend" qualities and negative consequences associated with the opposite, or "friendship-sinking," behaviors were repeatedly stressed. A poll of what friends each member had at that time revealed that they had very few. They were then asked to use the friendship-making skills presented so far either to further stabilize existing friendships or to make new ones. Finally, the following "Let's Make Friends" skill chart was distributed to each group member.

LET'S MAKE FRIENDS

DO....

	M	T	W	TH	F
1. Said nice things to my friend					
2. Was a helper					
3. Kept a secret					
4. Didn't tattle-tale					

5. Spent time with my friend after school   _____
6. Spent time with my friend in school   _____

DON'T. . . .
1. Don't boss your friend.
2. Don't hit your friend.
3. Don't tease your friend.
4. Don't lie.
5. Don't hurt your friend's feelings.

(Bring this with you when you next visit Mr. Labak)

Staff Training Programs

An ongoing component of the job of the behavioral school social worker is training other staff in the setting, including professionals and aides. Labak developed and carried out specific programs focusing on, praise, clear instruction, positive feedback, and playground procedures.

Praise Program

The following basic components should be considered when developing and implementing an effective behavior change program (BCP), primarily utilizing praise:

Specifically target teacher and student behaviors to be changed or increased (teachers praising students and teachers praising teachers).

Make praise statements descriptive. Praise statements should describe specific target behaviors you want to see increased.

　　Target behavior: Sitting Quietly

　　　　Good example: "I like the way you're sitting quietly, Brian" (specific).

　　　　Poor example: "Good working" (too general).

Praise statements must be made frequently to communicate your behavior expectations to students (sitting quietly is desired) or to remind teachers of what specific behaviors they should demonstrate in order to encourage.

When delivering praise,

　　establish initial eye contact (most optimal);

　　stand relatively close (approximate) to the student being praised;

　　be sincere in your delivery;

　　consider simultaneous tactile complements such as a touch on the shoulder; and

　　be consistent.

Consider using "across the room praise" to reinforce students showing desired behaviors but with whom you are not working directly.

Management Skills

Structuring the environment of a school to allow every child to perform at his maximum capacity is an important goal and teaching tool. To do this best, a clear plan has to be developed to help the school faculty understand and acquire needed skills. Rules designed to implement these purposes have to be drafted, understood, and carried out by all the pupils and adults. Therefore, at LADSE careful and detailed instructions have been prepared and taught to members of the school staff.

Management skills have the added benefit of offering consistency to the child for whom a specific program has been implemented. If every person dealing with a pupil has the same expectations and uses the same techniques, that child will have a better chance to develop the behavior sought by a plan tailored to his needs.

Giving Clear Instructions

The more specific the directions, the better the chances are that the student will be able to follow the directions.

As the teacher masters the skill of giving clear instructions, she becomes more effective in teaching, her optimism and confidence grow, and the child learns cooperation.

There are several key elements in giving clear directions:

Get the child's attention.
Look at the child (your eyes should be looking at his eyes).
Use a physical prompt (touch or nudge).
Lower the tone of your voice.
Repeat only one or two words from the original directions. "It's time to line up" becomes "Line up, now."
Reward cooperative response by praising the child when he begins to follow the direction.

Several additional important points should be remembered:

The younger the child, the fewer the words in the direction.

The more important the demand, the clearer the *statement* must be. (Do not use a question such as "Would you please stop that?") Say, "Please stop that."

Give directions that state what you want; don't assume he knows what you mean. (Avoid statements like "Behave yourself," "Act your age," and "Be good."

When introducing any change strategies, be consistent.

Delivering Positive Feedback and Discouraging Inappropriate Behavior

Positive feedback can be delivered in many ways. Select examples are:

Clearly delivered verbal praise. Give effective praise using descriptive language at the time the desired behaviors are observed (e.g., "Good sitting quietly, Gil," while Gil is seen sitting quietly).

Positive tactile feedback. Rest a comforting supportive hand on Gil's shoulder or arm to show approval while he is exhibiting desired behaviors (e.g., waiting quietly in line at a fast-food restaurant). Add a praise statement to strengthen the feedback.

Presentation of a reinforcer. Provide Gil with a proven/genuine reward (e.g., a toy or activity) contingent/dependent upon first observing his exhibiting a wanted behavior.

A variety of effective strategies, including time out, cost, verbal reprimand, and exclusion procedures, can be used to decrease unwanted behaviors.

The following example illustrates how both positive and negative feedback might be implemented effectively in a given program.

Playground Program

Goal: To gain control over student behavior(s) on the playground.

Tools: A plan to encourage good/desirable student behavior and another plan to discourage bad/undesirable student behavior.

Program philosophy: Student behavior is influenced by feedback.

Type: Positive feedback which encourages desirable behavior. Negative feedback which discourages undesirable behavior

Frequency: As often as either type of feedback is communicated.

Implementation:

Watch to see whether students are exhibiting good or bad behaviors.

Take time to verbally compliment or acknowledge students playing the right way.

Deliberately walk over and make positive verbal comments to students behaving appropriately.

Give a small piece of laminated paper, serving as a token reward with later payoff value, to a student to present to his teacher. A specified number of tokens can earn a special acknowledgement or privilege.

Catch a student displaying bad behavior.

Approach him and state exactly what you saw him do that was bad or unacceptable playground behavior.

Inform him authoritatively that his unacceptable behavior has earned him _____ minutes of TAP (time away from play) against a designated wall or within a designated (chalk-marked) area. No more than one warning should be given before delivering TAP.

Tell him he can return to play only after compliantly serving TAP.

Reward him, as practical, after he returns and exhibits good behavior.

Note: When a student refuses to go to the TAP area or tries to leave without permission, you can gain compliance by adding a minute for each refusal to his already assigned time. Say, "That's five minutes, Al. . . . Now it's six minutes. . . . Now seven."

A form for classroom teacher follow-up can be developed, to record student behavior on the playground and give additional power to the use.

Playground Report Form

Date:

Student(s) receiving warnings:

Name   Teacher

_____

_____

_____

Student(s) given TAP time:

_____

_____

_____

Student(s) given tokens for good behavior (reward for a job well done):

(This draft prepared for Review and later discussion by Bob Labak)._____

_____

_____

BIBLIOGRAPHY

Aaron, B. A., and Bostow, D. F. (1978). "Indirect Facilitation of On-Task Behavior Produced by Contingent Free-Time for Academic Productivity." *Journal of Applied Behavior Analysis* 11: 197.

Abbott, Martha (1969). "Modification of the Classroom Behavior of a 'Disadvantaged' Kindergarten Boy by Social Reinforcement and Isolation." *Journal of Education* 151: 31–44.

Abel, Gene G.; Becker, Judith V.; Murphy, William D.; and Flanagan, Barry U. (1981). "Identifying Dangerous Child Molesters." In *Violent Behavior: Social Learning Approaches to Prediction, Management and Treatment,* edited by R. B. Stuart. New York: Brunner/Mazel.

Abel, Gene G.; Mittleman, Mary S.; and Becker, Judith V. (1985). "Sexual Offenders: Results of Assessment and Recommendations for Treatment." In *Clinical Criminology: The Assessment and Treatment of Criminal Behavior,* edited by M. H. Ben-Aron, S. J. Hucker, C. D. Webster. Toronto, Canada: M and M Graphics.

Adams, Janis; Conn, Maureen; Fiscus, Shawn; Gilmore, Carlye; Kelley, Mark; Klotz, Brenda; Sulsar-Stuart, Cindy; and Flanagan, Pat (1987). *Classwide Peer Tutoring.* Unpublished manual, Junction City, Kans.

Addams, Jane (1893). "The Subjective Necessity for Social Settlements," *Philanthropy and Social Progress.* New York: New Republic.

Alden, Lynn (1980). "Preventive Strategies in the Treatment of Alcohol Abuse: A Review and a Proposal." In *Behavioral Medicine: Changing Health Lifestyles,* edited by P. O. Davidson and S. M. Davidson. New York: Brunner/Mazel.

Alexander, James, and Parsons, Bruce (1973). "Short-Term Behavioral Intervention with Delinquent Families: Impact on Family Process and Recidivism," *Journal of Abnormal Psychology* 81: 219–25.

Allen, K. Eileen; Henke, Lydia B.; Harris, Florence R.; Baer, Donald M.; and Reynolds, Nancy J. (1967). "Control of Hyperactivity by Social Reinforcement of Attending Behavior," *Journal of Educational Psychology* 58: 231–37.

Allen-Meares, Paula; Washington, Robert O.; and Welsh, Betty L. (1986). *Social Work Services in Schools.* Englewood Cliffs, N.J.: Prentice Hall.

Arkava, Morton L. (1973). *Behavior Modification: A Procedural Guide for Social Workers.* Missoula, Mont.: University of Montana.

Atkeson, B. M., and Forehand, R. (1978). "Parent Behavioral Training: An Example of Studies Using Multiple Outline Measures," *Journal of Abnormal Child Psychology* 6: 449–60.

Ayllon, Teodoro, and Azrin, Nathan (1968). *The Token Economy, A Motivational System for Therapy and Rehabilitation.* New York: Appleton-Century-Crofts.

Ayllon, Teodoro D.; Layman, Dale; and Burke, Sandra (1972). "Disruptive Behavior and Reinforcement of Academic Performance," *Psychological Record* 22: 315–23.

Ayllon, Teodoro D.; Layman, Dale; and Kandel, H. (1975). "A Behavioral-Educational Alternative to Drug Control of Hyperactive Children," *Journal of Applied Behavior Analysis* 8: 137–46.

Ayllon, Teodoro D., and Roberts, M. D. (1974). "Eliminating Discipline Problems by Strengthening Academics," *Journal of Applied Behavior Analysis* 7: 71–76.

Ayllon, Theodoro; Smith, D.; and Rogers, M. (1970). "Behavioral Management of School Phobia," *Journal of Behavior Therapy and Experimental Psychiatry* 1: 125–38.

Azrin, Nathan H. (1989). "Community-Reinforcement Treatment of Alcoholism." Paper delivered at the Association for Behavior Analysis Convention in Milwaukee, May 1989.

——— (1976). "Improvements in Community-Reinforcement Approach to Alcoholism," *Behavior Research and Therapy* 14: 339–48.

Azrin, Nathan H.; Flores, T.; and Kaplan, S. J. (1975). "Job-Finding Club: A Group-Assisted Program for Obtaining Employment," *Behavior Research and Therapy* 13: 17–26.

Azrin, Nathan H., and Nunn, R. Gregory (1977). *Habit Control in a Day.* New York: Simon and Schuster.

Azrin, Nathan H.; Sisson, R. W.; Meyers, R.; and Godley, M. (1982). "Alcoholism Treatment By Disulfiram and Community-Reinforcement Therapy," *Journal of Behavior Therapy and Experimental Psychiatry* 13: 105–12.

Azrin, N. H.; Sneed, T. J.; and Foxx, R. M. (1974). "Dry-Bed Training: Rapid Elimination of Childhood Enuresis," *Behavior Research and Therapy* 12: 147–56.

Azrin, N. H., and Thienes, P. M. (1978). "Rapid Elimination of Enuresis by Intensive Learning Without a Conditioning Apparatus," *Behavior Therapy* 9: 342–54.

Azrin, N. H.; Thienes-Hontos, P.; and Besalel-Azrin, V. (1979). "Elimination of Enuresis Without a Conditioning Apparatus: An Extension by Office Instruction of the Child and Parent," *Behavior Therapy* 10: 14–19.

Baer, Donald M. (1982). "Applied Behavior Analysis." In G. T. Wilson and C. M. Franks, eds., *Contemporary Behavior Therapy.* New York: Guilford Press.

Baer, Donald M., and Guess, R. (1971). "Receptive Training of Adjective Inflections in Mental Retardates," *Journal of Applied Behavior Analysis* 4: 129–40.

Baer, Donald M.; Wolf, Montrose M.; and Risley, Todd R. (1968). "Some Current Dimensions of Applied Behavior Analysis," *Journal of Applied Behavior Analysis*, 1: 91–97.

Baker, Bruce L. (1969). "Symptom Treatment and Symptom Substitution in Enuresis," *Journal of Abnormal Psychology* 74: 42–49.

Bakken, Joel; Miltenberger, Raymond; and Schauss, Scott (1989). "Training Mentally Retarded Parents: Knowledge vs. Skills." Paper presented at the fifteenth annual convention of the Association for Behavior Analysis, Milwaukee, May 1989.

Bandura, Albert (1969). *Principles of Behavior Modification.* New York: Holt, Rinehart and Winston.

(1971). "Psychotherapy Based Upon Modeling Principles." In *Handbook of Psychotherapy and Behavior Change*, edited by A. E. Bergin and S. L. Garfield. New York: Wiley.

Bandura, Albert; Blanchard, Edward; and Ritter, Brunhilde (1969). "Relative Efficacy of Desensitization and Modeling Approaches for Inducing Behavioral, Affective, and Attitudinal Changes," *Journal of Personality and Social Psychology* 13: 173–99.

Barrish, Harriet H.; Saunders, Muriel; and Wolf, Montrose M. (1969). "Good Behavior Game: Effects of Individual Contingencies for Group Consequences on Disruptive Behavior in a Classroom," *Journal of Applied Behavior Analysis* 2: 119–24.

Bass, Roger F. (1987). "Computer Assisted Observer Training," *Journal of Applied Behavior Analysis* 20: 83–85.

Becker, Judith V. (1989). "Teen-age Sexual Abusers." Talk to Maryville Academy and Chicago Association for Behavior Analysis, April 10, 1989, Chicago.

Becker, Judith V., and Coleman, Emily M. (1988). "Incest." In *Handbook of Family Violence*, edited by V. B. Van Hasselt, R. L. Morrison, A. S. Bellack, and M. Hersen. New York: Plenum Press.

Becker, Wesley C. (1971). *Parents are Teachers: A Child Management Program*. Champaign, Ill.: Research Press.

Ben-Aron, M. H.; Hacker, S. J.; and Webster, C. D., eds. (1985). *Clinical Criminology: The Assessment and Treatment of Criminal Behavior*. Toronto: M. and M. Graphics.

Berkowitz, B. P., and Graziano, A. M. (1972). "Training Parents as Behavior Therapists: A Review," *Behavior Research and Therapy* 10: 297–317.

Bernal, Martha; Duryee, John; Pruett, Harold; and Burns, Beverlee (1968). "Behavior Modification and the Brat Syndrome," *Journal of Consulting and Clinical Psychology* 4: 447–55.

Bigelow, G.; Liebson, I.; and Lawrence, C. (1973). "Prevention of Alcohol Abuse by Reinforcement of Incompatible Behavior." Paper presented at the Association for Advancement of Behavior Therapy, Miami, December 1973.

Bootzin, Richard R. (1975). *Behavior Modification and Therapy: An Introduction*. Cambridge, Mass.: Winthrop Publishers.

(1973). "Stimulus Control of Insomnia." Paper presented at the Symposium on the Treatment of Sleep Disorders, American Psychological Association Convention, Montreal, July 1973.

Bootzin, R. R., and Nicassio, P. M. (1978). "Behavioral Treatments for Insomnia," *Progress in Behavior Modification* 6: 1–45.

Boudin, H. M. (1972). "Contingency Contracting as a Therapeutic Tool in the Deceleration of Amphetamine Use," *Behavior Therapy* 3: 604–8.

Boudin, H. M., and Valentine, V. E. (1972). "Behavioral Techniques as an Alternative to Methadone Maintenance." Paper read at the Association for Advancement of Behavior Therapy, New York, October 1972.

Bourne, P. G.; Alford, J. A.; and Bowcock, J. Z. (1966). "Treatment of Skid Row Alcoholics With Disulfiram," *Quarterly Journal of Studies on Alcohol* 27: 42–48.

Broden, Marcia; Hall, R. Vance; and Mitts, Brenda (1971). "The Effect of Self-Recording on the Classroom Behavior of Two Eighth Grade Students," *Journal of Applied Behavior Analysis* 4: 191–99.

Brophy, Jere, and Good, Thomas (1970). "Teachers' Communications of Differential Expectations for Children's Classroom Performance: Some Behavioral Data," *Journal of Educational Psychology* 61: 365–74.

Brown, P., and Elliott, R. (1965). "Control of Aggression in a Nursery School Class," *Journal of Experimental Child Psychology* 2: 103–7.

Buckley, Nancy K., and Walker, Hill M. (1978). *Modifying Classroom Behavior.* rev. ed. Champaign, Ill.: Research Press.

Budd, Karen S., and Baer, Donald M. (1976). "Behavior Modification and the Law: Implications of Recent Judicial Decisions," *Journal of Psychiatry and Law* 4: 171–244.

Budd, Karen S., and Greenspan, Stephen (1984). "Parameters of Successful and Unsuccessful Interventions With Parents Who Are Mentally Retarded," *Mental Retardation* 23, 6: 269–73.

Budziak, Tom (1988). *Dealing with Substance Abuse.* Presentation given to the Chicago Association for Behavior Analysis. Chicago, 15 November 1988.

     (1989). *Substance Abuse Intervention: The Matching Hypothesis.* Oak Brook, Ill.: Thomas J. Budziak.

Buechin, N.; Nielsen, C.; Notier, V.; Slaughter, R.; and Thomas, T. (1983). *Students in Class Behavior: Momentary Time Sampling Recording System.* Form copyrighted by LaGrange Area Department of Special Education, LaGrange, Ill.

Buell, Joan; Stoddard, Patricia; and Harris, Florence (1968). "Collateral Social Development Accompanying Reinforcement of Outdoor Play in a Preschool Child," *Journal of Applied Behavior Analysis* 1: 167–75.

Bushell, Don Jr.; Wrobel, Patricia; and Michaels, Mary (1968). "Applying 'Group' Contingencies to the Classroom Study Behavior of Preschool Children," *Journal of Applied Behavior Analysis* 1: 55–61.

Byers, R. K., and Lord, E. E. (1943). "Late Effects of Lead Poisoning on Mental Development," *American Journal of Diseases of Children* 66: 471–94.

Carter, Ron (1972). *Help! These Kids are Driving Me Crazy.* Champaign, Ill.: Research Press.

Chassen, J. B. (1967). *Research Design in Clinical Psychology and Psychiatry.* New York: Appleton-Century-Crofts.

Christianson, A.; Miller, W. R.; and Muñoz, R. F. (1978). "Paraprofessionals, Peers, Partners, Paraphernalia, and Parent," *Professional Psychology* May 1978, 249–69.

Clancy, J.; Vanderhoof, E.; and Campbell, P. (1967). "Evaluation of an Aversive Technique as a Treatment for Alcoholism: Controlled Trial With Succinylcholine-induced Apnea," *Quarterly Journal of Studies on Alcohol* 28: 476–85.

Clark, Hewitt B.; Boyd, Sandra B.; and MacRae, John W. (1975). "A Classroom Program Teaching Disadvantaged Youths to Write Biographic Information," *Journal of Behavior Analysis* 8: 67–75.

Cohen, M.; Liebson, I. A.; Faillace, L. A.; and Allen, R. P. (1971). "Moderate Drinking by Chronic Alcoholics," *The Journal of Nervous and Mental Disease* 53: 434–44.

Conner, T., and Kremen, E. (1971). "Methadone Maintenance—Is It Enough?" *International Journal of the Addictions* 6: 279–98.

Constable, Robert T., and Flynn, John P., eds. (1982). *School Social Work: Practice and Research Perspectives.* Homewood, Ill.: Dorsey Press.

Copeland, Rodney; Brown, Ronald; and Hall, R. Vance (1974). "The Effects of Prin-cipal-Implemented Techniques on the Behavior of Pupils," *Journal of Applied Behavior Analysis* 7: 77–86.

Cornille, T. A.; Bayer, A. E.; and Smyth, C. K. (1983). "Schools and Newcomers: A National Survey of Innovative Programs," *Personnel and Guidance Journal* 62: 229–36.

Corsi, E. S.; Jones, A. D.; Sipes, M. L.; Gierich, K. B.; Daniels, M. E.; and Greene, B. F. (1989). "Maintenance of Self-Help Skills: A Clinical Update." Poster presen-tation at the fifteenth annual convention of the Association for Behavior Analy-sis, Milwaukee, May 1989.

Couch, Richard W. (1989). "Large vs. Small N Applicatons of Ecobehavioral Obser-vations Strategies." Presentation to the fifteenth annual meeting of the Associ-ation for Behavior Analysis, Milwaukee, May 1989.

Craighead, W. Edward; Kazdin, Alan E.; Mahoney, Michael J. (1976). *Behavior Mod-ification*. Boston: Houghton Mifflin.

Crary, Elizabeth (1979). *Without Spanking or Spoiling, a Practical Approach to Tod-dler and Preschool Guidance*. Seattle: Parenting Press.

Crowley, C. P., and Armstrong, P. M. (1977). "Positive Practice, Overcorrection and Behavior Rehearsal in the Treatment of Three Cases of Encoparesis," *Journal of Behavior Therapy and Experimental Psychiatry* 8: 411–16.

Cuvo, A. J. (1979). "Multiple-Baseline Design in Instructional Research: Pitfalls of Measurement and Procedural Advantages," *American Journal of Mental Defi-ciency* 84: 219–28.

Dangel, Richard F., and Polster, Richard A., eds. (1984). *Parent Training—Founda-tions of Research and Practice*. New York: Guilford.

Dangel, Richard F., and Polster, Richard A. (1988). *Teaching Child Management Skills*. New York: Pergamon.

Daoust, P. M.; Hamm, S. I.; and Roehler, D. T. (1989). "The Application of a Behav-ioral Intervention to Improve Athletic Performance Amongst Twelve Year Old Boys Playing Baseball: A Preliminary Study." Poster presentation at the fif-teenth annual convention of the Association for Behavior Analysis, Milwaukee, May 1989.

David, O. J. (1974). "Association Between Lower Level Lead Concentrations and Hy-peractivity," *Environmental Health Perspective* 7: 17–25.

Davidson, Park O., and Davidson, Sheena M. (1980). *Behavioral Medicine: Changing Health Lifestyles*. New York: Brunner/Mazel.

Davison, Gerald (1968). "Systematic Desensitization as a Counterconditioning Pro-cess," *Journal of Abnormal Psychology* 73, 2: 91–99.

de la Burdi, B., and Choate, M. (1972). "Does Symptomatic Lead Exposure in Chil-dren Have Latent Sequelae?" *Journal of Pediatrics* 8: 1088–91.

Delquadri, J. C.; Greenwood, C. R.; Stretton, K.; and Hall, R. V. (1983). "The Peer Tutoring Spelling Game: A Classroom Procedure for Increasing Opportunity to Respond and Spelling Performance," *Education and Treatment of Children* 6: 225–39.

Delquadri, Joe; Greenwood, Charles R.; Whorton, Debra; Carta, Judith J.; and Hall, R. Vance (1986). "Classwide Peer Tutoring," *Exceptional Children*, 52, 6: 535–42.

Dinsmoor, James A. (1970). *Operant Conditioning: Experimental Analysis of Behavior.* Dubuque, Iowa: William C. Brown.

Doleys, D. M. (1977). "Behavioral Treatments for Nocturnal Enuresis in Children: A Review of the Recent Literature," *Psychological Bulletin* 8: 541–48.

Dougherty, Richard; Friedman, Benjamin S.; and Pinkston, Elsie M. (1982). "An Analysis of Time-Out and Response-Cost Procedures in a Special Education Class." A practice illustration in *Effective Social Work Practice,* edited by E. M. Pinkston, J. L. Levitt, G. R. Green, N. L. Linsk, and T. L. Rzepnicki. San Francisco: Jossey-Bass.

Drager, Susan, and Hanrahan, Patricia (1979). "Training the Parents of Aggressive Children." Joint thesis, University of Chicago.

Dumas, Jean E., and Wahler, Robert G. (1983). "Predictors of Treatment Outcome in Parent Training: Mother Insularity and Socioeconomic Disadvantage," *Behavioral Assessment* 3: 301–13.

Epstein, Laura (1980). *Helping People: The Task-Centered Approach.* St. Louis, Mo.: C. V. Mosby.

Farrar, C. H.; Powell, B. J.; and Martin, L. K. (1968). "Punishment of Alcohol Consumption by Amnesic Paralysis," *Behavior Research and Therapy* 6: 13–16.

Feldman, Maurice A.; Case, Laurie; Garrick, Maria; and MacIntyre-Grande, Wanda (1989). "Using Picture Books to Teach Child-Care Skills to Low-IQ, Illiterate Parents." Poster presentation at the fifteenth annual convention of the Association of Behavior Analysis, Milwaukee, May 1989.

Ferber, Richard (1985). *Solve Your Child's Sleep Problems.* New York: Simon and Schuster.

Ferritor, D. R.; Buckholdt, D.; Hamblin, R. L.; and Smith, L. (1972). "The Non-Effects of Contingent Reinforcement for Attending Behavior on Work Accomplished," *Journal of Applied Behavior Analysis* 5: 7–17.

Ferster, C. B. (1967). "Arbitrary and Natural Reinforcement," *The Psychological Record* 17: 341–47.

Ferster, C. B.; Culbertson, Stuart; Boren, Mary Carol Perrott (1975). *Behavior Principles.* 2nd ed. Englewood Cliffs, N. J.: Prentice-Hall.

Fisen, Dean; Phillips, Elery; and Wolf, Montrose (1973). "Achievement Place: Experiments in Self-Government with Predelinquents," *Journal of Applied Behavior Analysis* 6: 31–47.

Fisen, Dean; Wolf, Montrose; Phillips, Elery (1973). "Achievement Place: A Teaching-Family Model of Community-Based Group Homes for Youth in Trouble." In *Behavior Change: Methodology, Concept and Practice,* edited by Leo S. Hamerlynck, Lee C. Handy, Eric J. Mash. Champaign, Ill.: Research Press.

Forehand, R. L. (1977). "Child Noncompliance to Parental Commands: Behavior Analysis and Treatment." In *Progress in Behavior Modification (Vol. 5),* edited by M. Hersen, R. M. Eisler, and P. M. Miller. New York: Academic Press.

Forehand, R. L, and Atkeson, B. M. (1977). "Generality of Treatment Effects with Parents as Therapists: A review of Assessments and Implementation Procedures," *Behavior Therapy* 8: 575–93.

Forehand, R. L., and King, H. E. (1977). "Noncompliant Children: Effects of Parent Training on Behavior and Attitude Change," *Behavior Modification* 1: 93–108.

Fromm-Steege, Lisa; Wacher, David P.; Berg, Wendy K.; Scebold, Kathy (1989). "School vs. Community Instruction: Increasing Opportunities for Collateral

Behavior Acquisition." Poster presentation at the fifteenth annual convention of the Association for Behavior Analysis, Milwaukee, May 1989.

Gambrill, E. D. (1977). *Behavior Modification: Handbook of Assessment, Intervention, and Evaluation*. San Francisco: Jossey-Bass.

Gelfand, Donna M., and Hartman, Donald P. (1984). *Child Behavior Analysis and Therapy*. New York: Pergamon.

Ginsburg, Evelyn Harris (1989). *School Social Work, A Practioner's Guidebook, A Community-Integrated Approach to Practice*. Springfield, Ill.: Thomas.

Goldsmith, J. B., and McFall, R. M. (1975). "Development and Evaluation of an Interpersonal Skill-Training Program for Psychiatric Inpatients," *Journal of Consulting and Clinical Psychology* 84: 51–58.

Graubard, P. S.; Rosenberg, H.; and Miller, M. (1971). "Student Applications of Behavior Modification to Teachers and Environments or Ecological Approaches to Social Deviancy." In E. A. Ramp and B. L. Hopkins, eds., *A New Direction for Education: Behavior Analysis*, vol. 1. Lawrence, Kans.: University of Kansas, Support and Development Center For Follow-Through, Department of Human Development.

Graziano, A. M., and Kean, J. (1968). "Programmed Relaxation and Reciprocal Inhibition with Psychotic Children," *Behaviour Research and Therapy* 6:433–37.

Graziano, Anthony M., and Mooney, Kevin C. (1984). *Children and Behavior Therapy*. New York: Aldine.

Greenwood, C. R.; Delquadri, J.; Stanley, S.; Terry, B.; and Hall, R. V. (1985). "Assessment of Eco-Behavioral Interaction in School Settings," *Behavior Assessment* 7: 331–47.

Greenwood, Charles R.; Dinwiddie, Granger; Bailey, Voris; Carta, Judith J.; Dorsey, Don; Kohler, Frank W.; Nelson, Chris; Rotholz, David; and Schulte, Dan (1987). "Field Replication of Classwide Peer Tutoring," *Journal of Applied Behavior Analysis* 20: 151–60.

Hall, Marilyn C. (1976, 1982). *Parent Manual for the Responsive Parenting Program*. rev. ed. Overland Park, Kans.: Marilyn Clark Hall.

Hall, R. Vance (1971). *Managing Behavior, Behavior Modification Applications in School and Home*. Lawrence, Kans.: H and H Enterprises.

Hall, R. Vance; Cristler, Connie; Cranston, Sharon S.; and Tucker, Bonnie (1970). "Teachers and Parents as Researchers Using Multiple Baseline Designs," *Journal of Applied Behavior Analysis* 3: 247–55.

Hall, R. V.; Delquadri, J.; Greenwood, J.; Greenwood, C. R.; and Thurston, L. (1982). "The Importance of Opportunity to Respond in Children's Academic Success." In *Mentally Handicapped Children: Education and Training*, edited by E. Edgar, N. Haring, J. Jenkins, and C. Pious. Baltimore, Md.: University Park Press.

Hall, R. Vance; Lund, D.; Jackson, D. (1968). "Effects of Teacher Attention on Study Behavior," *Journal of Applied Behavior Analysis* 1: 1–12.

Harper, Gregory F., and Mallette, Barbara (1968). "Classwide Peer Tutoring to Teach Spelling to Students Enrolled in a Primary Special Education Classroom." Poster presentation at the fifteenth annual convention of the Association for Behavior Analysis, Milwaukee, May 1989.

Hart, Betty, and Risley, Todd (1968). "Establishing Use of Descriptive Adjectives in the Spontaneous Speech of Disadvantaged Preschool Children," *Journal of Applied Behavior Analysis* 1: 109–20.

Haskett, Gary, and Lenfestey, William (1974). "Reading-Related Behavior in an Open Classroom: Effects of Novelty and Modeling on Preschoolers," *Journal of Applied Behavior Analysis* 7: 233–41.

Hauri, Peter (1982). *Current Concepts, The Sleep Disorders.* 2nd ed. Kalamazoo, Mich.: Upjohn.

Hawkins, Robert; Peterson, Robert; Schweid, Edda; and Bijou, Sidney (1964). "Behavior Therapy in the Home: Amelioration of Problem Parent-Child Relations with the Parent in a Therapeutic Role," *Journal of Experimental Child Psychology* 4: 99–107.

Haynes, Stephen (1973). "Contingency Management in a Municipally-Administered Antabuse Program for Alcoholics," *Journal of Behavior Research and Experimental Psychiatry* 4: 31–32.

Heather, Nick (1986). "Changes Without Therapists, The Use of Self-Help Manuals by Problem Drinkers." In *Treating Addictive Behaviors*, edited by W. R. Miller and N. Heather. New York: Plenum Press.

Hedberg, Allen, and Campbell, Lowell (1974). "A Comparison of Four Behavioral Treatments of Alcoholism," *Journal of Behavior Therapy and Experimental Psychiatry* 5: 251–56.

Heneggler, Scott W., ed. (1982). *Delinquency and Adolescent Psychopathology: A Family-Ecological Systems Approach.* Boston: John Wright-PSG.

Herbert, E. W.; Pinkston, E. M.; Hayden, M. L.; Sajwaj, T. E.; Pinkston, S.; Cordua, G.; and Jackson, D. (1973). "Adverse Effects of Differential Parental Attention," *Journal of Applied Behavior Analysis* 6: 15–30.

Hersen, Michael, and Barlow, David H. (1976). *Single Case Experimental Designs; Strategies for Studying Behavior Change.* New York: Pergamon Press.

Hester, Reid K., and Miller, William R., eds. (1989). *Handbook of Alcoholism Treatment Approaches.* New York: Pergamon Press.

Hinds, William, and Roehlke, Helen (1970). "A Learning Theory Approach to Group Counseling with Elementary School Children," *Journal of Counseling Psychology* 17: 49–55.

Homme, Lloyd E.; Csanyi, Attila P.; Gonzales, Mary Ann; and Rechs, James R. (1973). *How to Use Contingency Contracting in the Classroom.* rev. ed. Champaign, Ill.: Research Press.

Honig, W. K., and Staddon, J. E. R., eds. (1977). *Handbook of Operant Behavior.* Englewood Cliffs, N.J.: Prentice-Hall.

Houlihan, Daniel, and Jones, Robert N. (1989). "Treatment of a Boy's School Phobia With *In Vivo* Systematic Desensitization," *Professional and School Psychology* 6, in press.

Hsu, J. J. (1965). "Electroconditioning Therapy of Alcoholics: A Preliminary Report," *Quarterly Journal of Studies on Alcohol* 26: 449–59.

Hundert, J.; Bucher, B.; and Henderson, M. (1976). "Increasing Appropriate Classroom Behavior and Academic Performance by Reinforcing Correct Work Alone," *Psychology in the Schools* 13: 195–200.

Hunt, G. M., and Azrin, N. H. (1973). "A Community-Reinforcement Approach to Alcoholism," *Behaviour Research and Therapy* 11: 91–104.

Iwata, Brian (1987). "Negative Reinforcement in Behavior Analysis: An Emerging Technology," *Journal of Applied Behavior Analysis* 20: 361–78.

Jacobs, James B. (1989). *Drunk Driving: An American Dilemma*. Chicago: University of Chicago Press.

Jacobson, E. (1938). *Progressive Relaxation*. Chicago: University of Chicago Press.

Jason, Leonard A.; Betts, David; Johnson, Joseph H.; Smith, Suzanne; Newson, Lisa; Filappelli, A.; and Cradock, Mary (1989). "Developing a Preventive Intervention for High Risk Transfer Children." Unpublished paper. DePaul University.

Jason, L. A.; Betts, D.; Johnson, J.; Kruckeberg, S.; and Cradock, M. (1989). "An Evaluation of an Orientation Plus Tutoring School Based Prevention Program," *Professional School Psychology*, in press.

Jason, L. A., and Bogat, G. A. (1983). "Preventive Behavioral Interventions." In *Preventive Psychology: Theory, Research, and Practice*, edited by R. D. Felner, L. A. Jason, J. N. Mortisugu, and S. S. Farber. New York: Pergamon.

Jason, Leonard A.; Ginsburg, Evelyn H.; Rucker, Walter; Merbitz, Charles; Tabon, Daniel; and Harkness, Margaret (1985). "A Support System for Behavior Analysts in an Urban Area," *The Behavior Therapist* 8: 138–40.

Jehu, Derek; Hardiker, Pauline; Yelloly, Margaret; and Shaw, Martin (1972). *Behaviour Modification in Social Work*. London: Wiley-Interscience.

Jones, Allen D.; Tucker, Roy A.; Hernandez, Michele M.; Corsi, Eduardo S.; Lubeck, Roger C.; Wesch, David W.; and Greene, Brandon F. "Training an Adolescent with Behavior Disorders to Socially Initiate in Games." Poster presentation at the Association for Behavior Analysis, Milwaukee, May 1989.

Jones, D. P., and McGraw, J. M. (1987). "Reliable and Fictitious Accounts of Sexual Abuse to Children," *Journal of Interpersonal Violence* 2(1): 27–45.

Juniper Gardens Childrens' Project (1989). Unpublished reports, Kansas City, Kans.

Kazdin, A. E. (1982). *Single-Case Research Designs, Methods for Clinical and Applied Settings*. New York: Oxford.

——— (1982). "Symptom Substitution, Generalization, and Response Covariation: Implications for Psychotherapy Outcome," *Psychological Bulletin* 91: 349–65.

——— (1977). *The Token Economy: A Review and Evaluation*. New York: Plenum.

Kifer Robert; Lewis, Martha A.; Green, Donald R.; Phillips, Elery L. (1974). "Training Predelinquent Youths and Their Parents to Negotiate Conflict Situations," *Journal of Applied Behavior Analysis* 7: 354–57.

Kimmel, H. D., and Kimmel, Ellen (1970). "An Instrumental Conditioning Method for the Treatment of Enuresis," *Journal of Behavior Therapy and Experimental Psychiatry* 1: 121–23.

Kirigin, K. A.; Braukmann, C. J.; Atwater, J. D.; and Wolf, M. M. (1982). "An Evaluation of Teaching-Family (Achievement Place) Group Homes for Juvenile Offenders," *Journal of Applied Behavior Analysis* 15: 1–16.

Kirk, Stuart A., and Corcoran, Kevin J. (1989). "The $12,000 Question: Does it Pay to Publish?" *Social Work* 34: 4, 379–81.

Kleber, H. (1970). "The New Haven Methadone Program," *International Journal of the Addictions* 5: 457–58.

Klein, Roger D.; Hapkiewicz, Walter G.; and Roden, Aubrey H. (1973). *Behavior Modification in Educational Settings*. Springfield, Ill.: Thomas.

Kosloff, Martin A. (1979). *A Program for Families of Children with Learning and Behavior Problems*. New York: Wiley and Sons.

Kurkjian, J. A., and Scotti, J. R. (1989). "An Analysis of the Child Sexual Abuse Literature: Are Psychologists Ignoring the Problem?" Poster presentation at the fifteenth annual convention of the Association for Behavior Analysis, Milwaukee, May 1989.

Kurtz, P. David, and Barth, Richard P. (1989). "Parental Involvement: Cornerstone of Social Work Practice," *Social Work* 34: 5, 407–13.

Last, Cynthia G. (1985). "School Phobia." In *Behavior Therapy Case Book*, edited by M. Hersen and C. G. Last. New York: Springer.

Lauren, Kathryn Le, and Risley, Todd (1968). "The Organization of Day-Care Environments: 'Zone' versus 'Man-to-Man' Staff Assignments," *Journal of Applied Behavior Analysis* 5: 225–32.

Laxer, Robert; Quarter, Jack; Kooman, Ann; and Walker, Keith (1969). "Systematic Desensitization and Relaxation of High Test-Anxious Secondary School Students," *Journal of Counseling Psychology* 16: 446–51.

Lazarus, A. A. (1965). "Towards the Understanding and Effective Treatment of Alcoholism," *South African Medical Journal* 39: 736–41.

Lehrer, P. M., and Woolfolk, R. L. (1984). "Are All Stress-Reduction Techniques Interchangeable, or Do They Have Specific Effects? A Review of the Comparative Empirical Literature." In *Principles and Practices of Stress Management*, edited by R. L. Woolfolk and P. M. Lehrer. New York: Guilford Press.

——— (1985). "The Relaxation Therapies." In *Evaluating Behavior Therapy and Outcome*, edited by R. M. Turner and L. M. Ascher. New York: Springer .

Leiby, James (1978). *A History of Social Welfare and Social Work in the United States*. New York: Columbia University Press.

Lemere, F., and Voegtlin, W. L. (1950). "An Evaluation of the Aversion Treatment of Alcoholism," *Quarterly Journal of Studies on Alcoholism* 11: 199–204.

Liberman, Robert Paul (1972). *A Guide to Behavioral Analysis and Therapy*. New York: Pergamon.

Liberman, R. (1969). "Aversive Conditioning of Drugs: A Pilot Study," *Behavior Research and Therapy* 6: 229–31.

Libet, J., and Lewinsohn, P. M. (1973). "Concept of Social Skill With Reference to the Behavior of Depressed Persons," *Journal of Consulting and Clinical Psychology* 40: 303–12.

Liebson, I.; Bigelow, G.; and Flamer, R. (1973). "Alcoholism Among Methadone Patients: A Specific Treatment Method," *American Journal of Psychiatry* 130: 483–85.

Lovaas, O. Ivar, and Bucher, Bradley D., eds. (1974). *Perspectives in Behavior Modification with Deviant Children*. Englewood Cliffs, N. J.: Prentice-Hall.

Lutzker, J. R. (1984). "Project 12-Ways: Treating Child Abuse and Neglect from an Ecobehavioral Perspective." In *Parent Training: Foundations of Research and Practice*, edited by R. R. Dangel and R. A. Polster. New York: Guilford.

Lutzker, J. R.; Frame, R. E.; and Rice, J. M. (1982). "Project 12-Ways: An Ecobehavioral Approach to the Treatment and Prevention of Child Abuse and Neglect,"*Education and Treatment of Children* 5: 141–55.

Lutzker, John R.; Wesch, David; and Rice, James M. (1984). "A Review of Project '12-Ways': An Ecobehavioral Approach to the Treatment and Prevention of Child Abuse and Neglect," *Advanced Behavioral Research and Therapy* 6: 63–73.

Macnab, Alexander G. (1979). "Project Earn and Learn." In *The Career Education Workshop*. West Nyack, N.Y.: Parker.

Marcus, Marsha D. (1985). "Obesity." In *Behavior Therapy Case Book*, edited by M. Hersen and C. G. Last. New York: Springer.

Marholin, D.; Steinman, W.; McInnis, E.; and Heads, T. (1975). "The Effect of Teacher's Presence in the Classroom Behavior of Conduct Problem Children," *Journal of Abnormal Child Psychology* 3: 11–24.

Martin, Marian; Burkholder, Rachel; Rosenthal, Ted; Tharp, Roland; and Thorne, Gaylord (1968). "Programming Behavior Change and Reintegration into School Milieux of Extreme Adolescent Deviates," *Behavior Research and Therapy* 6: 371–83.

Mash, Eric J., and Barkley, Russell A., eds. (1989). *Treatment of Childhood Disorders*. New York: Guilford.

McAllister, Loring W.; Stachowiak, James G.; Baer, Donald M.; and Conderman, Linda (1969). "The Application of Operant Conditioning Techniques in a Secondary School Classroom," *Journal of Applied Behavior Analysis* 2: 277–85.

McFall, R. M., and Marston, A. (1970). "An Experimental Investigation of Behavior Rehearsal in Assertive Training," *Journal of Abnormal Psychology* 76: 295–303.

McGill, Nancy Buechin, and Robinson, Liz (1989). "Regular Education Teacher Consultant," *Teaching Exceptional Children* Winter 1989, 71–73.

McKenzie, Hugh; Clark, Marilyn; Wolf, Montrose; Kothera, Richard; and Benson, Cedric (1968). "Behavior Modification of Children with Learning Disabilities Using Grades as Tokens and Allowances as Back-Up Reinforcers," *Exceptional Children* 34: 745–53.

McKeown, Douglas Jr.; Adams, Henry; and Forehand, Rex (1975). "Generalization to the Classroom of Principles of Behavior Modification Taught to Teachers," *Behavior Research and Therapy* 13: 85–92.

McMahon, Robert J., and Wells, Karen C. (1989). "Conduct Disorders." In *Treatment of Childhood Disorders*, edited by E. J. Mash and R. A. Barkley. New York: Guilford.

Mendelson, Wallace B. (1987). *Human Sleep*. New York: Plenum.

Messier, Paul R. (1989). "A Brief to the White House Staff." Unpublished paper, Washington, D. C., 28 February 1989.

Michael, J. (1975). "Positive and Negative Reinforcement: A Distinction That Is No Longer Necessary; Or a Better Way To Talk about Bad Things," *Behaviorism* 3: 33–44.

Miller, P. M. (1972). "The Use of Behavioral Contracting in the Treatment of Alcoholism: A Case Report," *Behavior Therapy* 3: 593–96.

Miller, P. M., and Hersen, M. (1972). "Quantitative Changes in Alcohol Consumption as a Function of Electrical Aversive Conditioning," *Journal of Clinical Psychology* 28: 590–93.

Miller, William R. (1989). "Matching Individuals with Interventions." In *Handbook of Alcoholism Treatment Approaches*, edited by R. K. Hester and W. R. Miller. New York: Pergamon Press.

Miller, William R., and Heather, Nick, eds. (1986). *Treating Addictive Behaviors*. New York: Plenum.

Modgil, Sohan, and Modgil, Celia, eds. (1986). *B. F. Skinner, Consensus and Controversy*. New York: Falmer.

Mowrer, O. H., and Mowrer, W. M. (1938). "Enuresis: A Method for Its Study and Treatment," *American Journal of Orthopsychiatry* 8: 436–59.

Neale, D. H. (1963). "Behaviour Therapy and Encopresis in Children," *Behavior Research and Therapy* 1: 139–49.

Nederhouser, Deborah M., and Labak, Robert A. (1988). "Fostering Accepting Environments, a Program for the Integration of Students with Moderate Impairments into a Public School Setting." Poster presentation at the Association for Behavior Analysis, Milwaukee, 1988.

Neisworth, John, and Moore, Florese (1972). "Operant Treatment of Asthmatic Responding with the Parent as Therapist," *Behavior Therapy* 3: 95–99.

Nichols Middle School, School District 65 (1988). *A Handbook for Parents and Students*. Evanston, Ill., 1988–1989.

Ninness, H. A. Chris, and Glenn, Sigrid S. (1988). *Applied Behavior Analysis and School Psychology*. New York: Greenwood.

Oden, Sherri (1983). "The Applicability of Social Skills Training Research." In *Social Skills Training for Children and Youth*, edited by C. W. LeCroy. New York: Haworth.

O'Donnell, J. A. (1965). "The Relapse Rate in Narcotic Addiction: A Critique of Follow-up Studies." In *Narcotics*, edited by D. M. Wilner and G. C. Kassebaum. New York: McGraw-Hill.

O'Leary, K. Daniel, and Becker, Wesley (1967). "Behavior Modification of an Adjustment Class: A Token Reinforcement Program," *Exceptional Children* 33: 637–42.

O'Leary, K. Daniel, Kaufman, Kenneth; Kass, Ruth; and Drabman, Ronald (1970). "The Effects of Loud and Soft Reprimands on the Behavior of Disruptive Students," *Exceptional Children* 36: 145–55.

O'Leary, K. Daniel, and Wilson, G. Terence (1975). *Behavior Therapy, Application and Outcome*. Englewood Cliffs, N.J.: Prentice-Hall.

Ormsby, Diane E., and Deitz, Diane E. D. (1989). "A Systematic Analysis of Peer Interactions of Elementary-Aged Students With Learning Disabilities." Poster presentation at the fifteenth annual convention of the Association for Behavior Analysis, Milwaukee, May 1989.

Osnes, Pamela G.; Stokes, Trevor F.; and DaVerne, Kristina C. (1989). "An Assessment of Mainstreamed Preschoolers' Interactions." Poster presentation at the fifteenth annual convention of the Association for Behavior Analysis, Milwaukee, May 1989.

Page, D. P., and Edwards, R. P. (1978). "Behavior Change Strategies for Reducing Disruptive Classroom Behavior," *Psychology in Schools* 15: 413–18.

Pappenfort, Donnell M., and Young, Thomas M. (1980). *Use of Secure Detention for Juveniles and Alternatives to its Use*. Washington, D.C.: U.S. Department of Justice.

Parsons, H. M. (1989). "Lying." An invited address at the 1989 meeting of the Association for Behavior Analysis, Milwaukee, May 1989.

Patterson, Gerald R. (1982). *A Social Learning Approach*, vol. 3 of *Coercive Family Process*. Eugene, Ore.: Castalia.

——— (1973). "Changes in Status of Family Members as Controlling Stimuli: A Basis for Describing Treatment Process." In *Behavior Change: Methodological Con-*

cepts and Practice, edited by Leo A. Hamerlynck, Lee C. Handy, and Eric J. Mash, Champaign, Ill.: Research Press.

(1971). *Families' Applications of Social Learning to Family Life*. Champaign, Ill.: Research Press.

(1976). *Living With Children*. rev. ed. Champaign, Ill.: Research Press.

Patterson, Gerald R., and Gullion, M.E. (1968). *Living With Children*. Champaign, Ill.: Research Press.

Patterson, Gerald R., and Reid, J. B. (1973). "Intervention for Families of Aggressive Boys: A Replication Study," *Behavior Research and Therapy* 11 (4): 383–94.

Perlstein, M. A., and Attala, R. (1966). "Neurologic Sequelae of Plumbism in Children," *Clinical Pediatrics* 5: 292–98.

Piazza, Cathleen C., and Fisher, Wayne (1989). "Utilizing Behavioral Principles and Circadian Rhythms in the Treatment of Pediatric Sleep Disorders: The Faded Bedtime Protocol With Response Cost." Address to the fifteenth annual meeting of the Association for Behavior Analysis, Milwaukee, May 1989.

Pierce, Charles, and Risley, Todd (1974). "Improving Job Performance of Neighborhood Youth Corps Aides in an Urban Recreation Program," *Journal of Applied Behavior Analysis* 7: 207–15.

Pigott, H. Edmund; Fantuzzo, John W.; and Gorsuch, Richard L. (1987). "Further Generalization Technology: Accounting for Covariation in Generalized Assessment," *Journal of Applied Behavior Analysis* 20: 273–78.

Pinkston, Elsie M.; Freidman, B. S.; and Polster, R. A. (1981). "Parents as Agents of Behavior Change." In *Behavior Methods in Social Welfare*, edited by S. P. Schinke. Hawthorne, New York: Aldine.

Pinkston, Elsie M., and Herbert-Jackson, Emily W. (1975). "Modification of Irrelevant and Bizarre Verbal Behavior Using Mother as Therapist," *The Social Service Review* 49: 46–63.

Pinkston, Elsie M.; Levitt, John L.; Green, Glenn R.; Linsk, Nick L.; and Rzepnicki, Tina L., eds. (1982). *Effective Social Work Practice, Advanced Techniques for Behavioral Intervention With Individuals, Families, and Institutional Staff*. San Francisco: Jossey-Bass.

Pinkston, Elsie M.; Polster, Richard A.; Freidman, Benjamin S.; and Lynch, Mary Ann (1982). "Intervention for Coercive Family Interactions." In *Effective Social Work Practice*, edited by E. M. Pinkston, J. L. Levitt, G. R. Green, N. L. Linsk, and T. Rzepnicki. San Francisco: Jossey-Bass.

Pinkston, Elsie M.; Reese, Nancy M.; LeBlanc, Judith M.; and Baer, Donald M. (1973). "Independent Control of a Preschool Child's Aggression and Peer Interaction by Contingent Teacher Attention," *Journal of Applied Behavior Analysis* 1 (6): 115–24.

Polster, Richard A. (1977). "Self-Control Procedures in the Development of a Delivery System To Improve the Academic Performance of Seventh- and Eighth-Grade Underachievers." Unpublished dissertation, University of Chicago.

Polster, Richard A., and Pinkston, Elsie M. (1979). "A Delivery System for the Treatment of Underachievement," *Social Service Review* 49:35–55.

Poppin, Roger (1988). *Behavioral Relaxation Training and Assessment*. New York: Pergamon.

Poulin, J. E.; Levitt, J. L.; Young, T. M.; and Papenfort, D. M. (1980). "Juveniles in Detention Centers and Jails: An Analysis of State Variations during the Mid-

Seventies." *Reports of the National Juvenile Justice Centers*. Washington, D.C.: Government Printing Office, August 1980.

Premack, D. A. (1959). "Toward Empirical Behavior Laws: I. Positive Reinforcement," *Psychological Review* 66: 219–33.

Pressy, Sidney L. (1926). "A Sample Device for Teaching, Testing, and Research in Learning," *School Sociology*, 23: 373–76.

Raymond, M. J. (1964). "The Treatment of Addiction by Aversion Conditioning with Apomorphine," *Behaviour Research and Therapy* 1: 287–91.

Redd, William H.; Porterfield, Albert L.; and Andersen, Barbara L. (1979). *Behavior Modification: Behavioral Approaches to Human Problems*. New York: Random House.

Reese, Ellen P. (1966). *The Analysis of Human Operant Behavior*. Dubuque, Iowa: William C. Brown.

Reid, J. B., and Hendriks, A. F. (1973). "Preliminary Analysis of the Effectiveness of Direct Home Intervention for the Treatment of Predelinquent Boys Who Steal." In *Behavior Change: Methodological Concepts and Practice*, edited by L. A. Hamerlynck, L. C. Handy, and E. J. Mash. Champaign, Ill.: Research Press.

Reid, William J. (1978). *The Task-Centered System*. New York: Columbia University Press.

Reid, William J., and Epstein, Laura (1972). *Task-Centered Casework*. New York: Columbia University Press.

Reid, William J., and Epstein, Laura (1977). *Task-Centered Practice*, New York: Columbia University Press.

Reid, William J., and Shyne, Ann (1969). *Brief and Extended Casework*. New York: Columbia University Press.

Rhodes, Jean E., and Jason, Leonard A. (1988). *Preventing Substance Abuse Among Children and Adolescents*. New York: Pergamon.

Richards, Virginia (1989). "Guidelines for Assertiveness Training." Unpublished document, Chicago, Ill.

Rickel, A. U., and Allen, L. (1987). *Preventing Maladjustment from Infancy through Adolescence*. Newbury Park, Calif.: Sage.

Risley, Todd, and Wolf, Montrose (1967). "Establishing Functional Speech in Echolalic Children," *Behavior Research and Therapy* 5: 73–88.

Roberts, N. C., and Peterson, L. eds., (1984). *Prevention of Problems in Childhood: Psychological Research and Applications*. New York: Wiley.

Rose, S. D., and others (1972). "Group Training of Parents as Behavior Modifiers of Their Own Mentally Retarded Children." Mimeograph, School of Social Work, University of Wisconsin.

Rosett, Henry L., and Weiner, Lyn (1984). *Alcohol and the Fetus: A Clinical Perspective*. New York: Oxford.

Ross, Alan O. (1981). *Child Behavior Therapy: Principles, Procedures, and Empirical Basis*. New York: John Wiley.
———. (1967). "The Application of Behavior Principles in Therapeutic Education," *The Journal of Special Education* 1: 275–86.

Ryback, David, and Staats, Arthur, W. (1970). "Parents as Behavior Therapy-Technicians in Treating Reading Deficits (Dyslexia)," *Journal of Behavior Therapy and Experimental Psychiatry* 1: 109–19.

Rzepnicki, Tina, and Bremer, Jeanne (1977). "Home-Based Reinforcement and Skills Training: An Approach to Mainstreaming." Unpublished paper.

Sachs, Henrietta K.; Krall, Vita; McCraughran, Donald G.; Rozenfeld, Irving H.; Youngsmith, Nillawan; Growe, Glenn; Lazar, Billie S.; Novar, Lenore; O'Connell, Linda; and Rayson, Barbara (1978). "I.Q. Following Treatment of Lead Poisoning: A Patient-Sibling Comparison," *The Journal of Pediatrics* 93 (3): 428–31.

Sachs, Henrietta K.; McCaughran, Donald A.; Krall, Vita; Rozenfeld, Irving H.; and Youngsmith, Nillawan. "Lead Poisoning With Encephalopathy: Effect of Early Diagnosis on Neurologic and Psychologic Salvage," *Journal of Diseases of Children* 133: 786–90.

Salter, Anna C. (1988). *Treating Child Sex Offenders and Victims, A Practical Guide*. Newbury Park, Calif. : Sage.

Schumaker, Jean B.; Hovell, Melbourne; and Sherman, James A. (1977). "An Analysis of Daily Report Cards and Parent-Managed Privileges in the Improvement of Adolescents' Classroom Performance," *Journal of Applied Behavior Analysis* 10: 449–64.

Schwartz, Arthur; Goldiamond, Israel; and Howe, Michael W. (1975). *Social Casework: A Behavioral Approach*. New York: Columbia University Press.

Scott, E. (1977). "A Desensitization Program for the Treatment of Mutism in a Seven Year Old Girl," *Journal of Child Psychology and Psychiatry and Applied Disciplines* 18: 263–70.

Selinske, Jane E.; Greer, R. Douglas; and Lodhi, Seema (1989). "A Functional Analysis of the Comprehensive Application of Behavior Analysis to Schooling," under revision for *Journal of Applied Behavior Analysis*.

Shapiro, M. B. (1961). "The Single Case in Fundamental Clinical Psychological Research," *British Journal of Medical Psychology* 34: 255–63.

Shapiro, M. B., and Ravenette, A. T. (1959). "A Preliminary Experiment of Paranoid Delusions," *Journal of Mental Science* 105: 295–312.

Sheldon, Brian (1982). *Behavior Modification*. London: Tavistock.

Sidman, Murray (1960, 1988). *Tactics of Scientific Research, rev. ed*. New York: Basic Books.

Sidman, Murray (1960). *Tactics of Scientific Research*. New York: Basic Books.

Sisson, R. W., and Azrin, N. H. (1986). "Family-Member Involvement To Initiate and Promote Treatment of Problem Drinkers," *Journal of Behavior Therapy and Experimental Psychiatry* 17: 15–21.

Skiba, Russell, and Raison, Jeffrey (1989). "The Relationship Between the Use of Time Out and Academic Achievement." Paper presented at the fifteenth annual meeting of the Association for Behavior Analysis, Milwaukee, May 1989.

Skinner, B. F. (1969). *Contingencies of Reinforcement: A Theoretical Analysis*. New York: Appleton-Century-Crofts.

  (1982). "Contrived Reinforcement," *The Behavior Analyst* 5: 3–8.

  (1953). *Science and Human Behavior*. New York: Macmillan.

  (1938). *The Behavior of Organisms: An Experimental Analysis*. New York: Appleton-Century-Crofts.

  (1968). *The Technology of Teaching*. New York: Appleton-Century-Crofts.

Skinner, B. F., and Epstein, Robert (1982). *Skinner for the Classroom*. Champaign, Ill.: Research Press.

Slaughter, Renata (1988). "The Spelling Game Procedural Guide." Unpublished paper, LaGrange, Ill.

Snyder, J. C., and Newberger, E. H. (1986). "Consensus and Difference Among Hospital Professionals in Evaluating Child Maltreatment," *Violence and Victims* 1: 125–39.

Sobell, M. B., and Sobell, L. C. (1973). "Individualized Behavior Therapy for Alcoholics," *Behavior Therapy* 4: 49–72.

Sontag, Arthur (1988). "Case Study of a Profoundly Retarded Girl." Unpublished document, Evanston, Ill.

Sparrow, S. S.; Balla, D. A.; and Cicchetti, D. V. (1984). "Vineland Adaptive Behavior Scales," *Interview Edition Survey Form Manual*. Circle Pines, Minn.: American Guidance Service.

Spielman, A. J.; Saskin, P.; and Thorpy, M. J. (1987). "Treatment of Chronic Insomnia by Restriction of Time in Bed," *Sleep* 10: 45–56.

Stanley, S. O., and Greenwood, C. R. (1983). "How Much 'Opportunity to Respond' Does the Minority Disadvantaged Student Receive in School?" *Exceptional Children* 49: 370-73.

Stedman, James M.; Patton, William F.; and Walton, Kay F. (1973). *Clinical Studies in Behavior Therapy with Children, Adolescents, and Their Families*. Springfield, Ill.: Thomas.

Stedman, James M., and Peterson, Travis (1971). "Application of a Token System in a Pre-Adolescent Boys' Group," *Journal of Behavior Therapy and Experimental Psychiatry* 323–29.

Stokes, T. F., and Baer, D. M. (1977). "An Implicit Technology of Generalization," *Journal of Applied Behavior Analysis* 10: 349–67.

Strain, Philip S.; Steele, Peggy; Ellis, Toni; and Timm, Matthew A. (1982). "Long-Term Effects of Oppositional Child Treatment with Mothers as Therapists and Therapist Trainers," *Journal of Applied Behavior Analysis* 15: 163–69.

Streissguth, Ann Pytkowicz (1986). "Alcohol and Motherhood: Physiological Findings and the Fetal Alcohol Syndrome." In Research Monograph No. 16, *Women and Alcohol: Health-Related Issues*. Rockville, Md.: U.S. Dept. of Health and Human Services, 215–25.

Streissguth, Ann Pytkowicz, and Giunta, Carole (1986). "Mental Health and Health Needs of Infants and Preschool Children with Fetal Alcohol Syndrome," *International Journal of Family Psychiatry* 9 (1): 29–47.

Streissguth, Ann Pytkowicz, and LaDue, Robin (1987). "Fetal Alcohol Teratogenic Causes of Developmental Disabilities." In *Toxic Substances and Mental Retardation*, edited by S. R. Schroeder. Washington, D.C.: American Association on Mental Deficiency.

Streissguth, Ann Pytkowicz, and Randels, Sandra (1988). "Long Term Effects of Fetal Alcohol Syndrome." In *Alcohol and Child/Family Health*, edited by G. C. Robinson and R. W. Armstrong. Vancouver: University of British Columbia.

Stuart, Richard B. (1971). "Behavioral Contracting Within the Families of Delinquents," *Journal of Behavior Therapy and Experimental Psychiatry* 2: 1–11.

Stuart, Richard B., ed. (1981). *Violent Behavior: Social Learning Approaches to Prediction, Management, and Treatment*. New York: Brunner/Mazel.

Sulzer-Azaroff, Beth, and Mayer, G. Roy (1977). *Applying Behavior-Analysis Procedures with Children and Youth*. New York: Holt, Rinehart and Winston.

Switzer, E. B.; Deal, T. E.; and Bailey, J. S. (1977). "The Reduction of Stealing in Second Graders Using a Group Contingency," *Journal of Applied Behavior Analysis* 10: 267–72.

Tharp, R. G., and Wetzel, R. J. (1969). *Behavior Modification in the Natural Environment*. New York: Academic Press.

Thimann, J. (1949). "Conditioned-Reflex Treatment of Alcoholism," *New England Journal of Medicine* 241: 368–70.

Thomas, Edwin J. (1984). *Designing Interventions for the Helping Professions*. Beverly Hills, Calif.: Sage.

Thompson, I. G., and Rathod, N. H. (1968). "Aversion Therapy for Heroin Dependence," *Lancet* 2: 382–84.

Thyer, Bruce A. (1987). "Contingency Analysis: Toward a Unified Theory of Social Work Practice," *Social Work* 32 (2): 150–56.

Thyer, Bruce A. (1981). "Behavioral Social Work: A Bibliography," *International Journal of Behavioral Social Work and Abstracts* 1 (3): 229–51.

Thyer, Bruce, and Maddox, Kim (1988). "Behavioral Social Work: Results of a National Survey on Graduate Curricula," *Psychological Reports* 63: 239–42.

Timm, Matthew A. (1988). "RIP: A Parent-Implemented Treatment Model for Families with Behaviorally Disordered and/or Developmentally Delayed Young Children." In *Mental Retardation and Mental Health*, edited by J. A. Stark, F. J. Mendlascion, M. H. Albarelli, and V. C. Gray. New York: Springer-Verlag.

Towle, Charlotte (1957). *Common Human Needs*. New York: National Association of Social Workers. First presented in 1947 in a bulletin by the Social Security Administration.

Townsley, Bruce (1989). "Negative Reinforcement and School Behavior." Unpublished paper for LaGrange Area Dept. of Special Education, Career Development Award.

Van Hasselt, V. B.; Hersen, M.; Whitehill, M. B.; and Bellack, A. S. (1979). "Social Skill Assessment and Training for Children: An Evaluative Review," *Behaviour Research and Therapy* 17: 413–37.

Van Hasselt, Vincent B.; Morrison, Randall L.; Bellack, Alan S.; and Hersen, Michael (1988). *Handbook of Family Violence*. New York: Plenum.

Vargas, Julie S. (1977). *Behavioral Psychology for Teachers*. New York: Harper and Row.

Voegtlin, Walter (1940). "The Treatment of Alcoholism by Establishing Conditioned Reflex," *British Journal of Medical Sciences* 199: 802–10.

Wahler, Robert G. (1989). "An Interbehavioral Model of Child Abuse and Neglect." Invited address at the annual meeting of the Association for Behavior Analysis, Milwaukee, May 1989.

——— (1969). "Oppositional Children: A Quest for Parental Reinforcement Control," *Journal of Applied Behavior Analysis* 2: 159–70.

——— (1969). "Setting Generality: Some Specific and General Effects of Child Behavior Therapy," *Journal of Applied Behavior Analysis* 2: 239–46.

——— (1980). "The Insular Mother: Her Problems in Parent-Child Treatment," *Journal of Applied Behavior Analysis* 13: 207–19.

Wahler, R. G., and Nordquist, V. M. (1973). "Adult Discipline as a Factor in Childhood Imitation," *Journal of Abnormal Psychology* 1: 40–56.

Wahler, R. G.; Winkel, G. H.; Peterson, R. F.; and Morrison, D. C. (1965). "Mothers as Behavior Therapists for Their Own Children," *Behavior Research and Therapy* 3: 113–14.

Walker, C. Eugene; Kenning, Mary; and Faust-Campanile, Jan (1989). "Enuresis and Encopresis." In *Treatment of Childhood Disorders*, edited by E. J. Mash and R. A. Barkley. New York: Guilford.

Waltzer, Fred (1984). "Using a Behavioral Group Approach with Chronic Truants," *Social Work in Education* 6 (3): 193–200.

Weil, G., and Goldfried, M. R. (1973). "Treatment of Insomnia in an Eleven-Year-Old Child Through Self-Relaxation," *Behavior Therapy* 4: 282–84.

Weinrott, M. R.; Corson, J. A.; and Wilchesky, M. (1979). "Teacher-Mediated Treatment of Social Withdrawal," *Behavior Therapy* 10: 281–94.

Weinrott, M. R.; Jones, R. R.; and Howard, J. R. (1982). "Cost-Effectiveness of Teaching Family Programs for Delinquents: Results of a National Evaluation," *Evaluation Review* 6: 173–201.

Weist, M. D., and Ollendick, T. H. (1989). "Empirical Validation of Assertive Behaviors in Boys." Paper presented at the fifteenth annual meeting of the Association for Behavior Analysis, Milwaukee, May 1989.

Werner, John; Minkin, Neil; Minkin, Bonnie; Fixsen, Dean; Phillips, Elery; and Wolf, Montrose (1975). "Intervention Package: An Analysis to Prepare Juvenile Delinquents for Encounters with Police Officers," *Criminal Justice and Behavior* 2: 5–84.

Westling, Kathleen (1986). *Supportive Home Teaching, A Parent Training Program Designed to Strengthen the Parent/School Relationship in Special Education.* LaGrange, Ill.: LaGrange Area Dept. of Special Education.

White, Alicia G., and Bailey, Jon S. (1989). "Reducing Disruptive Behaviors of Elementary Physical Education Students with Sit and Watch." Poster presentation at the fifteenth annual meeting of the Association for Behavior Analysis, Milwaukee, May 1989.

Williamson, D.; Sewell, W.; Sanders, S.; Haney, J.; and White, D. (1977). "The Treatment of Reluctant Speech Using Contingency Management Procedures," *Journal of Behavior Therapy and Experimental Psychiatry* 8: 151–56.

Willis, Jerry, and Giles, Donna (1976). In *Great Experiments in Behavior Modification*, edited by B. R. Bugelski. Indianapolis: Hackett.

Wilson, C. T.; Leaf, R. C.; and Nathan, P. E. (1975). "The Aversive Control of Excessive Alcohol Consumption by Chronic Alcoholics in the Laboratory Setting," *Journal of Applied Behavior Analysis* 8: 13–26.

Wilson, G. Terence, and Franks, Cyril M. (1982). *Contemporary Behavior Therapy.* New York: Guilford Press.

Winett, R. A., and Winkler, R. C. (1972). "Current Behavior Modification in the Classroom: Be Still, Be Quiet, Be Docile," *Journal of Applied Behavior Analysis* 5: 499–504.

Wolf, M. M.; Phillips, E. L.; Fixsen, D. L.; Braukmann, C. J.; Kirigin, K. A.; Willner, A. G.; and Schumaker, J. (1976). "The Teaching-Family Model," *Child Care Quarterly* 5: 92–103.

Woll, Robert (1989). "Interactive Educational and Training Networks." Unpublished paper, San Jose, Illinois.

Wolpe, Joseph (1958). *Psychotherapy by Reciprocal Inhibition.* Stanford: Stanford University Press.

———— (1973). *The Practice of Behavior Therapy.* 2nd ed. New York: Pergamon.

Yen, Sherman (1989). "Behaviorally Treating Cocaine Addicts in an Outpatient Setting: A Preliminary Report." Invited address presented at the fifteenth annual convention of the Association for Behavior Analysis, Milwaukee, May 1989.

Yen, Sherman; McDonough, Joseph; Payrot, Mark; and Steinback, Cindy (1989). "Application of a Raffle System to Increase Cocaine Outpatients' Calling-In." Paper presented at the fifteenth annual convention of the Association for Behavior Analysis, Milwaukee, May 1989.

AUTHOR INDEX

SUBJECT INDEX

ABOUT THE AUTHOR

EVELYN HARRIS GINSBURG is a school social worker with the Chicago Public Schools. Over the past twenty years she has supervised some sixty social work interns for the University of Chicago; School of Social Service Administration; University of Illinois at Chicago; Jane Addams School of Social Work; and Loyola University School of Social Work. She had previously supervised social work interns in other settings (group work) and countries (Iran). For four years, she served as president of the Chicago Association for Behavior Analysis, a chapter of the Association for Behavior Analysis. In 1989, she authored *School Social Work, A Practitioner's Guidebook, A Community-Integrated Approach to Practice*.